Benefits Realisation Management

The Benefit Manager's Desktop Step-by-Step Guide

Mr Stuart C Wilde MBE

III Clink
Street

Published by Clink Street Publishing 2023

Copyright © 2023

First edition.

ISBN:
978-1-915785-25-1 - paperback
978-1-915785-26-8 - ebook

The images and templates throughout this book can be downloaded,
reviewed and exploited via the 'Resources' page
that can be accessed from this website:

https://stuartcwilde.com

V1.5
22 May 2023

Benefits are "the measurable improvement from change, which is perceived as positive by one or more stakeholders, and which contributes to organisational (including strategic) objectives".

Managing Benefits *by Steve Jenner.*

Table of Contents

SECTION 4

Benefit Profile Categorisations   67

SECTION 5

Benefit Register   77

Abbreviations

AO	Administrative Officer		MOD	Ministry of Defence
BAEs AI	BAE Systems Applied Intelligence		MoP	Management of Portfolios
BaU	Business as Usual		MS	Microsoft
BCHG	Business Change		MSP	Managing Successful Programmes
BCIA	Business Change Impact Assessment		OB	Optimisation Bias
BCM	Business Change Manager		OBC	Outline Business Case
BC&EM	Business Change & Engagement Manager		OGL	Oracle Guided Learning
BM	Benefit Manager		P3O	Project, Programme and Portfolio Offices
BMS	Benefit Management Strategy		pa	Per-Annum
BRM	Benefits Realisation Management		PaaS	Platform as a Service
BRRD	Benefit Realisation Report Date		PBS	Product Breakdown Structure
BRP	Benefit Realisation Plan		pd	Per-Day
BT	Benefit Tracker		Ph/Bh	Public and Bank Holidays
CF	Conditional Formatting		PMO	Programme Management Office
CI	Change Initiative		pm	Per-Month
Combo	Combination		POTI	Processes, Organisation, Technology, Information
CQC	Care Quality Commission			
CT	Control Total		PPM	Project and Programme Management
DDBTD	Design, Develop, Build, Test and Deploy		PSO	Project Support Office
EBP	Economic Benefit Profile		Pw	Per-Week
EPM	Enterprise Performance Management		RAG	Red, Amber, Green
ERP	Enterprise Resource Planning		RBAC	Role Based Access Control
FBC	Full Business Case		RR	Rate of Return
FBP	Finance Business Partner		SaaS	Software as a Service
FCDO	Foreign Commonwealth and Development Office		SME	Subject Matter Expert
			SO	Strategic Objectives
FTE	Full-Time Equivalent		SOC	Strategic Outline Case
HMT	His Majesty's Treasury		SQEP	Suitably Qualified and Experienced Personnel
HO	Home Office			
HR	Human Resource		SRO	Senior Responsible Owner
Hr	Hour(s)		TED	Test Execution Document
IaaS	Information as a Service		TWS	Test Witnessing Session
IPA	Infrastructure and Projects Authority		UAT	User Acceptance Testing
IT	Information Technology		VAT	Value-Added Tax
K	Thousands		VfM	Value for Money
LoD	Lines of Development		WBS	Work Breakdown Structure
M	Millions		WPT	Workforce Planning Team
MI	Management Information		WWW	World Wide Web
ML	Maturity Level		YtD	Year to Date
MoA	Method of Approach			

Introduction

The Benefit Manager's Desktop Step-by-Step Guide provides a new approach and practical application of Benefits Realisation Management (BRM) for Project, Programme and Portfolio Offices (P3O) professionals, Benefit Managers (BM)[1] and In-Service/Business as Usual Capability Managers working in private and public sector bodies and organisations.

It brings together successful approaches to BRM that have been implemented by Benefit led change initiatives[2] in the Ministry of Defence (MOD), Care Quality Commission (CQC), Home Office (HO), BAE Systems Applied Intelligence (BAEs AI) and the Foreign Commonwealth and Development Office (FCDO), into a single, coherent approach and reference. It is cognisant of guidance from the Infrastructure and Projects Authority (IPA), Managing Successful Programmes (MSP), Prince 2, Management of Portfolios (MoP) and *Managing Benefits* by Steve Jenner. The approach can be applied to large- and small-scale Change Initiatives (CIs) including information technology, digital, transformation, people, equipment among others and can be tailored by those organisations to suit their information requirements and priorities.

The reader will learn how to identify and quantify Benefits with ownership and at pace. Where to record them and in what format. The formulas and templates to be used (including examples of quantified Benefit Profiles) improve knowledge and enable the BMs to deliver their work effectively and coherently. The approach in this guide, and the Benefits generated from its application, informs the CIs Benefit Realisation Plan (see para 1.14.1 c), Benefit Register/Profiles, the Business Case and, assist the CIs during the IPA Gateway Review process. Targeted and significant new information has been incorporated to educate the reader, boost performance and achieve better results.

When adopted by the portfolio office and applied to the CIs beneath them, you will see a consistent approach that will standardise the reporting of time savings (calculated in days), cash and Non-Cash Releasing Benefits and people savings[3]. It will significantly improve the confidence and quality of information reported across the P3O communities and beyond.

---

1   Qualities of a BM: Self-starter; team worker; negotiator; influencer; listener; communicator; confident; persuasive; industrious; energetic; resilient. Good with PowerPoint; Excel; Word.

2   Reference to 'change initiatives' can mean a project, programme or work package.

3   The Business Case is likely to target savings in the context of time, money and people. While other soft descriptive Benefits are also important and not to be overlooked (i.e. reputation, satisfaction etc.), priority of work naturally shifts to the quantitative values targeted in the business case.

There is an appropriate balance between structured information, examples and visualisations[4] to help the reader to understand and learn from it so it can be applied. If stakeholders across the organisation can see an approach that is supported, consistent and working, those stakeholders will adopt it. Collaboration (and trust) between the stakeholders, in the application of BRM will improve significantly and the extraordinary shift in culture will be felt by you too.

The author seeks to close the knowledge gap between the significant information that already exists on this subject (i.e. the www; information and guidance received during formal/informal training; coffee shop chat), and the confusion so often seen in the workplace where its practical application is less clear or confused. *The Benefit Manager's Desktop Step-by-Step Guide* consists of approaches that have been tried and tested in the organisations listed. Significant engagements with Economic Advisors, IPA, Finance Business Partners (FBPs), Commercial, Programme Directors and End Users have de facto contributed and shaped the approach that has been documented below for you.

Kevin Lyons, Deputy Director, Hera Programme, FCDO:
"This is the best approach I have ever seen."
01 November 2022.

---

4   Most images show the BM how to create and populate a Benefit Register in Excel. The images are generated from the templated/populated Benefit Register in sections 5 and 9. The Benefit Register can be provided if requested by emailing this address: BRM.Mngr@hotmail.com

SECTION 1

Benefit Management Process

1.1 Introduction

1.1.1 The End Benefits captured by a CI on its Benefit Map[5], are realised incrementally when beneficiaries across an organisation receive new products and services and/or start employing new business processes delivered by subsidiary work packages/projects. The work packages/projects will therefore contribute to the achievement of the End Benefits through their deliverables. The deliverables (i.e. outputs) generate improvements felt by the End User known as 'Benefit Indicators' that can be quantified/metricised thus capturing low level Intermediate (anticipated) or Emergent (new) Benefits and Dis-Benefits which, when aggregated, inform and quantify the End Benefits of the CI and enable performance reporting and tracking. See example below (quantification looks complicated at first glance; follow the logic – it will make sense):

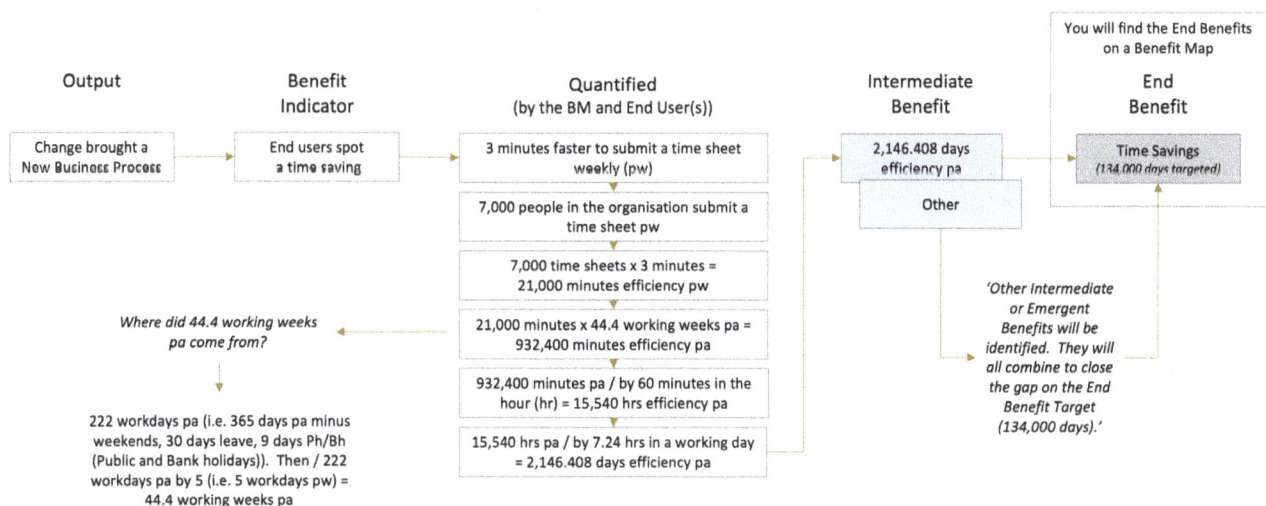

IMAGE 1 *Time Quantified.*

---

5   A CI will have too many Intermediate and Emergent Benefits to capture on the Benefit Map; the End Benefits that do sit on the Benefit Map are the 'main things' (i.e. themes) the CI intends to deliver. They are also 'buckets' in which to group lower level intermediate and emergent Benefits.

1.1.2 Image 1 represents the BM working with the End Users to quantify a time efficiency resulting from an improved business process. The time efficiency (2,146.408 workdays pa) is an intermediate Benefit that is informing an End Benefit. Hold this thought and read the next paragraph.

1.1.3 Consider this scenario: you are a BM with some Benefit Management experience; you recently arrived on a complicated programme; the Business Case targeted for delivery across the 10-year life of the programme circ. 134,000 Gross workdays savings, circ. £8.4M Gross Non-Cash Releasing and circ. £7.3M Gross Cash Releasing Benefits pa commencing year 3 and circ. 700 Gross Full-Time Equivalents (FTEs) workforce savings; these Business Case Benefits are high level; they were informed by personnel who have mostly left their roles; some Benefit Management work had been completed but the information is vague; the Benefit Profiles have limited or no ownership; Benefits Management is underdeveloped within the organisation. *I paint a worst-case scenario but this is not uncommon.* Your role as BM is to unpick the detail and work with stakeholders across the organisation to spot the Benefit Indicators to then quantify them, assign ownership and reach the Gross Benefits targeted in the Business Case. This is a significant undertaking that is extremely difficult unless you have an approach/process to help you achieve it. The process at image 1 is a starter that provides a logical approach to quantify time. But how can we take advantage of it...

1.2 3 Benefit Profiles from 1

1.2.1 An approach has been adopted whereby multiple values can be identified and reported for a single Benefit activity and multiple Benefits can be derived from a single activity. For example, time savings when quantified enable the capture of monetised time and the FTE. In this example, 3 quantitative Benefit Profiles are derived from one. Moreover, these time savings can be an 'indirect' proxy indicator and generate secondary and tertiary associations with other Benefits (i.e. improved user experience, simplicity, more automation; see para 9.6.1 – 9.6.2). In the example below, you will see how quantified time is used to capture monetised time and the FTE:

Step 1 Time Efficiency Intermediate Benefit	Step 2 Monetised Time Intermediate Benefit	Step 3 FTE Intermediate Benefit
2,146.408 work days efficiency pa	£484,403.01k efficiency pa	9.668 FTE efficiency pa

See Image 1 (Time Quantified). Now you have the logic behind quantifying time, use that to inform step 2 and 3.

2,146.408 work days x average daily cap rate for grade undertaking the work *(i.e. average cap rate £33,290 pa) / 222 work days pa (i.e. 365 days pa minus weekends, 30 days leave, 9 days Ph/Bh (Public and Bank holidays) = £149.954 pd).* **So £2,146.408 work days x £149.954 pd = £321,862.465k pa.**

'The £321,862.465k pa = monetised in the context of salary only. To calculate 'total cost on resource' the BM captures the organisations contribution to an employees National Insurance, Pension and 'Location' Allowances. This information can be received from the Workforce Planning Team (WPT) in the Human Resource (HR) Directorate or equivalent within your organisation. If these elements are not already factored into average salary provided to the BM, the WPT need provide them separately so they can be calculated using the example below. So, continuing from £321,862.465k pa above':

Add (a) Employer National Insurance Contribution @ 11% of Average Salary (b) Employer Pension Contribution @ 27.5% of Average Salary (c) London & Milton Keynes Location Allowances @ 12% of Average Salary. 11% + 27.5% + 12% = 50.5%. 50.5% of £321,862.465k = £162,540.545k. Add £321,862.465k to £162,540.545k = £484,403.01k pa.

2,146.408 work days / 222 work days pa for a single FTE (i.e. 365 days pa minus weekends, 30 days leave, 9 days Ph/Bh (Public and Bank holidays)) = 9.668 FTE pa.

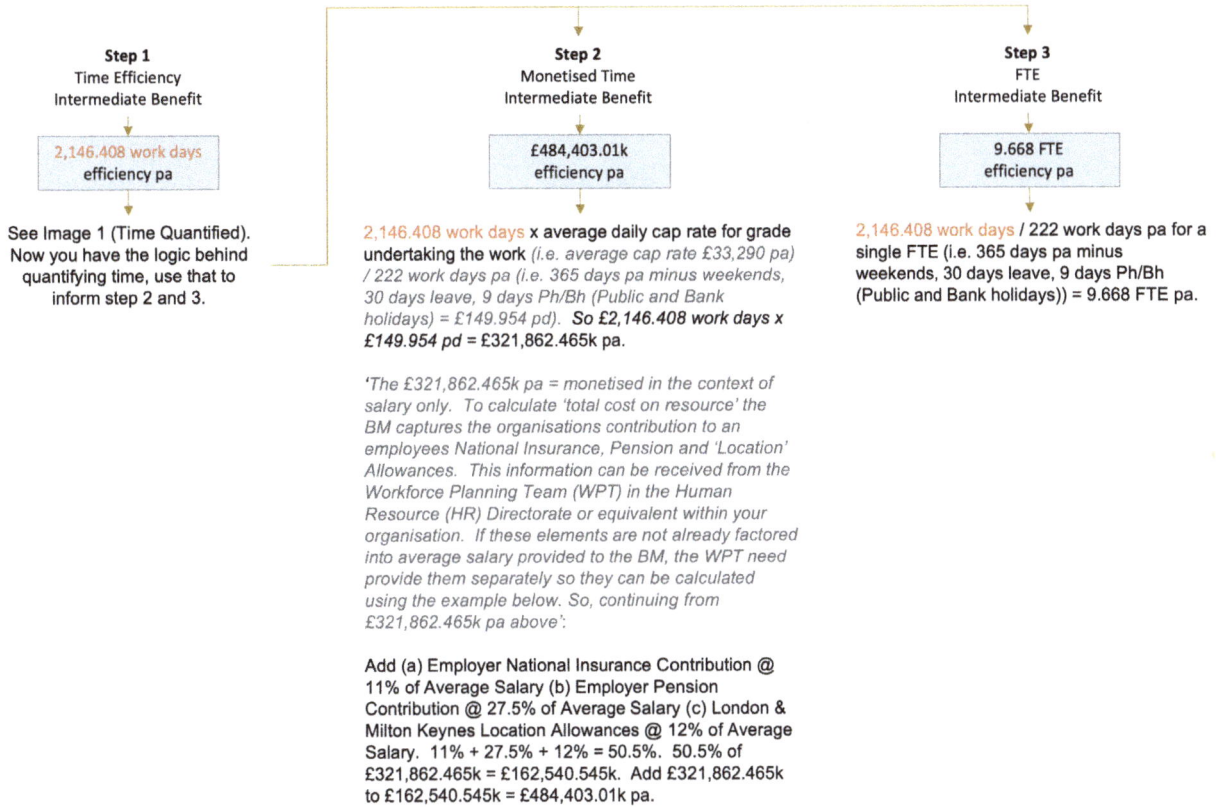

IMAGE 2 *Monetised Time and the FTE Quantified.*

1.2.2 Images 1 and 2 show the 3 steps used to quantify 3 developing Benefit Profiles in this order: time, monetised time, FTE. To achieve it, the BM:

a. Quantified step 1 first, with the End Users who spotted the time saving.

b. Agreed the ownership of step 1. The End Users assisting the BM to quantify the step(s) are usually best placed to own them. Confirming ownership is more successful during this process of collaboration/quantification.

c. Quantified steps 2 and 3 separately by following the process/formula provided.

1.2.3 Notes:

a. Using a step-by-step approach to quantifying the Benefits in the order shown provides logic and understanding for the owner of the Benefit Profiles and the BM. The BM/owner generated 3 Benefit Profiles from 1.

b. Agreeing ownership and achieving support for the profiles is less likely if the order is changed because the logic is broken, and the understanding is lost.

c. The formulas used in the examples can be adapted to meet the scenario, but it will be important to retain the logic. Formulas have been templated at para 1.10. The BM is advised to seek agreement/approval for their use as early as possible in the approach to enable consistency and avoid revisiting calculations downstream which could be time consuming. A way to achieve this is through the Benefit Realisation Plan (BRP)[6].

d. Each of the 3 steps can have more than 1 owner if it helps to improve confidence in the information.

e. The BM quantifies steps 2 and 3 separately to better prepare the 3 profiles. This saves the owners time and demonstrates the BM's consideration for them by taking work off-line[7].

f. Dis-Benefits are quantified in the same way but are expressed as negative rather than positive values.

g. These steps have been explained in detail; use them as a reference to assist you. It may appear complicated at first glance, but a little practice will see the BM being able to achieve it for varied and different scenarios at pace.

1.2.4 The BM can present the Benefit Profiles in the format shown at para 1.3 (i.e. a Word document enclosed within an email or a face-to-face/Teams meeting – whatever is appropriate), so the owner of the Benefit Profiles can agree them. The Word document can be stored in a filing system (i.e. SharePoint) and the data uploaded into the Benefit Profiles in the Benefit Register (see para 5.5 and 5.6).

1.3 Benefit Profile Template

1.3.1 The information below can be sent to the owner of the Benefit Profiles to seek their support and endorsement[8]. Structure the information in a way that

---

6 The BRP contains the 'how' (i.e. how we identify, quantify, measure, and report Benefits).

7 The BM is advised to seek opportunities to develop a good working relationship with the stakeholders. Taking work off-line; providing logic to the formulas; and communicating using salient information (not giving too much detail) builds trust and fosters a positive working relationship to enable success.

8 This is not a 'full' Benefit Profile. It contains salient information required by the owner of the Benefit Profile to take an informed decision to support it or not. When endorsed, the information will be transferred into the Benefit Register by the BM and populated with other data fields and categorisations to mature the full Benefit Profile. See para 5.6.

helps the owner of the Benefit Profiles to better interpret the information. By helping them, you will be gaining trust/confidence and helping yourself.

a. <u>Owner of the Benefit Profiles</u>: M Bloggs; south-west Human Resource (HR) Hub Team Leader.

b. <u>Description</u>[9]: During a User Acceptance Test (UAT), to check a new business process 'complete/submit time sheet' in the new system, the End Users were able to spot an improvement. It now takes, on average, 3 minutes faster to complete the process in the new system, vs the legacy system because time is now automated/calculated within the new system. The End Users do not need to calculate time manually. The Benefit indicator was confirmed by 4 personnel completing UAT within the south-west HR Hub and validated by the team leader. UAT Test Execution Document No.: UAT-CTS-004/1 refers. Time, Monetised Time, and FTE efficiencies are reinvested. The frequency of the Benefits is 'year-on-year' across the profile of the CI[10]. The Benefits were anticipated (i.e. not new, Emergent Benefits).

c. <u>Start of Improvement</u>: 01 Dec 22 (i.e. new system go live). The 1st Benefit Report Milestone is 31 Mar 23, then annually thereafter.

d. <u>Benefit 1/Formula (Efficiency – Time)</u>: 3 minutes faster to submit a time sheet weekly (pw). 7,000 people in the organisation submit a time sheet pw. 7,000 time sheets x 3 minutes = 21,000 minutes pw. 21,000 minutes x 44.4 working weeks pa (i.e. 222 work days pa (i.e. 365 days pa minus weekends, 30 days leave, 9 days Ph/Bh (Public and Bank holidays)) / 5 (i.e. 5 work days pw) = 44.4 working weeks pa) = 932,400 minutes pa / 60 minutes in the hour (hr) = 15,540 hrs pa. 15,540 hr pa / 7.24 hrs in a working day = (a) 2,146.408 days efficiency pa or (b) / by 12 mths pa then x 4 (Dec 22–Mar 23 which is the remaining 4 months to the end of the financial year) = 715.469 days. The time efficiency can be reinvested on other value-added tasks).

e. <u>Benefit 2/Formula (Economic – £)</u>:

---

9 The importance of the 'description' cannot be emphasised enough. This is the formation, context and logic behind the Benefit Indicator. The BM (assisted by the owner of the Benefit Profile) is to articulate the description in simple English to enable the stakeholders to better understand it.
10 The frequency of the Benefits is explained in para 1.4.

- 2,146.408 workdays x daily cap rate for grade undertaking the work (i.e. average cap rate £33,290 pa) / 222 work days pa (i.e. 365 days pa minus weekends, 30 days leave, 9 days Ph/Bh = £149.954 pd). So, £2,146.408 workdays x £149.954 pd = £321,862.465k pa.

- Add[11] (a) Employer National Insurance Contribution @ 11% of Average Salary (b) Employer Pension Contribution @ 27.5% of Average Salary (c) London & Milton Keynes Location Allowances @ 12% of Average Salary. 11% + 27.5% + 12% = 50.5%. 50.5% of £321,862.465k = £162,540.545k. Add £321,862.465k to £162,540.545k = (a) £484,403.01k efficiency pa Non-Cash Releasing or (b) / by 12 mths pa then x 4 (Dec 22–Mar 23 which is the remaining 4 months to the end of the financial year) = £161,467.67k. The spend on resource can be reinvested on other value-added tasks).

f. <u>Benefit 3/Formula (Efficiency – FTE)</u>: 2,146.408 workdays / 222 work days pa for a single FTE (i.e. 365 days pa minus weekends, 30 days leave, 9 days Ph/Bh) = (a) 9.668 FTE efficiency pa or (b) / by 12 mths pa then x 4 (Dec 22–Mar 23 which is the remaining 4 months to the end of the financial year) = 3.222 FTE. The FTE efficiency can be reinvested on other value-added tasks).

g. <u>Benefit Realisation Report Date</u>: 31 March 2023 (i.e. the Benefit Realisation Report was determined to be at the end of the financial year).

h. <u>Date of Next Review</u>: 20 March 2023 (i.e. ideally before the Benefit Realisation Report is due).

i. <u>Remarks/Comments</u>[12]: Average salary rates have been provided by the HR MI/Planning Team. Size of the organisation has been provided by the HR Directorate MI Team. Total spend on resource (i.e. Pension, National Insurance and Location Allowances) have been provided by the WPT in the HR Directorate.

---

11 If not already included within av. salary/cap rates – see para 1.10.2.

12 This element can be added to the profiles, to provide context behind the values used in the formula, so the owner of the Benefit Profiles, and the stakeholders reading them, can take confidence in the information. See para 1.10.

1.4 Frequency of the Benefits

1.4.1 When the 3 Benefit Profiles have been endorsed by their owner, they can be transferred into the Benefit Register. The 3 Benefit Profiles can be (a) a one-off saving. For example, an automated intervention removed a need to manually clear a backlog of work once only or (b) year-on-year savings. For example, an improved business process reduced an aspect of a team's work, the time efficiency was determined to be year-on-year because if the improved business process was not delivered, the team would be undertaking the additional work enduringly. In other words, without intervention, it is not known when the additional work would cease.

1.4.2 Reviewing the 3 Benefit Profiles at para 1.3.1, sub paras d, e, f (and the 'description' at sub para b), the BM can see they are year-on-year efficiencies[13]. The Benefit Register will calculate the total year-on-year efficiencies for you but, this next exercise shows, for your information, how the aggregated values provide a greater contribution to the End Benefits of the CI.

1.4.3 First, consider this scenario: the new business process was implemented Nov 22; the Benefits are calculated from 01 Dec 22 (01 Dec 22 is year 3 in the life of the CI); each year calculation is 01 Apr–31 Mar. So:

a. <u>2,146.408 days Efficiency pa</u>: (a) calculate the 01 Dec 22–31 Mar 23 efficiency in year 3 by dividing 2,146.408 days by 12 months in the year, then multiply by the 4 months (Dec 22–Mar 23) = 715.469 days (b) multiply 2,146.408 by 7 (i.e. year 4 to year 10 incl.) = 15,024.856 days. Now add a+b = 15,740.325 days Gross Benefit across the life of the CI. This will generate 8 Benefit Profiles in the Benefit Register (i.e. 715.469 days reported at end of year 3 and 2,146.408 days reported at end of each financial years 4–10 incl).

b. <u>£484,403.01k Economic pa</u>: (a) calculate the 01 Dec 22–31 Mar 23 efficiency in year 3 by dividing £484,403.01k by 12 months in the year, then multiply by the 4 months (Dec 22–Mar 23) = £161,467.67k (b) multiply £484,403.01k by 7 (i.e. year 4 to year 10 incl.) = circ. £3.391M. Now add a+b = circ. £3.552M Non-Cash Releasing Gross Benefit across the life of the CI.

---

13 HM Treasury Green Book (https://www.gov.uk/government/publications/the-green-book-appraisal-and-evaluation-in-central-governent/the-green-book-2020) states: "Costs and Benefits should be calculated over the lifetime of an intervention. As a guideline, a time horizon of 10 years is a suitable working assumption." The 10 years are usually expressed in financial years; certainly, in respect to monetised values (i.e. 01 Apr–31 Mar).

This will generate 8 Benefit Profiles in the Benefit Register (i.e. £161,467.67k reported at end of year 3 and £484,403.01k reported at end of each financial year 4–10 incl.).

c. <u>9.668 FTE Efficiency pa</u>: (a) calculate the 01 Dec 22–31 Mar 23 efficiency in year 3 by dividing 9.668 FTE by 12 months in the year, then multiply by the 4 months (Dec 22–Mar 23) = 3.222 FTE (b) multiply 9.668 FTE by 7 (i.e. year 4 to year 10 incl.) = 67.676 FTE. Now add a+b = 70.898 FTE Gross Benefit across the life of the CI. This will generate 8 Benefit Profiles in the Benefit Register (i.e. 3.222 FTE reported at end of year 3 and 9.668 FTE reported at end of each financial year 4–10 incl.).

1.4.4 In summary, this exercise shows that a Benefit indicator was identified (time efficiency) when using a new business process. From that, the BM worked with the End Users to, initially, quantify 3 Benefit Profiles from 1. The annual, year-on-year frequency of the Benefits led to 24 Benefit Profiles; each profile with an owner; 15,740.325 days Gross Benefit; circ. £3.552M Non-Cash Releasing Gross Benefit; 70.898 FTE Gross Benefit – each being a significant contribution toward 3 primary[14] End Benefits on the CIs Benefit Map. See further examples of quantified Benefits at Section 11.

1.4.5 You will see these values/Benefits again at para 5.6 where you will be shown how to record them in an Excel Benefit Register document (Benefit Profiles worksheet and Economic Benefit Profiles worksheet)[15].

1.5 Dis-Benefits

1.5.1 Benefits Management is a generic term incorporating the management of Benefits and Dis-Benefits. The following examples show how Dis-Benefits are quantified in the same way as a Benefit but, on this occasion, the End User's time to complete an action has increased because there is more complexity in the new system resulting in a disadvantage.

---

14 Primary, secondary, and tertiary End Benefits are explained at para 1.9.

15 The P3Os may have another software preference in which to record the Benefits. For example, at the time of writing MOD organisations are using Microsoft (MS) Project with adaptations to suit data collection and reporting requirements. Whatever the software being used, the approach, structure and categorisations in this guide can be used to develop that software to ensure consistency and standardisation of data collection and reporting requirements. This guide uses the Excel application in Office 365. The BM should confirm the tooling used to record Benefits Data with the portfolio office BM to ensure the CI is aligned with the portfolio office approach from the outset.

a. <u>Owner of the Dis-Benefit Profiles</u>: P Smith (Central HR Hub Support Team) and A Goldsmith (Appointments and Inter Change Team).

b. <u>Description</u>: UAT Test Execution Document (TED) No. XPT-17734 in respect to 'Manage my Move' recorded the following statement: 'There are now more steps in the business processes. There are additional fields to be populated requiring more information and different screens to navigate through; there is a lot of going back/forth between the screens.' During a review with the End Users in the HR Directorate undertaking the UAT, it was further confirmed that, when populating the data fields and navigating between screens to complete the transactions in an employee's record, a significant time increase was identified when compared to the same process in the previous system. A conservative estimate/count of transactions pa taken from the associated teams is as follows: The Central HR Hub Support Team x 700 records; the Appointments and Inter Change Team x 150 records. The observed time increase is 15 minutes per transaction. The data input is usually undertaken by an Administrative Officer (AO) in both teams. These are new, Emergent Dis-Benefits not previously anticipated.

c. <u>Start of the Disadvantage</u>: 01 Jul 22 (i.e. new system go live). The 1st Benefit Report Milestone in year 3 of the CI is 31 Mar 23, then annually thereafter until a solution is found.

d. <u>Dis-Benefit 1/Formula (Time)</u>:

- Central HR Hub: 15 minutes time increase to process 700 records pa. 700 records x 15 minutes = 10,500 minutes pa. 10,500 minutes / 60 minutes in the hour (hr) = 175 hrs pa. 175 hrs pa / 7.24 hrs in a working day = (a) 24.171 days pa or (b) / by 12 mths pa then x 9 mths (Jul 22–Mar 23 incl. which is the remaining 9 mths to the end of the financial year) = 18.128 days. The Dis-Benefit has an annual frequency so 24.171 days pa x 7 (i.e. years 4–10) = 169.197 days plus 18.128 days in year 3 = 187.325 days Dis-Benefit across the life of the CI.

- Appointments and Inter Change Team: 15 minutes time increase to process 150 records pa. 150 records x 15 minutes = 2,250 minutes pa. 2,250 minutes / 60 minutes in the hr = 37.5 hrs pa. 37.5 hrs pa / 7.24 hrs in a working day = (a) 5.179 days pa or (b) / by 12 mths pa then x 9 mths (Jul 22–Mar 23 incl. which is the remaining 9 mths to the end of the financial year) = 3.884 days. The Dis-Benefit has an annual frequency so 5.179 days pa x 7 (i.e. years 4–10) = 36.253 days plus 3.884 days in year 3 = 40.137 days Dis-Benefit across the life of the CI.

- Total Dis-Benefit = 187.325 days + 40.137 days = 227.462 days additional work across the life of the CI.

e. <u>Dis-Benefit 2/Formula (£)</u>:

- Central HR Hub: 24.171 workdays pa x average daily cap rate for grade undertaking the work (i.e. average cap rate for an AO @ £35,048 pa (incl. the organisations contributions to Pension, National Insurance and Location Allowances)) / 222 work days pa (i.e. 365 days pa minus weekends, 30 days leave, 9 days Ph/Bh = £157.873 pd). So, 24.171 workdays pa x £157.873 pd = (a) £3,815.948k pa or (b) / by 12 mths pa then x 9 mths (Jul 22–Mar 23 incl. which is the remaining 9 mths to the end of the financial year) = £2,861.961k. The Dis-Benefit has an annual frequency so £3,815.948k pa x 7 (i.e. years 4–10) = £26,711.636k plus £2,861.961k in year 3 = £29,573.597k Dis-Benefit across the life of the CI.

- Appointments and Inter Change Team: 5.179 workdays pa x average daily cap rate for grade undertaking the work (i.e. average cap rate for an AO @ £35,048 pa (incl. the organisations contributions to Pension, National Insurance and Location Allowances)) / 222 work days pa (i.e. 365 days pa minus weekends, 30 days leave, 9 days Ph/Bh = £157.873 pd). So, 5.179 workdays pa x £157.873 pd = (a) £817.624 pa or (b) / by 12 mths pa then x 9 mths (Jul 22–Mar 23 incl. which is the remaining 9 mths to the end of the financial year) = £613.218. The Dis-Benefit has an annual frequency so £817.624 pa x 7 (i.e. years 4–10) = £5,723.368k plus £613.218 in year 3 = £6,336.586k Dis-Benefit across the life of the CI.

- Total Dis-Benefit = £29,573.597k + £6,336.586k = £35,910.183k spend on resource on the increased workload across the life of the CI.

f. <u>Dis-Benefit 3/Formula (FTE)</u>:

- Central HR Hub: 24.171 workdays / 222 workdays pa (i.e. 365 days pa minus weekends, 30 days leave, 9 days Ph/Bh) = (a) 0.108 of an FTE pa or (b) / by 12 mths pa then x 9 mths (Jul 22–Mar 23 incl. which is the remaining 9 mths to the end of the financial year) = 0.081 FTE. The Dis-Benefit has an annual frequency so 0.108 FTE pa x 7 (i.e. years 4–10) =

0.756 FTE plus 0.081 FTE in year 3 = 0.837 FTE Dis-Benefit across the life of the CI.

- Appointments and Inter Change Team: 5.179 workdays / 222 workdays pa (i.e. 365 days pa minus weekends, 30 days leave, 9 days Ph/Bh) = (a) 0.023 of an FTE pa or (b) / by 12 mths pa then x 9 mths (Jul 22–Mar 23 incl. which is the remaining 9 mths to the end of the financial year) = 0.017 FTE. The Dis-Benefit has an annual frequency so 0.023 FTE pa x 7 (i.e. years 4–10) = 0.161 FTE plus 0.017 FTE in year 3 = 0.178 FTE Dis-Benefit across the life of the CI.

- Total Dis-Benefit = 0.837 FTE + 0.178 FTE = 1.015 FTE resource consumption on the increased workload across the life of the CI.

g. <u>Benefit Realisation Report Date</u>: 31 March 2023 (i.e. the 1st Benefit Realisation Report was determined to be at the end of the financial year).

h. <u>Date of Next Review</u>: 20 March 2023 (i.e. ideally before the Benefit Realisation Report is due).

i. <u>Remarks/Comments</u>: Average salary rates have been provided by the HR MI/Planning Team. They incorporate the total spend on resource (i.e. Pension, National Insurance and Location Allowances) provided by the WPT in the HR Directorate.

1.5.2 The Dis-Benefit Profiles will be associated with the time, monetised time, and FTE End Benefits on the CIs Benefit Map but rather than adding to the Gross Benefit values of those End Benefits, they will be subtracted from them until the additional burdens have been removed.

1.5.3 When the 24 Dis-Benefit Profiles are incorporated into the Benefit Profiles worksheet in the Benefit Register, the values will be entered with a '–' so they can be subtracted from the Gross Benefits.

1.6 Is it worth it?

1.6.1 A stakeholder considers: Time saved as a result of change to fix a problem with a new system (i.e. an unintended outcome of the new system increased burdens on the End User) reverted the End User back to the start point, thus there was no Benefit and quantification would be time wasted. The example below explains why Benefit Management should be applied:

a. The future 'to-be' state brought additional housekeeping requirements resulting in increased manual data processing burdens for the End User. A Dis-Benefit is quantified to capture the increased time to deliver the output; the new baseline is revised upwards.

b. Subsequently, a CI was able to treat/remove the Dis-Benefit and revise the baseline back down. The difference between the baselines is quantified as follows:

- An 'efficiency' Benefit: The End User felt a disadvantage/increased time (i.e. the baseline had been revised up) and, the End User then subsequently felt an advantage/time reduction (i.e. the baseline was then revised down) resulting from change or adjustments to the system. The efficiency Benefit can be reinvested.

- An 'avoidance' Benefit: The End User felt no disadvantage/increased time because the baseline had not been revised up/down (i.e. treatment of the Dis-Benefit took place before the End User burdens had increased). The avoidance Benefit cannot be reinvested.

1.7 Workforce Reductions

1.7.1 Unless it has been directed to do so, a CI is not likely to remove/reduce internal resources and take the equivalent Cash Releasing Benefits. Such approaches come from wider change and strategic/economic direction from inside the organisation, not the CI itself. FTE Benefits generated by a CI with no mandate to remove posts can only inform the organisation of the scale/scope of efficiencies generated by the CI, enabling the organisation to take strategic decisions on the size and structure of its workforce.

1.8 Reinvestment

1.8.1 When maturing the Benefit Profiles, the BM can categorise which Benefits can/cannot be reinvested. For example (and as a rule for those CIs with no mandate to remove posts)[16]:

---

16 This is a useful exercise to practise and understand when maturing/categorising the Benefit Profiles in the Benefit Register. When the logic is applied correctly, it helps to ensure the accuracy of information being reported (i.e. PivotTables and visualisations generated from aggregated information sourced from the Benefit Profiles themselves).

a. Time saved inside the organisation is reinvested[17]. See example yellow entry Table 1.

b. Outsourced Subject Matter Experts (SMEs), for example contractors or consultants who sit outside the organisation: time savings in respect to these people (i.e. a planned activity to bring consultants into the organisation to deliver a product that is no longer required) cannot be reinvested. See example green entry Table 1.

c. Spend (i.e. salary) on internal resources when allocated new work due to time savings is considered reinvested, on the new work.

d. Planned spend on outsourced SMEs no longer required (if funds had not been secured/contracted) cannot be reinvested because there was no uplift to the Control Total (CT). This would be an avoidance Benefit, that is non-cash releasing; see grey entry Table 1. The reverse is true if funds had been secured/contracted but the work was no longer required, in which case this would be an efficiency Benefit that is cash releasing and can be reinvested. See example orange entry Table 1.

e. FTEs saved inside the organisation are reinvested on other priorities; they can also be used to inform strategic decisions on internal restructuring. See example blue entry Table 1.

1.8.2 The logic in Table 1 can be used to help the BM mature/categorise each of the Benefit Profiles to better understand the 'intent' of the Benefit and remove confusion. In addition, please note: an Efficiency Benefit will have a numeric value (i.e. time or percentage), not a monetised value. Monetised values are associated with the Economic Benefits. Objective and/or qualitative descriptors (i.e. soft Benefits) are Effectiveness Benefits, not Economic/Efficiency. This guidance will help to improve the accuracy of information in the Benefit Register that is used to draw visuals/insights to inform strategic decisions.

---

17 There is one exception to this rule. That is when time to achieve an action is mostly spent waiting, not doing. In this example, the quantified time will not be reinvested and should not be monetised, nor should the FTE be taken from it. The idea being, in the context of this example, the time saving is merely recording the time in which an action can be achieved now, as opposed to previously. The quantified time can still be added to the Gross Time forecast/Benefit.

3E Category	Benefit Category	Assessment	Contract	Efficiency/ Avoidance	Reinvested
(a)	(b)	(c)	(d)	(e)	(f)
Economic	£ cash releasing	Quantitative (Monetised)	Contracted; Started	Efficiency	Yes
	£ Non-Cash Releasing	Quantitative (Monetised)	Contracted; Started	Efficiency	Yes
	£ Non-Cash Releasing	Quantitative (Monetised)	Not contracted; not started	Avoidance	No
Efficiency	Time saving	Quantitative (Numeric)	Contracted; Started	Efficiency	Yes
	Time saving	Quantitative (Numeric)	Not contracted; not started	Avoidance	No
Efficiency	FTE saving	Quantitative (Numeric)	Contracted; Started	Efficiency	Yes
	FTE saving	Quantitative (Numeric)	Not contracted; not started	Avoidance	No
Effectiveness	New capability (i.e. information advantage)	Objective (Descriptive)	N/A in this context		
	Opinion (i.e. improved reputation)	Qualitative (Descriptive / Subjective)	N/A in this context		

TABLE 1 *Understanding the intent of the Benefit Profile.*

1.9 Relationships Between the Benefits and Objectives.

1.9.1 'Direct' relationships between Intermediate/Emergent Benefits and Dis-Benefits, with a CI's End Benefits are primary associations. Indirect relationships are secondary and/or tertiary associations[18]. The same is true of the

---

18 See pictorial representation of these associations at Images 3 and 17.

relationships between the End Benefits and Strategic Objectives (SOs). The point being the BM can see (a) how Intermediate/Emergent Benefits and Dis-Benefits contribute to the wider End Benefits of the CI 'reducing work in the long run' and how that can be achieved at pace and (b) how the End Benefits contribute to the wider SOs 'reducing work in the long run' and how that can be achieved at pace.

1.9.2 When the associations have been 'connected' in the Benefit Profiles in the Benefit Register[19], visualisations can generate useful information. For example (a) quantify the End Benefits (b) count of associations between the Intermediate/Emergent Benefits, Dis-Benefits, and the End Benefits – see para 9.6 (c) quantify the SOs (d) count of associations between the End Benefits and the SOs – see para 9.7 (e) those End Benefits or SOs with fewer associations 'suggests more work can be done on them' so appropriate action/prioritisation can be taken.

1.9.3 Image 3 provides a pictorial representation of the primary, secondary and tertiary associations between an Intermediate Benefit, End Benefits and SOs[20]:

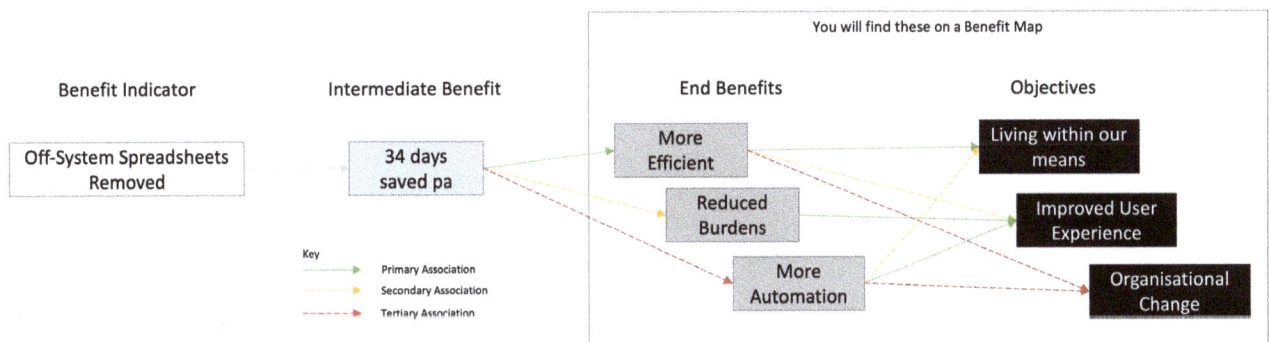

IMAGE 3 *Relationships between the Benefits and Objectives.*

1.10 Formulas (and Format of Numeric and Monetised Values)

1.10.1 P3Os will want to standardise, where possible, the formulas used to quantify time, monetised time, and FTE Benefits. The formulas and values should be

---

19 See example Image 39, columns t, u and v (primary, secondary, tertiary associations to the End Benefits) and columns w, x and y (primary, secondary, tertiary associations to the Strategic Objectives) and Images 101 and 102.

20 While this small-scale/simple visual provides an example of primary, secondary and tertiary associations and how a single Intermediate Benefit is playing a wider part and contribution to the End Benefits and Strategic Objectives, the connections complicate the Benefit Map. Para 3.8 provides a sensible workaround solution for your consideration and, when connecting the fields do not go to the nth degree otherwise the associations become meaningless and a waste of time.

sent to the appropriate team(s) within the organisations HR Directorate or their equivalent inside your organisation to seek their support, then replicate the information in the BRP for transparency – this will help to communicate the approach to the IPA, for example, during the Gateway Review process and demonstrate wider engagement between the BM and business functions to ensure accurate, current data is being used to quantify the Benefits. Completed examples of Benefit Profiles using these formulas have been demonstrated already. The formulas are as follows:

a. <u>Step 1 (Time)</u>: No of units x length of time (mins) / 60 mins in the hr = hrs / 7.24 hrs in a working day = no of workdays x frequency.

b. <u>Step 2 (Monetised Time)</u>[21]: No of workdays x daily cap rate for grade undertaking the work (i.e. average cap rate £ pa) / 222 work days pa (i.e. 365 days pa minus weekends, 30 days leave, 9 days Ph/Bh = £ pd) x frequency.

  • *Average daily cap rate for internal resource can be obtained from the Workforce Planning Team (WPT) in the HR Directorate.*

  • *Average daily cap rate for outsourced resource can be obtained online from this site for example: https://www.itjobswatch.co.uk/contracts/uk/software engineering.do*

c. <u>Step 3 (FTE)</u>: Either internal or external/contracted resource:

  • No of workdays / 222 overall workdays pa = no of FTE x frequency.

1.10.2 <u>Total Spend on Resource</u>: The organisations contribution to an employee's National Insurance, Pension and Location Allowances, when merged with average salary rates, provides the organisation's 'total spend' on 'internal resources'. When used in a Benefits context, the information will provide a 'true' picture of advantage (or disadvantage) when monetising time in relation to Benefits and Dis-Benefits. The following agreed values, for the purpose of this exercise, are being used in the FCDO, for example, at the time of writing. They were provided by the WPT in the HR Directorate:

---

21 It is better if the organisation captures average salary that includes the organisation's contribution to the employee's pension, national insurance and location allowances. This will reduce/simplify the step 2 formula. If the organisation is not capturing them together, the BM ought to extend the step 2 formula to include these additional elements. See 'total spend on resource' at para 1.10.2.

a. Employer National Insurance Contribution @ 11% of Average Salary.

b. Employer Pension Contribution @ 27.5% of Average Salary.

c. London & Milton Keynes Location Allowances @ 12% of Average Salary.

1.10.3 <u>Size of the Organisation</u>: For a large organisation, the HR Directorate Management Information (MI) team can provide a count of personnel working across the organisation broken down by location and numbers using legacy system(s). This information can help the BM when quantifying Benefits. For example, you saw an agreed time saving (3 minutes) resulting from an improved business process that was then multiplied across the size of the organisation (7,000 personnel) who all benefited from the new business process.

1.10.4 <u>Format (Numeric and Monetised Values)</u>: The format used to record/report numeric and monetised values should be cohered across the portfolio to remove confusion. The format should be agreed with the portfolio office BM to provide a consistent approach across the portfolio. For example, monetised values (millions) structured like this '£15,067,234.62M', can be simplified to '£15,067.234M'. The simple format is used in this document when recording monetised values in the Economic Benefit Profile (see para 2.1.2) and the Benefit Profiles in the Benefit Register (see blue boxes Image 38).

1.11 Benefit Process Model – Change Process

1.11.1 The Programme Management Office (PMO) or Project Support Office (PSO) manages the change management process for the CI, presenting change[22] to a design authority and board to cohere and progress change in the pipeline. The BM's role in this process is to sit in on the meetings, listen for 'Benefit Indicators', then subsequently work with the stakeholders to define and quantify the Benefit Indicators[23] for recording in the Benefit Register. This demonstrates Benefit Management as an integral part of the change process and enables cost-Benefit analysis and/or (VfM) assessments to be undertaken by the design authority and board. The work will be incremental and commensurate to the maturity of the change/Benefit thus ensuring a sustainable approach where the right information is captured at the right time.

---

22 For example, a tweak to an Information Technology (IT) System to improve it for the organisation and the End Users.

23 As shown at para 1.3.

1.11.2 The approach to change should be 'Benefits-led' to ensure maximum value for the change, the End Users and the Organisation as a whole. Managing Benefits by Steve Jenner 2nd edition states: 'Benefits are not just another dimension of project and programme management (PPM) – rather, they are the rationale for the investment of taxpayers' and stakeholders' funds in change initiatives. As such, Benefits should be the driver behind all change initiatives from initiation through to, and indeed beyond, integration into Business as Usual (BaU)'.

1.11.3 Requests for change (i.e. the template used to present change to the board) can be edited by the BM so it incorporates clear and simple direction as to what is required to be articulated in a Benefits context. The change request template will 'or should' contain the costs for implementing the change, and the BM is advised to assist the author of the change to incorporate the Rate of Return (RR) when possible to do so (i.e. quantified advantages or disadvantages in respect to time, monetised time and the FTE)[24]. **An effective change process in the context of Benefit Management, is a demonstration that the organisation is 'Benefits-led'.**

1.11.4 The process model contextualises this approach (i.e. how the Benefits are matured as they progress from an idea through to delivery in the change process).

Typical Benefit Management Process

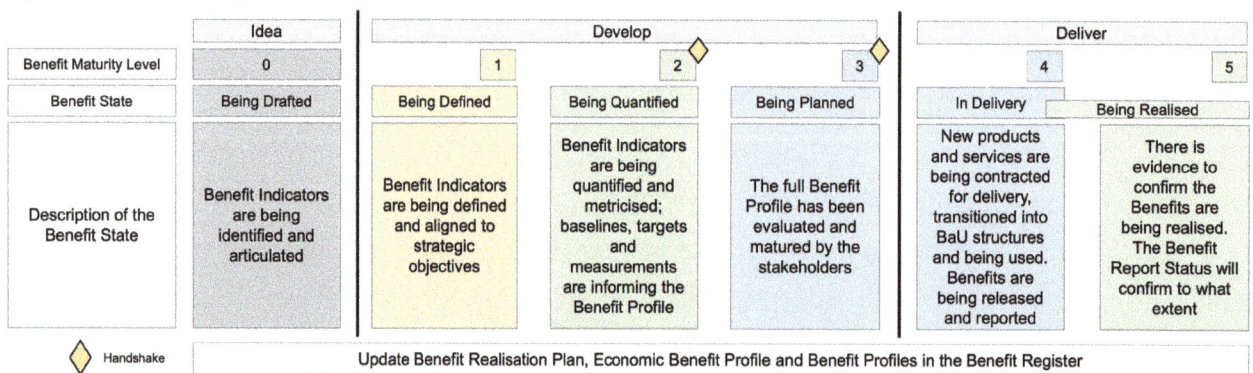

IMAGE 4 *Benefit Process Model*[25].

---

24 Collaboration between the BM and the initiator/author of the change request can identify wider advantages or disadvantages to other areas in the organisation.

25 As a Benefit progresses along the maturity levels or Benefit states, its progress can be fast or slow, depending on the situation. The descriptions merely help to categorise each Benefit that has been recorded in the Benefit Register into the most appropriate bucket, to be able to understand where the Benefit currently sits in the process. This will demonstrate the level of maturity of the Benefit and can be used to inform the prioritisation of work.

1.11.5 A breakdown of Benefits-related activities is as follows:

a. Draft the Benefits (Maturity Level (ML) 0): Benefit Indicators (i.e. the reason for change) are captured at the start of the change process. Benefit identification should be a collaborative task that is brokered between the End Users and Business Process Owners, for example, who are assisted by the BM.

b. Define and Quantify the Benefits (ML1&2): Identifying how these Benefits break down between each of the affected areas forms the basis of the first handshake[26]. '*You saw an example of this at para 1.5 when 2 different teams in the HR Directorate were disadvantaged by a new system.*' Clear and transparent identification of the beneficiary recipient and owner of the Benefit Profiles is key to the delivery of these Benefits. The top-level Benefits are broken down into realistic targets for each of the affected areas to realise. The agreement of apportionment should be brokered between the BM and owner of the Benefit Profiles across the functions of the business (i.e. Expenses, Commercial, Payroll, Travel Package, Accounts Payable, other) who are required to monitor, report and realise the Benefits.

c. Plan the Benefits (ML3): Once Benefits have been defined, quantified, and their breakdown between affected areas across the functions of the business have been agreed, this forms the basis of the second handshake between the business functions, owner of the Benefit Profiles and Benefits Authority (a pictorial representation of the handshake can be seen at Image 65); the Benefits are baselined at ML3.

d. Deliver the Benefits (ML4): During 'delivery', the functions of the business through the owner of the Benefit Profiles will be assisted by the BM to track and report the progress made towards the realisation of the Benefits. Progress reporting should be through established governance arrangements. It is essential to track and report Benefits after the CI has completed its delivery phase.

e. Benefits Realised (ML5): Once Benefits are realised, they will have reached ML5. Subsequent treatment will be in accordance with established governance arrangements. Prior to closure of the CI, residual Benefits and their owners, assisted by the BM, will transition to BaU areas/functions and governance

---

26 The handshake is a 'virtual' concept between the CI and the beneficiary recipient, that will occur as a Benefit matures through the Benefit State/Maturity levels, acting as a threshold to be satisfied to progress on to the next level.

arrangements; these arrangements are agreed in the final iteration of the BRP that is issued prior to closure of the CI. If Benefits are subsequently being eroded (i.e. capability gaps and risks materialise), they will inform the development of new CIs in the pipeline.

1.12 Benefit Ownership

1.12.1 When identifying the 'owner of a Benefit', experience shows how difficult it can be to achieve because a large cohort of stakeholders feel they do not 'own' the Benefit. It makes them feel 'culpable' for the Benefit and a 'failing' on their part if the target had not been achieved. A common response received when identifying ownership is 'the organisation owns the Benefit not me' so, there is a reluctance to take ownership with circular conversations and no end state, which stifles the application of Benefits Management.

1.12.2 Change the language. For example, when identifying the 'owner of the Benefit Profile' (not the Owner of the Benefit), experience has shown the BM is more likely to be successful.

1.12.3 Example: The FBP in the PMO who tracks and owns the information, worked with the BM to quantify an underspend in relation to the CI's implementation costs and generate a Benefit Profile for it. When the FBP responded to the BM's question at the end of the process 'are you content to own the Benefit Profile'? The FBP agreed because their understanding of their role improved when assisting the BM to quantify and develop the Benefit Profile. Confirming ownership appeared seamless, obvious even, for the FBP. The slight change in terminology and, raising the question at the right time in the process, provided a significant advantage for the BM and is drawn from experience. This example shows the owner of a Benefit Profile is not always the Beneficiary Recipient.

1.13 Identifying Benefit Indicators – Opportunities

1.13.1 The Business Case: Ensures investment on change is justified in terms of (a) the organisation's strategic direction and (b) forecast Benefits targeted for the organisation and the End Users. Significant Benefit Indicators can be found within the Business Case. If the BM had no part in the development of the Business Case, it is the BM's first port of call.

1.13.2 UAT and Test Witnessing Sessions (TWS). Both provide a unique opportunity for End Users, who are testing business processes in a new system, to draw comparisons with the system being terminated, and to be able to spot advantages and disadvantages between the business processes. The author incorporated the below text into UAT/TWS TEDs for a programme in the FCDO. The approach generated a rich source of information in which the BM was able to spot Benefit Indicators within 1000+ TEDs).

a. These words were used up front to plant the thought in the End Users' minds, before they undertook the UAT/TWS: '*UAT/TWS provides a unique opportunity for the End Users when testing [new system name], to draw comparisons with [old system name], to be able to spot advantages and disadvantages (i.e. benefits) of the new system. We would like to know, what are the time savings when using [new system name]. For example, what work can be achieved faster? Likewise, if time to undertake an activity in [new system name] has increased (i.e. an unintended consequence), we want to know that too. End Users undertaking UAT/TWS are to "take a note" of those advantages and disadvantages in respect to length of time to achieve an action; a question will be asked later in the document.*'

b. The user will then see the test script in the TEDs before reaching a series of questions for completion. The 2 questions below were incorporated into the TEDs by the BM[27]:

- *Please answer the following 2 questions in the context of advantages and/or disadvantages of [new system name] as a comparator to [old system name]:*

  - *Did you spot (a) a time saving/advantage or (b) a time increase/ disadvantage, to achieve the action in [new system name]. Answer (a) or (b) only?*

  - *A very rough order estimation: Will the time saving or time increase (a) impacting many users, (b) impacting medium numbers of users, (c) impacting just a few users. Answer (a), (b) or (c)?*'

---

27 UAT/TWS can be a time-consuming process for the End Users. For that reason, the questions/responses were kept simple to avoid taking up too much time. Post UAT/TWS, the BM interrogated the TEDs (they were stored in SharePoint), to find the Benefit Indicators. The BM prioritised the list, using it to engage with the associated End Users so that advantages and disadvantages could be quantified and recorded in the Benefit Register.

1.13.3 Change Process. See para 1.11. The change request template ought to include the costs to deliver the change and, costs for the delivery of alternative options if they have been identified. Comparisons/difference between these costs can identify 'avoidance' Benefits to be quantified with ownership in the Benefit Register. The template can also include the associated SO's to ensure alignment is achieved/understood at the outset. The template can be edited by the BM to ensure it captures the advantages and disadvantages of change. The following words have been used with a degree of success[28]:

Benefits: If you need help articulating this section of the form, contact the BM [email address].	We want to know as a matter of priority in the context of Benefits Management: • Does this change improve a business process that saves the End Users time? If yes, how much time is saved (i.e. per individual and how many individuals if known)? And, whose time is saved (i.e. in what team or area of the workforce)? And/or • Does this change save money?

1.13.4 Business Change Impact Assessment (BCIA). The BCIA starts the development of change planning and ensures the implications of change can be actively managed. The BCIA defines how change can impact on the End Users as they transition between the as-is and to-be states. The BCIA is produced by the Business Change (BCHG) Team, recording the advantages and disadvantages felt by the End Users. The BM uses the information to spot Benefit Indicators.functions of the business and can incorporate the 'length of time' to achieve an action in the [old system name] so the information is available for comparisons with [new system name] later.

1.13.5 HO Approach. Benefits Management in the HO identified several 'cost avoidance' Benefits when converging multiple systems into a single cloud infrastructure/solution. The work would be undertaken for each of the systems if not being converted into a single solution (i.e. avoidance of: re-engineering of on premise systems, procurement, annual security assurance, other). The work was successfully re-used in the FCDO to identify new, emergent Benefits that had not been previously captured for a CI[29].

---

28 If the section is being ignored by the author of the change request, the BM (while sitting in on the design authority and board) can remind the stakeholders that the organisation is Benefits Led and Benefits identification should be borne in mind. Para 1.11.2 refers.

29 Examples are provided at Section 11.

1.13.6 Underspend. Monitoring 'in-year' programme implementation costs can identify an underspend. Depending on the scenario the underspend can be recorded as a Cash or Non-Cash Releasing Benefit and be added to the Gross Benefit Forecast. See para 2.6.7.

1.13.7 Back-office Technology/Services. CIs and the portfolio office will want to ascertain/understand the cost breakdown of back-office technology and services, to help identify the Benefits of clustering, transformation, merger, integration. For example, working with the HR Function, the FTE baseline pre-merger of organisations can identify duplicated roles post-merger (i.e. 10 FBPs in department A, 10 FBPs in department B, all using separate systems and processes, when merged into a single system and process will identify savings opportunities).

1.13.8 Licensing. Commercial, finance and the software provider review spend on licensing to ensure VfM. Reduced run costs, for example, in respect to licensing, will increase the Gross and Net Benefit Profiles. See example at para 2.5.9. Regular reviews of the EBP (the EBP is explained in part 2) will capture the cost adjustments so that appropriate action is taken in the Benefit Register.

1.13.9 Finance and Cost Management (i.e. Cost Optimisation). There are opportunities to reduce the run costs. For example, all the environments need not be running 24/7, 365 days of the year. Controlling access to environments when they are needed reduces the associated costs. The software provider finance director can confirm (a) spend on environments prior to scheduling them (b) spend on environments after schedules had been implemented (c) the difference between both can consist of both Cash Releasing and Non-Cash Releasing Benefits. See para 2.5.7.

1.13.10 Guided Learning. Guided learning videos show the End Users how to operate a new system. The End Users, across the functions of the business, assist in the development of the videos. There could be many videos, business functions and End Users involved. The point being, those End Users are likely to have a good knowledge of new/old business processes between the new/old systems. They can be approached by the BM when identifying Benefit Indicators between the systems and processes.

1.13.11 The software provider finance director is able to confirm whether the CI/organisation has received reduced costs for the unit price of cloud services. If so, Benefits Management applies.

1.13.12 Image 5 situates some of the opportunities by framing them around the Business Case and delivery phases.

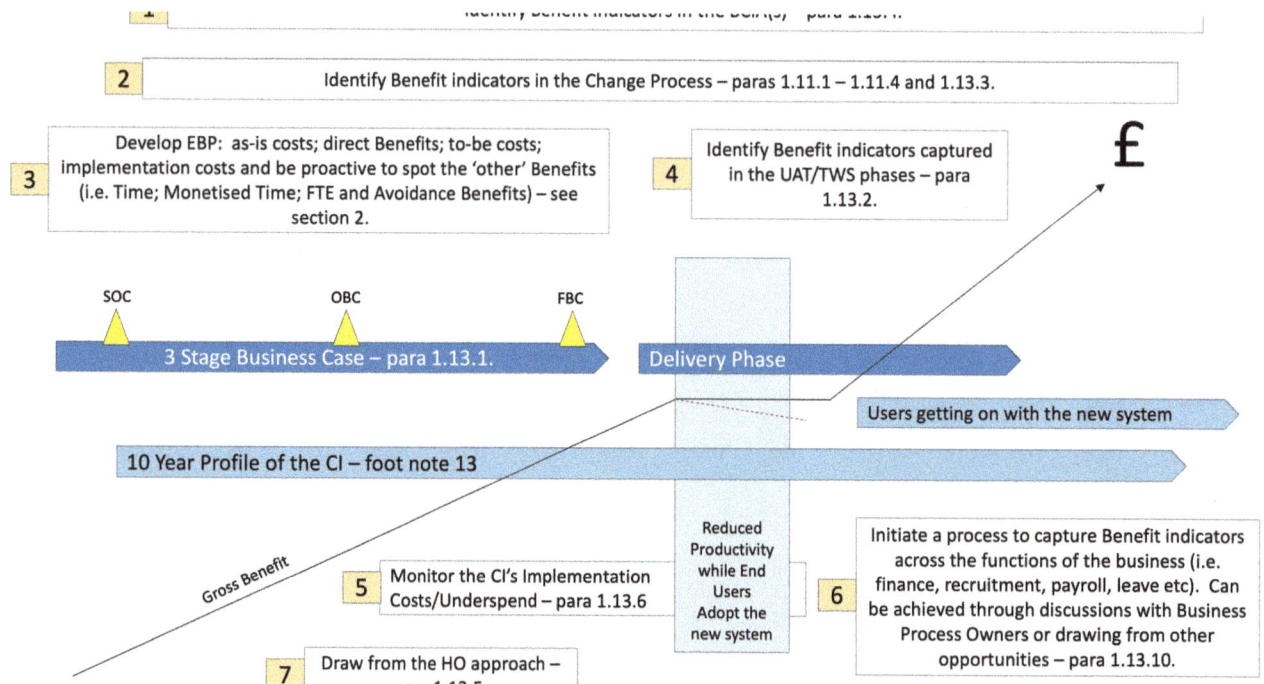

IMAGE 5 *Managing Benefits – Opportunities.*

1.14 Documentation

1.14.1 The following suite of Benefits-related documents are produced by the BM on behalf of the CI (i.e. a programme or, an independent work package or project that sits outside of a programme). An example of a BM work schedule can be seen at para 5.3; it shows the length of time that can be reasonably expected to produce the documents by an experienced BM and, is drawn from experience.

a. Benefit Management Strategy (BMS). The BMS addresses the 'what' and the 'why' for Benefits Management. It describes the approach, the strategic context, strategic alignment, frequency of reporting, roles and responsibilities and, defines how Benefits will be managed by the CI throughout the business-change lifecycle. The Benefit Map ought to be included within the strategy as an Annex because both Map/Strategy are strategic-facing documents. Producing them together is advised. The BMS is 'quite' static, therefore a good BMS need only change if the strategic context changes, but periodic reviews/checks are recommended.

b. Benefit Map. Produced as part of the BMS, the Benefit Map is a pictorial representation of the business and enabling changes on which Benefit realisation depends; it demonstrates how the CI contributes to the achievement of organisational (including strategic) objectives. The Benefit Map is 'quite' static therefore a good Map need only change if the strategic context changes, but periodic reviews/checks are recommended.

c. BRP. Contains the 'how' (i.e. how we identify, quantify, measure and report the Benefits). The BRP provides a consolidated view of all the Benefits, their dependencies and expected realisation timelines. It is the baseline against which the forecasting and realisation of Benefits is tracked and monitored[30]. The BRP is 'less' static therefore continuous reviews and iterations are expected.

d. Benefit Profiles. The Benefit Profiles describe the Benefits with their attributes and dependencies. The BM works closely with a range of stakeholders to identify, define and quantify the Benefit Profiles with ownership, recording them in the Benefit Register. Key attributes of a Benefit Profile include: ID; name; description; formula; baseline; target; Benefit. A detailed list with examples and explanations can be seen at section 4.

e. Benefit Register. A consolidation of all the Benefit Profiles and other Benefits-related data (see sections 5 and 9). The Benefit Register should be consistent with the portfolio office and is used to inform governance arrangements and reporting requirements (i.e. steering boards and transformation boards). It provides a central repository and single source of the truth, enabling dynamic updates when changes occur.

1.14.2 All documents are to be maintained in a digital repository so that they are readily available, accessible and version controlled.

---

30 Practically speaking: Summarised costs and Benefits generated using this guide will inform and structure the CI's BRP. The BRP is iterative, so the information provides a baseline (i.e. where we are now) that is recorded at the time of writing or updating the BRP document. Experience shows a good BRP is informed through aggregated Benefits data pulled from the Benefit Register; otherwise, the BRP can become an underwhelming cut/paste and duplication of information from the BMS for example.

Economic Benefit Profile (EBP)

2.1 Introduction

2.1.1 Each CI will have its costs and Benefits recorded in different formats but the BM is advised to develop the EBP in the format presented in this guide. The EBP consists of structured/owned monetised values including Costs, Benefits and Dis-Benefits. The EBP is an important tool for the BM because it calculates the Gross and Net[31] Benefit Actual and Forecast (i.e. the EBP is the Benefits Calculation for the CI). The BM works with finance/commercial departments, the PMO/PSO FBP, and the portfolio office, drawing information from them to inform the EBP. This section of *The Benefit Manager's Desktop Step-by-Step Guide* builds an EBP by incorporating examples from live scenarios to demonstrate its use.

2.1.2 A template EBP containing populated examples can be seen at Image 6. The format of each monetised field has been simplified as follows: £MMM,TTT. HHH.

2.1.3 Its use reaches beyond the CI. For example, portfolio offices in the CQC and MOD directed their CIs to use the EBP to bring consistency of reporting monetised values across their portfolios and the FCDO is using it currently. The EBP is used by the PMO FBP when undertaking quarterly reports to the IPA/GMPP. Confidence, trust, and access to the information improved as a result. The template itself is quite simple and can be adapted to suit the needs of the CI or organisation (i.e. a BM decides 'because of the nature of the business' to incorporate 'income generation' as a new section, after the 'Other Benefits').

---

31 His Majesty's Treasury Green Book states: 'Estimating Benefits means they can be compared with costs and net benefit can be calculated (i.e. Benefits once costs have been taken into account or netted off).'

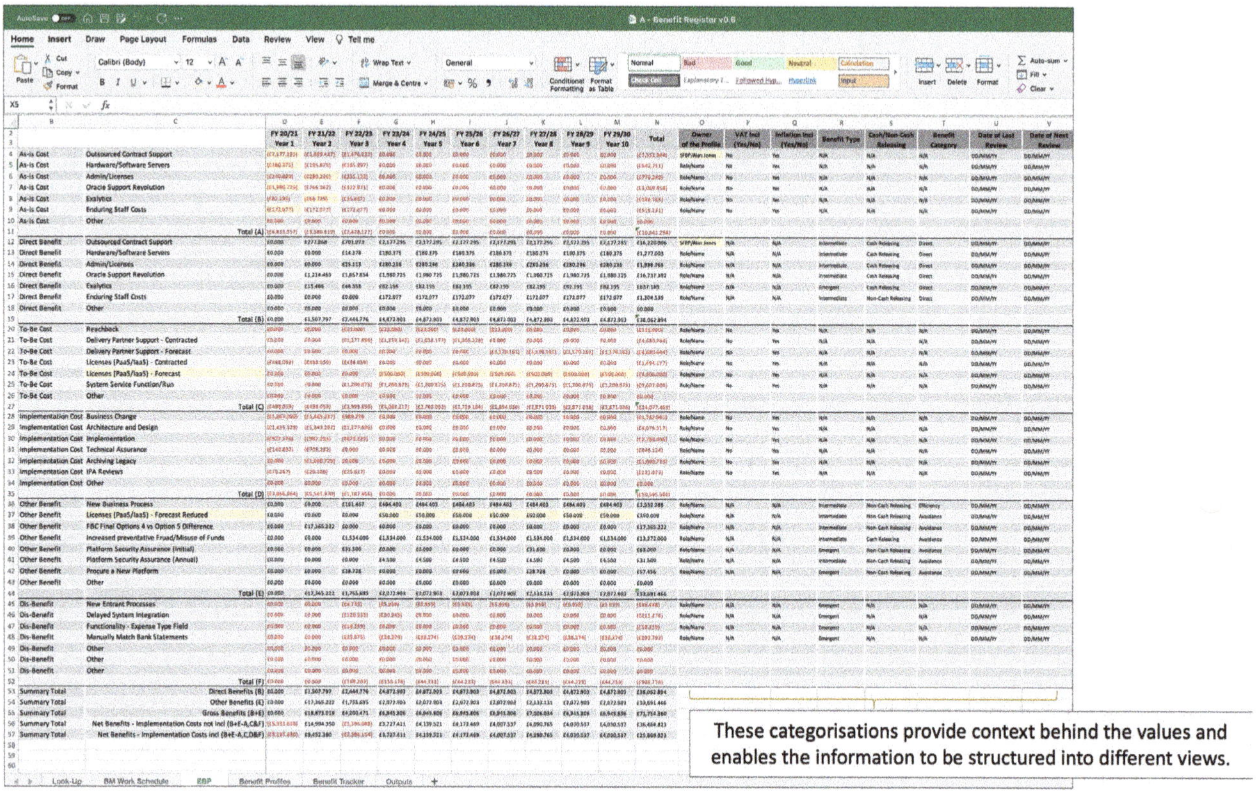

These categorisations provide context behind the values and enables the information to be structured into different views.

IMAGE 6 *Template EBP.*

2.2 Structure/Order of the EBP

2.2.1 The minimum structure/order of the EBP is as follows.

Section	Name	Description
(a)	(b)	(c)
A	Current 'as-is' Costs	Total spend on current contracts and associated support for legacy system(s) being replaced by a new system/solution.
B	Direct Benefits	When spend on 'as-is' contracts cease, the savings are recorded year-on-year. They can be Cash Releasing or Non-Cash Releasing. For example, savings on resources that were supporting the legacy system are likely to be Non-Cash Releasing if those resources are retained within the department and allocated work on other priorities. Savings from as-is costs are also called 'Direct Benefits'.
C	Future 'to-be' Costs	Spend on new contracts supporting the new system(s). Also called 'Run Costs'.
D	Implementation Costs	Money spent by the CI itself (i.e. project, programme, work package) to deliver new products and services (i.e. procure, design, develop, deliver a new IT system).

Section	Name	Description
(a)	(b)	(c)
E	Other Benefits	Other monetised Benefits resulting from the use or implementation of new system(s). For example, monetised time savings and cost-avoidance Benefits that are Cash Releasing or Non-Cash Releasing and not related to the Direct Benefits explained in row 'B' above.
F	Dis-Benefits	Disadvantages of the new system(s) that have been monetised.
G	Calculation	Used to identify Gross and Net Benefits.

TABLE 2 *Structure/Order of the EBP.*

2.2.2 The BM is responsible for the development and maintenance of the EBP.

2.2.3 The EBP sits in the Benefit Register document in its own worksheet called 'EBP'.

2.2.4 Gross and Net Benefit values generated by the EBP quantify the Economic End Benefit on the CI's Benefit Map. For example:

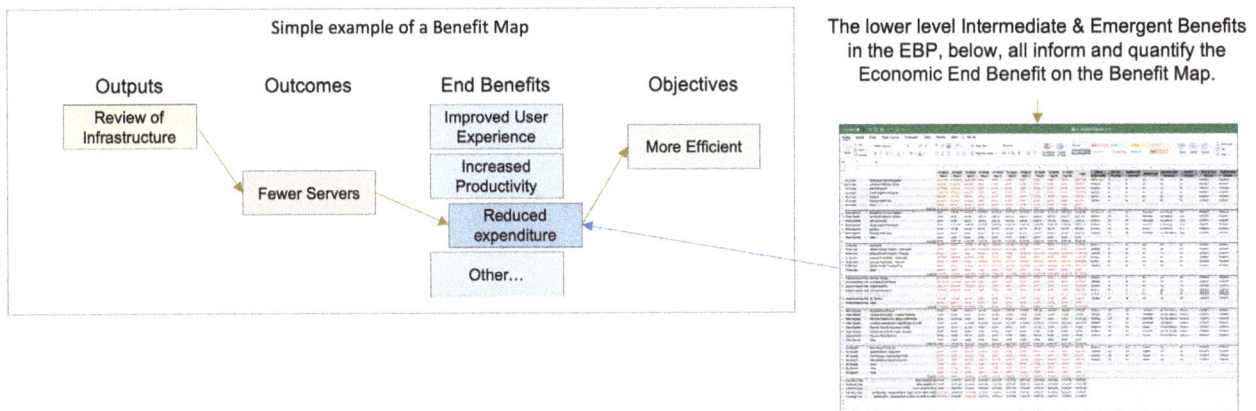

IMAGE 7 *EBP informing the Economic End Benefit on the CI's Benefit Map.*

2.2.5 Let us now look at each element of the EBP.

2.3 Current 'as-is' Costs (A)

2.3.1 The table at Image 8 is calculating the 'as-is' costs of the CI. As-is costs are the organisation's total, routine spend on current contracts and associated support for a legacy system that is being replaced by a new system, for example. The values are seen in red because they represent spend. They will be subtracted from the Gross Benefits to inform the Net Benefits.

		Previous Years
	Current Year (also called 'in-year')	
		Future Forecast

		FY 20/21 Year 1	FY 21/22 Year 2	FY 22/23 Year 3	FY 23/24 Year 4	FY 24/25 Year 5	FY 25/26 Year 6	FY 26/27 Year 7	FY 27/28 Year 8	FY 28/29 Year 9	FY 29/30 Year 10	Total	Owner of the Profile
As-is Cost	Outsourced Contract Support	(£2,177.295)	(£1,899.427)	(£1,476.222)	£0.000	£0.000	£0.000	£0.000	£0.000	£0.000	£0.000	(£5,552.944)	SFBP/Alan Jones
As-is Cost	Hardware/Software Servers	(£180.375)	(£195.879)	(£165.997)	£0.000	£0.000	£0.000	£0.000	£0.000	£0.000	£0.000	(£542.251)	Role/Name
As-is Cost	Admin/Licenses	(£240.890)	(£280.236)	(£255.123)	£0.000	£0.000	£0.000	£0.000	£0.000	£0.000	£0.000	(£776.248)	Role/Name
As-is Cost	Oracle Support Revolution	(£1,980.725)	(£766.262)	(£322.871)	£0.000	£0.000	£0.000	£0.000	£0.000	£0.000	£0.000	(£3,069.858)	Role/Name
As-is Cost	Exalytics	(£82.195)	(£66.729)	(£35.837)	£0.000	£0.000	£0.000	£0.000	£0.000	£0.000	£0.000	(£184.761)	Role/Name
As-is Cost	Enduring Staff Costs	(£172.077)	(£173.077)	(£172.077)	£0.000	£0.000	£0.000	£0.000	£0.000	£0.000	£0.000	(£516.231)	Role/Name
As-is Cost	Other	£0.000	£0.000	£0.000	£0.000	£0.000	£0.000	£0.000	£0.000	£0.000	£0.000	£0.000	
	Total (A)	(£4,833.557)	(£3,380.610)	(£2,428.127)	£0.000	£0.000	£0.000	£0.000	£0.000	£0.000	£0.000	(£10,642.294)	

IMAGE 8 *As-is Costs.*

2.3.2 There could be numerous stakeholders and departments across the business tracking different elements of as-is costs for varying reasons. The BM is to identify and liaise with them (i.e. the FBP embedded within the finance department who is responsible for tracking spend, other) to develop this part of the EBP.

2.3.3 Stakeholders contributing to the development of as-is costs (because they are the authoritative source of the information) own the information they provide to the BM. The BM undertakes reviews at agreed frequency with the owner to maintain the accuracy of the EBP. It is important to capture the role of the owner to be able to identify their successors when the owner leaves post. It is the role that owns the information that is provided by the current incumbent.

2.3.4 As-is costs are likely to reduce across the years. On occasion, they may increase for justified reasons provided by the owner. This point becomes pertinent in the next section of the EBP called the Direct Benefits.

2.3.5 The as-is costs inform the Economic Case within the Business Case. The Business Case breaks down the as-is costs for accountability/transparency; they can be structured in accordance with Image 8 and include the owner of the cost profiles. If this guidance is not followed, as-is costs come without ownership, they become subjective, and confidence in the information is eroded. Structuring them with agreed ownership as shown saves resources (time/cost) to achieve it later.

2.3.6 The BM reports variances between the EBP/Business Case as-is cost as directed by governance arrangements employed by the CI.

2.3.7 An endorsed Business Case triggers activities that see a reduction in as-is costs/ spend on legacy systems and associated support. The owner is best placed to confirm/agree with the BM when this happens. The highlighted fields in the table represent the agreed point in time. The BM can then calculate the subsequent year-on-year savings across the 10-year profile of the CI. The BM explains this process to the owner of the as-is cost profiles and presents them with the information for collaboration/agreement to develop the Direct Benefits within the EBP.

2.4 Direct Benefits (B)

2.4.1 The table at Image 9 is calculating the savings from closure of 'as-is' contracts and associated support for the legacy system(s). These savings are called 'Direct Benefits'. They can be either Cash Releasing or Non-Cash Releasing.

Previous Years													
Current Year (also called 'in-year')													
Future Forecast													

		FY 20/21 Year 1	FY 21/22 Year 2	FY 22/23 Year 3	FY 23/24 Year 4	FY 24/25 Year 5	FY 25/26 Year 6	FY 26/27 Year 7	FY 27/28 Year 8	FY 28/29 Year 9	FY 29/30 Year 10	Total	Owner of the Profile
Direct Benefit	Outsourced Contract Support	£0.000	£277.868	£701.073	£2,177.295	£2,177.295	£2,177.295	£2,177.295	£2,177.295	£2,177.295	£2,177.295	£16,220.006	SFBP/Alan Jones
Direct Benefit	Hardware/Software Servers	£0.000	£0.000	£14.378	£180.375	£180.375	£180.375	£180.375	£180.375	£180.375	£180.375	£1,277.003	Role/Name
Direct Benefit	Admin/Licenses	£0.000	£0.000	£25.113	£280.236	£280.236	£280.236	£280.236	£280.236	£280.236	£280.236	£1,986.765	Role/Name
Direct Benefit	Oracle Support Revolution	£0.000	£1,214.463	£1,657.854	£1,980.725	£1,980.725	£1,980.725	£1,980.725	£1,980.725	£1,980.725	£1,980.725	£16,737.392	Role/Name
Direct Benefit	Exalytics	£0.000	£15.466	£46.358	£82.195	£82.195	£82.195	£82.195	£82.195	£82.195	£82.195	£637.189	Role/Name
Direct Benefit	Enduring Staff Costs	£0.000	£0.000	£0.000	£172.077	£172.077	£172.077	£172.077	£172.077	£172.077	£172.077	£1,204.539	Role/Name
Direct Benefit	Other	£0.000	£0.000	£0.000	£0.000	£0.000	£0.000	£0.000	£0.000	£0.000	£0.000	£0.000	
	Total (B) £0.000		£1,507.797	£2,444.776	£4,872.903	£4,872.903	£4,872.903	£4,872.903	£4,872.903	£4,872.903	£4,872.903	£38,062.894	

IMAGE 9 *Direct Benefits.*

2.4.2 The BM is to review Images 8 and 9 to understand how the Direct Benefits are calculated. Generally, when spend on current contracts and associated support start reducing (the highlighted fields in Image 8 represent the agreed point in time with the owner of the cost profile), the savings can then be recorded year-on-year across the life of the CI as seen in Image 9. For example:

a. Hardware/Software Servers (Image 8): Year 1 start point £180.375k. Year 2 costs increased for a justified reason, so no saving is recorded in year 2 (Image 9). Back to Image 8, year 3 costs reduced below the start point in year 1 to £165.997k so £14.378k is recorded in year 3 (Image 9). Back to Image 8 again, year 4 costs are reduced to £0; the associated spend on this item is now removed; £180.375k can then be recorded in years 4–10 as shown in Image 9.

2.4.3 The owners of the Direct Benefit Profiles are the same individuals owning the as-is cost profiles. An example is provided in Images 8 and 9 'Owner of the Profile' column so the reader can understand what is meant by this.

2.4.4 New, Direct Benefits that were not identified in the Business Case will be categorised in the EBP as 'Emergent Benefits' (see Image 6 'Benefit Type' column). Direct Benefits that have been identified within the Business Case will be categorised 'Intermediate Benefits'. Emergent and Intermediate Benefits contribute to and quantify the Economic End Benefit of the CI as shown in Image 7.

2.4.5 The Direct Benefits inform the Economic Case within the Business Case. The Business Case breaks down the Direct Benefits/savings for accountability/ transparency; they can be structured in accordance with Image 9 <u>and include the owner of the Benefit Profiles</u>. If this guidance is not followed, 'perceived' benefits in the Business Case come without ownership, they become subjective and confidence in the information is eroded. Structuring them with agreed ownership as shown saves resources (time/cost) to achieve it later.

2.4.6 The Direct Benefits in Image 9 do not represent full Benefit Profiles. Each of the monetised value fields represent a single field of a Benefit Profile. For example, if you count the Direct Benefit values/fields, there are 50 of them. When they are copied into the Benefit Profiles worksheet in the Benefit Register and merged with the other metadata and categorisations (see Table 4), they become 50 Benefit Profiles[32].

2.4.7 When the Direct Benefits in the EBP have been updated with the owner of the Benefit Profiles, the Benefit Profiles themselves are to be updated concurrently. This is an important point to bear in mind in that the BM is to maintain the EBP worksheet and the Benefit Profiles worksheet in the Benefit Register together.

2.5 Future 'to-be' Costs (C)

2.5.1 The table at Image 10 is calculating the future to-be costs of the CI. The future to-be costs are also called run costs. Run costs are the organisation's total, routine spend on future contracts and associated support for the new systems or solutions. The values are seen in red because they represent spend. They will be subtracted from the Gross Benefits to inform the Net Benefits.

Previous Years														
Current Year (also called 'in-year')														
Future Forecast														
					FY 20/21 Year 1	**FY 21/22 Year 2**	**FY 22/23 Year 3**	**FY 23/24 Year 4**	**FY 24/25 Year 5**	**FY 25/26 Year 6**	**FY 26/27 Year 7**	**FY 27/28 Year 8**	**FY 28/29 Year 9**	**FY 29/30 Year 10**	**Total**	**Owner of the Profile**
To-Be Cost	Reachback	£0.000	£0.000	(£23.000)	(£23,000)	(£23,000)	(£23,000)	(£23,000)	£0.000	£0.000	£0.000	(£115.000)	Role/Name
To-Be Cost	Delivery Partner Support - Contracted	£0.000	£0.000	(£1,277.896)	(£1,359.342)	(£1,038.177)	(£1,005.229)	£0.000	£0.000	£0.000	£0.000	(£4,680,644)	Role/Name
To-Be Cost	Delivery Partner Support - Forecast	£0.000	£0.000	£0.000	£0.000	£0.000	£0.000	(£1,170.101)	(£1,170.101)	(£1,170.101)	(£1,170.101)	(£4,680,644)	Role/Name
To-Be Cost	Licenses (PaaS/IaaS) - Contracted	(£498.059)	(£498.059)	(£498.059)	£0.000	£0.000	£0.000	£0.000	£0.000	£0.000	£0.000	(£1,494.177)	Role/Name
To-Be Cost	Licenses (PaaS/IaaS) - Forecast	£0.000	£0.000	£0.000	(£500.000)	(£500.000)	(£500.000)	(£500.000)	(£500.000)	(£500.000)	(£500.000)	(£3,500.000)	Role/Name
To-Be Cost	System Service Function/Run	£0.000	£0.000	(£1,200.875)	(£1,200.875)	(£1,200.875)	(£1,200.875)	(£1,200.875)	(£1,200.875)	(£1,200.875)	(£1,200.875)	(£9,607.000)	Role/Name
To-Be Cost	Other	£0.000	£0.000	£0.000	£0.000	£0.000	£0.000	£0.000	£0.000	£0.000	£0.000		
	Total (C)	(£498.059)	(£498.059)	(£2,999.830)	(£3,083.217)	(£2,762.052)	(£2,729.104)	(£2,894.036)	(£2,871.036)	(£2,871.036)	(£2,871.036)	(£24,077.465)	

IMAGE 10 *Future 'to-be' Costs.*

---

32 Para 5.5 shows the BM how to create the Benefit Profiles. Para 5.6 shows the BM how to populate the Benefit Profiles.

2.5.2 There could be numerous stakeholders and departments across the business tracking different elements of run costs for varying reasons. The BM is to identify and liaise with them (i.e. a Commercial SME in the Commercial Department who is supporting the CI and has access to the associated contracts and spend forecast) to develop this part of the EBP.

2.5.3 Stakeholders contributing to the development of run costs (because they are the authoritative source of the information) own the information they provide to the BM. The BM undertakes reviews at agreed frequency with the owner to maintain the accuracy of the EBP. It is important to capture the role of the owner to be able to identify their successors when the owner leaves post. It is the role that owns the information that is provided by the current incumbent.

2.5.4 Run costs can include an element of what could be considered as-is costs (i.e. reach back) because access to information/archive in the legacy/closed systems, could be required post closure of those systems and the associated spend will continue; these are best structured in the run costs.

2.5.5 The run costs inform the Economic Case within the Business Case. The Business Case breaks down the run costs for accountability/transparency; they can be structured in accordance with Image 10 and include the owner of the cost profile. If this guidance is not followed, run costs come without ownership, they become subjective and confidence in the information is eroded. Structuring them with agreed ownership as shown saves resources (time/cost) in achieving it later.

2.5.6 The BM reports variances between EBP/Business Case run cost as directed by governance arrangements employed by the CI.

2.5.7 Convergence of on-premises systems into a single cloud solution provides opportunities to further reduce the run cost (i.e. the portfolio office may impose Cost Optimisation/Finance Cost Management targets to drive down cost of cloud solutions/computing across the portfolio). A CI in the HO employed this approach, targeting significant savings across the 10-year profile, and employed a Cost/Finance Management SME/Architect to implement change to deliver the targets[33]. For example, all the environments need not be running 24/7, 365 days of the year. Controlling access to environments when they

---

33 Savings from such approaches are deemed to be Cash-Releasing Efficiencies if money was secured/contracted for the purpose but then subsequently reduced.

are needed reduces the associated costs. A CI employing this approach could draw learning outcomes of use right across the portfolio.

2.5.8 Experience shows it is helpful to structure 'contracted' and 'forecasted' serials on separate lines. One example why is explained in the next paragraph.

2.5.9 Reference to 'Licences (PaaS/IaaS) – Forecast' in Image 10 – Scenario: During a review with the owner of the highlighted profile, the forecast was reduced from the £550k recorded in the Business Case, to £500k through negotiation between the authority and the service provider. The difference can be recorded as either (a) a Non-Cash Releasing Cost Avoidance Benefit if the value was a recorded/reported forecast but funds had not been secured/contracted for the purpose or (b) if funds had been secured/contracted the difference would be a Cash-Releasing Efficiency Benefit. If the Benefit was not the result of collaboration, for example, the funds were secured but overstated, the resulting Benefit would be Cash Releasing and Avoidance. The point being, when building the elements of the EBP, step back and draw insights/learning outcomes from them – you could be staring at Benefit opportunities but missing them.

2.6 Implementation Costs (D)

2.6.1 The table at Image 11 is calculating the implementation costs of the CI. Implementation costs are those costs associated with delivering the new systems and implementing change (i.e. they are costs incurred by the CI itself). The values are seen in red because they represent spend.

		Previous Years										
		Current Year (also called 'in-year')										
		Future Forecast										

		FY 20/21 Year 1	FY 21/22 Year 2	FY 22/23 Year 3	FY 23/24 Year 4	FY 24/25 Year 5	FY 25/26 Year 6	FY 26/27 Year 7	FY 27/28 Year 8	FY 28/29 Year 9	FY 29/30 Year 10	Total	Owner of the Profile
Implementation Cost	Business Change	(£3,267.000)	(£1,485.237)	£989.276	£0.000	£0.000	£0.000	£0.000	£0.000	£0.000	£0.000	(£1,762.961)	Role/Name
Implementation Cost	Architecture and Design	(£1,455.329)	(£1,343.292)	(£1,277.896)	£0.000	£0.000	£0.000	£0.000	£0.000	£0.000	£0.000	(£4,076.517)	Role/Name
Implementation Cost	Implementation	(£927.576)	(£987.291)	(£873.229)	£0.000	£0.000	£0.000	£0.000	£0.000	£0.000	£0.000	(£2,788.096)	Role/Name
Implementation Cost	Technical Assurance	(£140.892)	(£705.232)	£0.000	£0.000	£0.000	£0.000	£0.000	£0.000	£0.000	£0.000	(£846.124)	Role/Name
Implementation Cost	Archiving Legacy	£0.000	(£1,000.729)	£0.000	£0.000	£0.000	£0.000	£0.000	£0.000	£0.000	£0.000	(£1,000.729)	Role/Name
Implementation Cost	IPA Reviews	(£75.267)	(£20.189)	(£25.617)	£0.000	£0.000	£0.000	£0.000	£0.000	£0.000	£0.000	(£121.073)	Role/Name
Implementation Cost	Other	£0.000	£0.000	£0.000	£0.000	£0.000	£0.000	£0.000	£0.000	£0.000	£0.000	£0.000	
	Total (D)	(£3,866.064)	(£5,541.970)	(£1,187.466)	£0.000	£0.000	£0.000	£0.000	£0.000	£0.000	£0.000	(£10,595.500)	

IMAGE 11 *Implementation Costs.*

2.6.2 Implementation costs can be subtracted from the Gross Benefit to inform the Net Benefit, but some organisations decide not to do so because they represent 'one-off' spend. The BM is advised to take direction on the agreed approach from the portfolio office in conjunction with those individual(s) who track spend on implementation costs (i.e. the PMO/PSO FBP).

2.6.3 Contingency costs (i.e. an allowance for the cost of residual risks that cannot be avoided, shared or managed), can be built into the CI's implementation costs if required, when developing the Business Case. Advice can be taken from the Economic Advisors when developing the Business Case.

2.6.4 Stakeholders contributing to the development of implementation costs (because they are the authoritative source of the information) own the information they provide to the BM. The BM undertakes reviews at agreed frequency with the owner to maintain the accuracy of the EBP. It is important to capture the role of the owner to be able to identify their successors when the owner leaves post. It is the role that owns the information that is provided by the current incumbent.

2.6.5 The implementation costs inform the Economic Case within the Business Case. The Business Case breaks down the implementation costs for accountability/transparency; they can be structured in accordance with Image 11 and include the owner of the cost profile. If this guidance is not followed, implementation costs come without ownership, they become subjective and confidence in the information is eroded. Structuring them with agreed ownership as shown saves resources (time/cost) in achieving it later.

2.6.6 The BM reports variances between the EBP/Business Case implementation cost as directed by governance arrangements employed by the CI.

2.6.7 Monitoring 'in-year' programme implementation costs can identify an underspend. Depending on the scenario (see examples at para 1.8.1, sub para d) the underspend can be recorded as a Cash or Non-Cash Releasing Benefit and be added to the Gross Benefit Forecast.

2.6.8 The BM and owner of the implementation cost profiles are to monitor the information closely because they can frequently increase and/or decrease.

2.7 Other Benefits (E)

2.7.1 The table at Image 12 is calculating all the 'other' monetised Benefits that are not associated with the Direct Benefits in Image 9. The other Benefits consist of monetised time calculations (the process has been explained above) and any other Benefit with a monetary value that has been identified by the BM/CI. These other, monetised Benefits can be either Cash Releasing or Non-Cash Releasing.

		FY 20/21 Year 1	FY 21/22 Year 2	FY 22/23 Year 3	FY 23/24 Year 4	FY 24/25 Year 5	FY 25/26 Year 6	FY 26/27 Year 7	FY 27/28 Year 8	FY 28/29 Year 9	FY 29/30 Year 10	Total	Owner of the Profile
Other Benefit	New Business Process	£0.000	£0.000	£161.467	£484.403	£484.403	£484.403	£484.403	£484.403	£484.403	£484.403	£3,552.288	Role/Name
Other Benefit	Licenses (PaaS/IaaS) - Forecast Reduced	£0.000	£0.000	£0.000	£50.000	£50.000	£50.000	£50.000	£50.000	£50.000	£50.000	£350.000	Role/Name
Other Benefit	FBC Final Options 4 vs Option 5 Difference	£0.000	£17,365.222	£0.000	£0.000	£0.000	£0.000	£0.000	£0.000	£0.000	£0.000	£17,365.222	Role/Name
Other Benefit	Increased preventative Fruad/Misuse of Funds	£0.000	£0.000	£1,534.000	£1,534.000	£1,534.000	£1,534.000	£1,534.000	£1,534.000	£1,534.000	£1,534.000	£12,272.000	Role/Name
Other Benefit	Platform Security Assurance (Initial)	£0.000	£0.000	£31.500	£0.000	£0.000	£0.000	£0.000	£31.500	£0.000	£0.000	£63.000	Role/Name
Other Benefit	Platform Security Assurance (Annual)	£0.000	£0.000	£0.000	£4.500	£4.500	£4.500	£4.500	£4.500	£4.500	£4.500	£31.500	Role/Name
Other Benefit	Procure a New Platform	£0.000	£0.000	£28.728	£0.000	£0.000	£0.000	£0.000	£28.728	£0.000	£0.000	£57.456	Role/Name
Other Benefit	Other	£0.000	£0.000	£0.000	£0.000	£0.000	£0.000	£0.000	£0.000	£0.000	£0.000	£0.000	
	Total (£) £0.000	£17,365.222	£1,755.695	£2,072.903	£2,072.903	£2,072.903	£2,072.903	£2,133.131	£2,072.903	£2,072.903	£33,691.466		

Legend:
- Previous Years
- Current Year (also called 'in-year')
- Future Forecast

IMAGE 12 *Other Benefits.*

2.7.2 The first entry contains the monetised values generated from the new/improved business process captured at para 1.3.1 e and para 1.4.3 b. The second entry contains the Cost Avoidance Benefit that was explained at para 2.5.9 where you saw the PaaS/IaaS licences cost forecast revised down from £550k pa to £500k. The third entry is explained at para 2.7.8.

2.7.3 Stakeholders assisting the BM to quantify the Other Benefits (because they are the authoritative source of the information), own the information they provide to the BM. The BM undertakes reviews at agreed frequency with the owner to maintain the accuracy of the EBP. It is important to capture the role of the owner to be able to identify their successors when the owner leaves post. It is the role that owns the information that is provided by the current incumbent.

2.7.4 New, Other Benefits that were not identified in the Business Case will be categorised in the EBP as 'Emergent Benefits' (see Image 6 'Benefit Type' column). Other Benefits that have been identified within the Business Case will be categorised 'Intermediate Benefits'. Emergent and Intermediate Benefits contribute to and quantify the Economic End Benefit of the CI as shown in Image 7.

2.7.5 The Other Benefits inform the Economic Case within the Business Case. The Business Case breaks down the Other Benefits/savings for accountability/transparency; they can be structured in accordance with Image 12 and include the owner of the Benefit Profiles. If this guidance is not followed, 'perceived' benefits in the Business Case come without ownership, they become subjective and confidence in the information is eroded. Structuring them with agreed ownership as shown saves resources (time/cost) in achieving it later.

2.7.6 The Other Benefits in Image 12 do not represent full Benefit Profiles. Each of the monetised value fields represent a single field of a Benefit Profile. For example, if you count the Other Benefit values/fields, there are 40 of them. When they are copied into the Benefit Profiles worksheet in the Benefit Register and merged with the other metadata and categorisations (see Table 4), they become 40 Benefit Profiles[34].

2.7.7   When the Other Benefits in the EBP have been updated with the owner of the Benefit Profiles, the Benefit Profiles themselves are to be updated concurrently. This is an important point to bear in mind in that the BM is to maintain the EBP worksheet and the Benefit Profiles worksheet in the Benefit Register together.

2.7.8   Consider: A CI will likely have identified several options in the Business Case. The several options are down-selected to fewer, viable/final options as the Business Case matures. Eventually, one option (usually the recommended option) is approved. Let us assume there were 2 final options to select from. The difference between the approved option and the other final option (if the other final option cost more than the approved option) can be considered as a Non-Cash Releasing, Cost Avoidance Benefit that cannot be reinvested and be structured within the 'Other Benefits' section of the EBP. A CI in the FCDO applied this thinking, recording the avoidance Benefit in the FBC; a programme director agreed to own the Benefit Profile.

2.8 Dis-Benefits (F)

2.8.1   The table at Image 13 is calculating the Dis-Benefits of the CI. Dis-Benefits are the disadvantages or unintended outcomes resulting from change. For example, a new business process increased time taken by the End Users to complete an action because of additional steps in the new business process; an example has been shown at para 1.5 but those monetised values had not been incorporated in the Dis-Benefit examples in the EBP at Image 13 below, at the time of writing.

2.8.2   Dis-Benefits are captured and quantified in the same way as Benefits, but instead of being maximised, Dis-Benefits are minimised and kept below an agreed threshold.

2.8.3   The values are seen in red because, like spend, Dis-Benefits can be subtracted from the Gross Benefits to inform the Net Benefits. But, be careful because increased costs (i.e. run costs for example), are already netted off the Gross Benefits. If the BM also captures the increased run costs as a Dis-Benefit, the BM could inadvertently be netting them off twice.

---

34 Para 5.5 shows the BM how to create the Benefit Profiles. Para 5.6 shows the BM how to populate the Benefit Profiles.

		Previous Years												
		Current Year (also called 'in-year')												
		Future Forecast												

		FY 20/21 Year 1	FY 21/22 Year 2	FY 22/23 Year 3	FY 23/24 Year 4	FY 24/25 Year 5	FY 25/26 Year 6	FY 26/27 Year 7	FY 27/28 Year 8	FY 28/29 Year 9	FY 29/30 Year 10	Total	Owner of the Profile
Dis-Benefit	New Entrant Processes	£0.000	£0.000	(£4.725)	(£5.959)	(£5.959)	(£5.959)	(£5.959)	(£5.959)	(£5.959)	(£5.959)	(£46.448)	Role/Name
Dis-Benefit	Delayed System Integration	£0.000	£0.000	(£120.333)	(£90.945)	£0.000	£0.000	£0.000	£0.000	£0.000	£0.000	(£211.278)	Role/Name
Dis-Benefit	Functionality - Expense Type Field	£0.000	£0.000	(£18.259)	£0.000	£0.000	£0.000	£0.000	£0.000	£0.000	£0.000	(£18.259)	Role/Name
Dis-Benefit	Manually Match Bank Statements	£0.000	£0.000	(£25.875)	(£38.274)	(£38.274)	(£38.274)	(£38.274)	(£38.274)	(£38.274)	(£38.274)	(£293.793)	Role/Name
Dis-Benefit	Other	£0.000	£0.000	£0.000	£0.000	£0.000	£0.000	£0.000	£0.000	£0.000	£0.000	£0.000	
Dis-Benefit	Other	£0.000	£0.000	£0.000	£0.000	£0.000	£0.000	£0.000	£0.000	£0.000	£0.000	£0.000	
Dis-Benefit	Other	£0.000	£0.000	£0.000	£0.000	£0.000	£0.000	£0.000	£0.000	£0.000	£0.000	£0.000	
	Total (F)	£0.000	£0.000	(£169.202)	(£135.178)	(£44.233)	(£44.233)	(£44.233)	(£44.233)	(£44.233)	(£44.233)	(£569.778)	

IMAGE 13 *Dis-Benefits.*

2.8.4 Stakeholders assisting the BM to quantify the Dis-Benefits (because they are the authoritative source of the information), own the information they provide to the BM. The BM and owner of the Dis-Benefit Profiles are to monitor the information closely to help ensure they are minimised and kept below an agreed threshold. It is important to capture the role of the owner to be able to identify their successors when the owner leaves post. It is the role that owns the information that is provided by the current incumbent.

2.8.5 New, Dis-Benefits that were not identified in the Business Case will be categorised in the EBP as 'Emergent Dis-Benefits' (see Image 6 'Benefit Type' column). Dis-Benefits that have been identified within the Business Case will be categorised 'Intermediate Dis-Benefits'. Emergent and Intermediate Dis-Benefits contribute to and quantify the Economic End Benefit of the CI as shown in Image 7.

2.8.6 Dis-Benefits inform the Economic Case within the Business Case. The Business Case breaks down the Dis-Benefits for accountability/transparency; they can be structured in accordance with Image 13 <u>and include the owner of the Dis-Benefit profile</u>. If this guidance is not followed, 'perceived' Dis-Benefits in the Business Case come without ownership, they become subjective and confidence in the information is eroded. Structuring them with agreed ownership as shown saves resources (time/cost) in achieving it later.

2.8.7 The Dis-Benefits in Image 13 do not represent full Dis-Benefit Profiles. Each of the monetised value fields represent a single field of a Dis-Benefit profile. For example, if you count the Dis-Benefit values/fields, there are 19 of them. When they are copied into the Benefit Profiles worksheet in the Benefit Register and merged with the other metadata and categorisations (see Table 4), they become 19 Dis-Benefit Profiles[35].

---

35 Para 5.5 shows the BM how to create the Benefit Profiles. Para 5.6 shows the BM how to populate the Benefit Profiles.

2.8.8 When the Dis-Benefits in the EBP have been updated with the owner of the Dis-Benefit Profiles, the Dis-Benefit Profiles themselves are to be updated concurrently. This is an important point to bear in mind in that the BM is to maintain the EBP worksheet and the Benefit Profiles worksheet together.

2.9 Summary Totals (G)

2.9.1 The table at Image 14 consists of the summary totals of all the elements of the EBP so Benefits can be compared with Costs and Net Benefits can be calculated for the CI.

	FY 20/21 Year 1	FY 21/22 Year 2	FY 22/23 Year 3	FY 23/24 Year 4	FY 24/25 Year 5	FY 25/26 Year 6	FY 26/27 Year 7	FY 27/28 Year 8	FY 28/29 Year 9	FY 29/30 Year 10	Total
Summary Total — Direct Benefits (B)	£0.000	£1,507.797	£2,444.776	£4,872.903	£4,872.903	£4,872.903	£4,872.903	£4,872.903	£4,872.903	£4,872.903	£38,062.894
Summary Total — Other Benefits (E)	£0.000	£17,365.222	£1,755.695	£2,072.903	£2,072.903	£2,072.903	£2,072.903	£2,133.131	£2,072.903	£2,072.903	£33,691.466
Summary Total — Gross Benefits (B+E)	£0.000	£18,873.019	£4,200.471	£6,945.806	£6,945.806	£6,945.806	£6,945.806	£7,006.034	£6,945.806	£6,945.806	£71,754.360
Summary Total — Net Benefits - Implementation Costs not incl (B+E-A,C&F)	(£5,331.616)	£14,994.350	(£1,396.688)	£3,727.411	£4,139.521	£4,172.469	£4,007.537	£4,090.765	£4,030.537	£4,030.537	£36,464.823
Summary Total — Net Benefits - Implementation Costs incl (B+E-A,C,D&F)	(£9,197.680)	£9,452.380	(£2,584.154)	£3,727.411	£4,139.521	£4,172.469	£4,007.537	£4,090.765	£4,030.537	£4,030.537	£25,869.323

Legend:
- Previous Years
- Current Year (also called 'in-year')
- Future Forecast

IMAGE 14 *Summary Totals.*

2.9.2 The Net Benefits at row 4 do not include the implementation costs; the Net Benefits at row 5 do include the implementation costs. The reason for this has been explained at para 2.6.2.

2.9.3 The structure of the summary total fields can be adapted as necessary. For example, adding 2 additional rows, (a) the FBC Gross Benefit target and (b) the difference between the FBC Gross Benefit target and the actual, quantified Gross Benefits/Forecast captured in the EBP to date with ownership, as seen in the 3rd row, can show how well the CI is performing in the identification and quantification of monetised values in the EBP as a comparator with the FBC.

2.9.4 The CI BM is advised to agree the approach to recording summary totals in the EBP with the portfolio office BM to enable consistency of reporting across the portfolio.

2.10 Considerations

2.10.1 Value-Added Tax (VAT): Payable on sales of goods and services. Recovery depends on the VAT regime that applies to the organisation. If the organisation is recovering VAT, a decision may be taken to not include it within the EBP cost profiles. If VAT is not being recovered, it should be factored into the

EBP. The CI BM is to agree the approach to recording VAT in the EBP with the portfolio office BM to enable consistency of reporting across the portfolio.

2.10.2 Inflation: An agreed rate of inflation is applied to the CI cost profiles in the EBP. The initial rate can be agreed/determined through engagements with the Economic Advisors when developing the Business Case and subsequently reviewed post FBC with the Commercial SME and FBPs who are informing the cost profiles in the EBP with the BM. The CI BM is to agree the approach to recording inflation in the EBP with the portfolio office BM to enable consistency of reporting across the portfolio[36].

2.10.3 Optimism Bias (OB): Is the proven tendency for appraisers to be over-optimistic about key project parameters, including cost profiles and Benefit delivery due to the lack of evidence or understanding of the likely impact of new interventions. The aim of adjusting for OB is to provide a more realistic assessment of the initial estimates of costs and Benefits as the Business Case develops. Adjustments for OB may be reduced as more reliable estimates are underpinned with logic and evidence. Direction can be provided from the Economic Advisors when developing the Business Case. The CI BM is to agree the approach to recording OB in the EBP with the portfolio office BM[37] to enable consistency of reporting across the portfolio.

2.10.4 A portfolio office in the MOD had successfully employed a subjective 'Risk and Maturity' approach as an alternative to OB[38]. It was undertaken quarterly and, predominantly by those CIs who had not reached the FBC. The Risk and Maturity approach is explained below.

2.11 Risk and Maturity Approach

2.11.1 CIs will, at the point of their creation, forecast a set of Benefits which they aim to achieve. At this point, the CI is likely to exist only as a basic idea and there will be risks to the realisation of the Benefit. As the CI matures, the risks

36 For example, inflation can be factored into the cost profiles/lines themselves or sit in separate lines and named 'inflation' for transparency.

37 The portfolio office BM in turn receives direction from the Economic Advisors in His Majesty's Treasury (HMT).

38 The HM Treasury Green Book states in the context of OB: 'There are currently no generic values available to be applied to Benefits; however an adjustment should be applied based on an organisation's own evidence base.' The Risk and Maturity approach employed by the MOD demonstrates applied adjustment and an approach to achieve it.

surrounding them should reduce, reflecting that the information about the initiative will gradually improve and provide better fidelity as to how Benefits will be realised.

2.11.2 The Risk and Maturity approach recognises this logic and requires a risk adjustment to be applied to forecast Benefits to generate a more accurate picture of those financial Benefits which might realistically be realised.

2.11.3 Pre FBC, each CI would be evaluated against the three-criteria subjective model shown at Table 3. The cumulative risk output is applied to the expected financial Benefits to derive an adjusted assessment. A worked example of this process is shown below.

2.11.4 Post FBC, the CI is not required to be risk adjusted unless it is determined the CI will not deliver the full Financial Benefits forecast, or if there is limited evidence of Benefit realisation.

Risk and Maturity			
(a)	(b)	(c)	(d)
	Low	Medium	High
Rationale Strength	15%	10%	0%
Plan Strength	40%	20%	0%
Delivery Risk	5%	20%	40%
Descriptions **Rationale Strength**: The strength of the idea which underpins the initiative considered with the likely Benefits. **Plan Strength**: How coherently and effectively the initiative is planned considering ownership, delivery levers and timeframe. **Delivery Risk**: How easily the plan can be implemented considering inter-intuitive dependency and clarity of evidence.			

TABLE 3 *Risk and Maturity Model.*

2.11.5 **Rationale Strength**. The idea (the why) which underpins the CI is considered with the likely Benefits.

a. **Low**: The idea or hypothesis behind the CI is difficult to understand and/or the anticipated return on investment is likely to be very limited.

b. **Medium**: The idea behind the CI is understandable and the return on investment has either Financial or Non-Financial Benefit.

c. **High**: The idea behind the CI seems obvious and there are both Financial and Non-Financial benefits.

2.11.6 **Plan Strength**. How the CI is planned to be delivered – considered against ownership, delivery levers and the anticipated timeframe between validation and delivery.

a. **Low**: It is not clear who owns delivery of the CI and there are no obvious levers to enact the CI and/or the planned concept timeframe to delivery is greater than 12 months.

b. **Medium**: There is ownership, delivery levers have been identified and are clear and the timeframe to deliver is greater than 12 months.

c. **High**: There is a strong ownership chain, delivery levers are obvious and simple and/or the planned timeframe to delivery is less than 12 months.

2.11.7 **Delivery Risk**. How easily the plan can be implemented, considering the dependency on other CIs or degree of overlap and the ability to evidence delivery.

a. **Low**: The CI is assessed to have low dependency on other projects/programmes and the CI does not share the same financial baseline as other CIs, and the CI is likely to be easily evidenced.

b. **Medium**: The CI has dependencies with other projects/programmes or the CI is considering the same financial baseline as other CIs, or it is likely to be difficult to evidence successful delivery of the CI.

c. **High**: The CI is heavily dependent on other projects/programmes to deliver first and the CI is considering the same financial baseline as other CIs and it is likely to be difficult to evidence successful delivery of the CI.

Worked Example – Enterprise Resource Planning (ERP) Programme

The programme manager, portfolio governance lead and head of the PMO undertook a quarterly risk and maturity review for the ERP Programme, to derive an adjusted assessment.

Context: The Gross Benefit Forecast is £126M. The inclusive investment costs are £47M.

During the review, the following was noted:

Rationale strength: Rationale meets the criteria for HIGH. No reduction of Benefit forecast.

Plan strength: Plan strength meets the criteria for MEDIUM. 20% reduction in Benefit forecast.

Delivery risk: Delivery risk meets the criteria for LOW. 5% reduction in Benefit forecast.

The example shows a risk stack (25%). The remaining 75% would be applied to the Gross Benefit Forecast as follows.

Risk-adjusted Gross Benefit: Gross Benefit £126M @ 75% = £94.5M.

Risk-adjusted Net Benefit: Gross Benefit £126M @ 75% = £94.5M minus £47M investment costs = £47.5M.

The risk-adjusted Gross/Net Benefits can be incorporated as a new row in the EBP summary totals (Image 14).

SECTION 3

Benefit Map

3.1 Introduction

3.1.1 The Benefit Map is a pictorial representation of the business, showing changes on which Benefit realisation depends, and how those Benefits contribute to organisational (including Strategic) Objectives.

3.1.2 The BM coordinates the development of the Benefit Map through collaboration with a combination of stakeholders from the CI and business functions receiving the change. A good Benefit Map is produced through intelligent thinking, high energy, and appropriate involvement. Do not go to the nth degree; it should take approximately 2 weeks to achieve and be limited in size (i.e. the author prefers to use a single PowerPoint slide that can be printed on A3).

3.1.3 Development starts with 'top-down' strategic direction (i.e. organisational and SOs) on the right-hand side. It is then matured 'bottom up' from the left-hand side by structuring Outputs, Outcomes, End Benefits and aligning them to the Objectives[39].

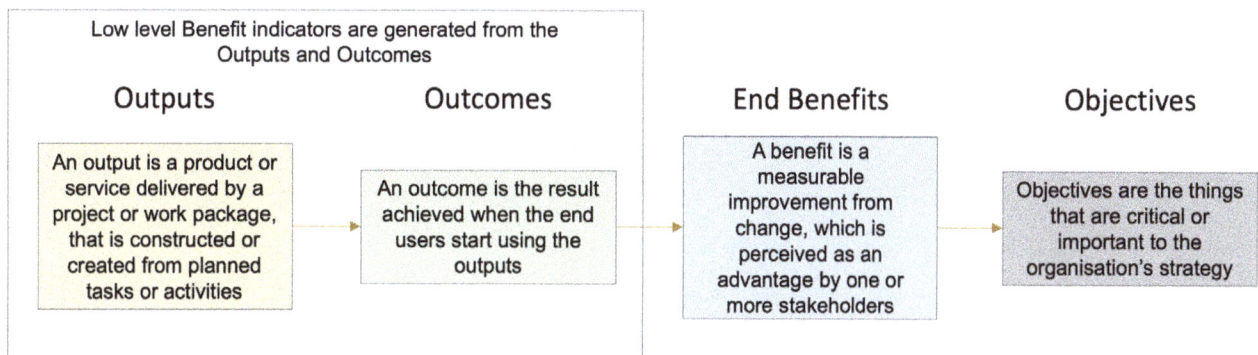

IMAGE 15 *Classic Benefit Map/Structure.*

---

39 When the End Benefits have been associated with Strategic Objectives, the alignment should be checked/reviewed with the portfolio office BM.

3.2 Template

3.2.1 Below you will find a template Benefit Map produced in PowerPoint to limit its size and help communication[40].

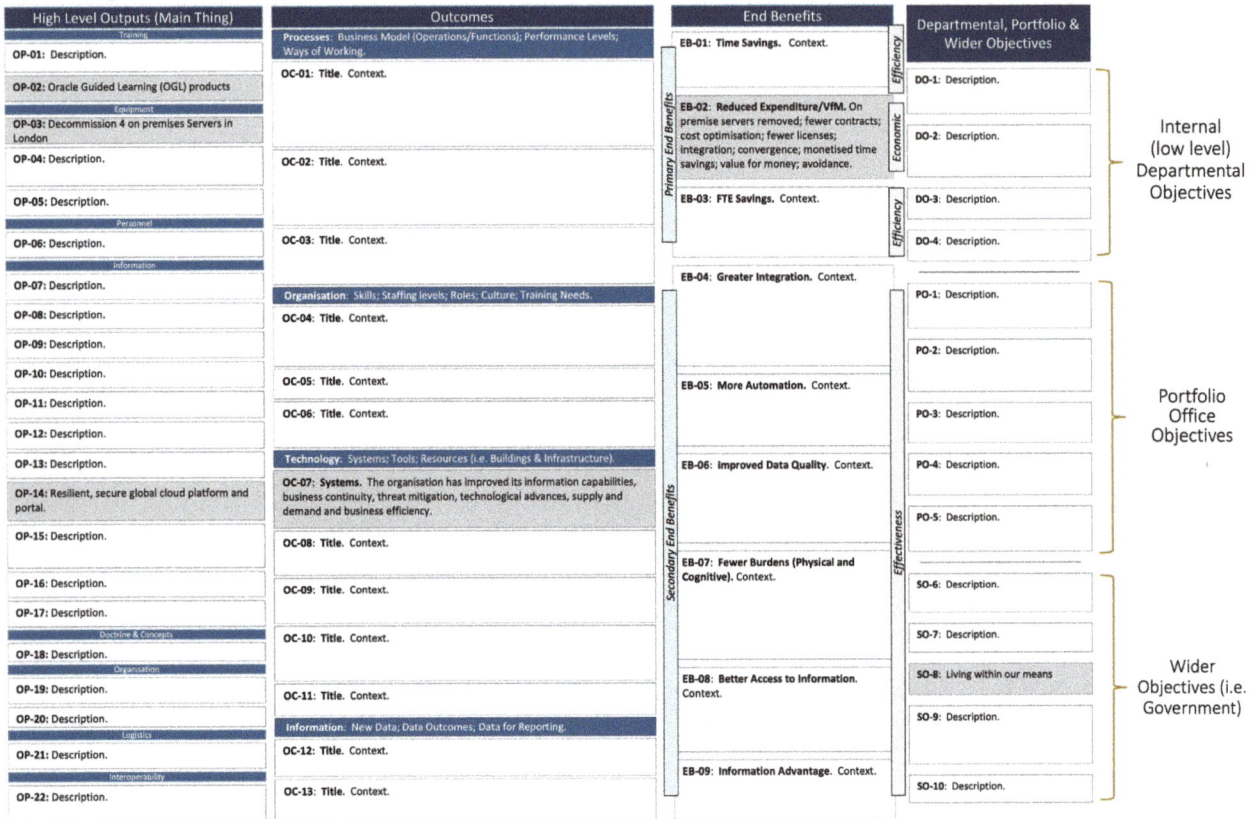

IMAGE 16 *Example - Template Benefit Map.*

3.3 Lines of Development (LoDs)

3.3.1 The outputs have been structured by LoDs. The LoDs are defined at para 3.3.3. The concept is widely used across Defence, who undertake capability management to shore up the delivery of outcomes, Benefits, and Objectives.

3.3.2 If the CI does not consider all the LoDs when defining the outputs to be delivered, it will not likely deliver the outcomes and associated End Benefits/ objectives. For example, End Users also need to be training on a new system to be able to use it competently; without training (or learning) Benefit realisation would be delayed at best or not happen at all in a worst-case scenario.

---

40 The template Benefit Map can be provided if requested by emailing this address: BRM.Mngr@hotmail.com

3.3.3 The LoDs:

    a. <u>Training</u>: The means to practise, develop and validate, the practical application of a common training/learning doctrine.

    b. <u>Equipment</u>: A physical entity (i.e. hardware, vehicle, on-premise servers).

    c. <u>Personnel</u>: The provision of personnel to deliver the organisation's outputs.

    d. <u>Information</u>: The provision of data, information and knowledge requirements and the processes designed to gather and handle data, information, and knowledge.

    e. <u>Concepts and Doctrine</u>: Concepts are the thoughts and beliefs of a capability to be used to accomplish an activity. Doctrine is an expression of the principles by which an organisation guides it actions and a codification of how activity is conducted.

    f. <u>Organisation</u>: Typically includes organisational structures (size and scope).

    g. <u>Infrastructure</u>: The provision of buildings and structures, land, estates, utilities, and facility management.

    h. <u>Logistics</u>: The planning, movement and maintenance of an entity including: acquisition, storage, transport, distribution, maintenance, evacuation and disposition of material; the transportation of personnel; the acquisition or furnishing of services, medical and health service support.

    i. <u>Interoperability</u>: Working together, connected, coherently, effectively, and efficiently to achieve an objective.

3.4 Outputs

3.4.1 An output[41] is constructed or created from planned tasks or activities[42]. The outputs have a direct relationship with the CI's outcomes and, indirect relationships with the CI's Benefits and objectives. The BM is to identify the

---

41 The outputs recorded on the left-hand side of a Benefit Map are high level (i.e. the main thing) being delivered by the work packages in a CI.

42 Outputs categorised by LoDs help to inform and capture Product Breakdown Structures (PBS) and Work Breakdown Structures (WBS) in a project delivery schedule/plan.

stakeholders working in and around the CI to capture the high-level outputs to be incorporated on the Benefit Map. For example, the CI will have structured work packages delivering products and services; to the BM these are called outputs. The work packages own the outputs they are delivering. They can be described at a high level and be structured on the left-hand side of the Benefit Map. When the Benefit Map has been endorsed, the outputs can be incorporated into their own worksheet in the Benefit Register for reporting purposes; see para 5.8.3.

3.5 Outcomes

3.5.1 The outcomes have been structured under POTI (Processes, Organisation, Technology, Information). The idea was taken from MSP but other ideas can be used/developed. The structure selected should be static where possible and not subject to future change; otherwise, the Benefit Map may need revisiting later which could have been avoided.

3.6 End Benefits

3.6.1 The End Benefits on the CI's Benefit Map are high-level, large buckets, in which to group lower-level Intermediate, Emergent and Dis-Benefits. The lower-level Benefits consists of the detail; they are the Benefit Profiles in the Benefit Register.

3.6.2 Define the End Benefits so they are very clear. Theme them up and include additional text/context. This will help to group the lower-level Benefits into the right End-Benefits buckets and reduce the number of End Benefits on the Benefit Map to provide control. For example:

   a. EB-01 (Time Savings): Do something faster; less complicated; fewer steps in the process; resourceful; not wasting time. *Efficiency.*

   b. EB-02 (Reduced Expenditure): On-premise servers removed; fewer contracts; cost optimisation; fewer licences; integration; convergence; monetised time savings; value for money. *Economic.*

   c. EB-03 (FTE Savings): Spare capacity; structured; organised; reinvestment; prioritisation; productivity; better use of resources. *Efficiency.*

d. EB-04 (More Automation): Robotics; straight-through processing; seamless electronic transactions without manual interventions; complexity hidden from the End User). *Effectiveness.*

3.7 SOs

3.7.1 SOs are the things that are critical or important to the organisation's strategy. They are delivered through a combination of BaU activities and strategic-level changes that address specific business drivers or evolving circumstances. The way in which a CI contributes to the SOs is described in the form of one or more Benefits.

3.7.2 SOs can consist of (a) internal, low level departmental objectives, (b) portfolio office objectives, (c) other. See para 5.2.2 d.

3.8 Complicated

3.8.1 The grey fields in Image 16 highlight a logical thread 'they relate to an arrow'. When the fields have been connected with arrows, the Benefit Map can appear complicated, and the logical thread cannot be seen because the fields are close together. The BM can get around that by adding additional slides to the PowerPoint pack. Each additional slide could be used to generate and communicate the connections between the outputs and outcomes, outcomes and Benefits and so on. The arrows themselves can be adapted with different colours, weighting (i.e. thickness) or dashes to add additional detail/dimensions as seen in the next image.

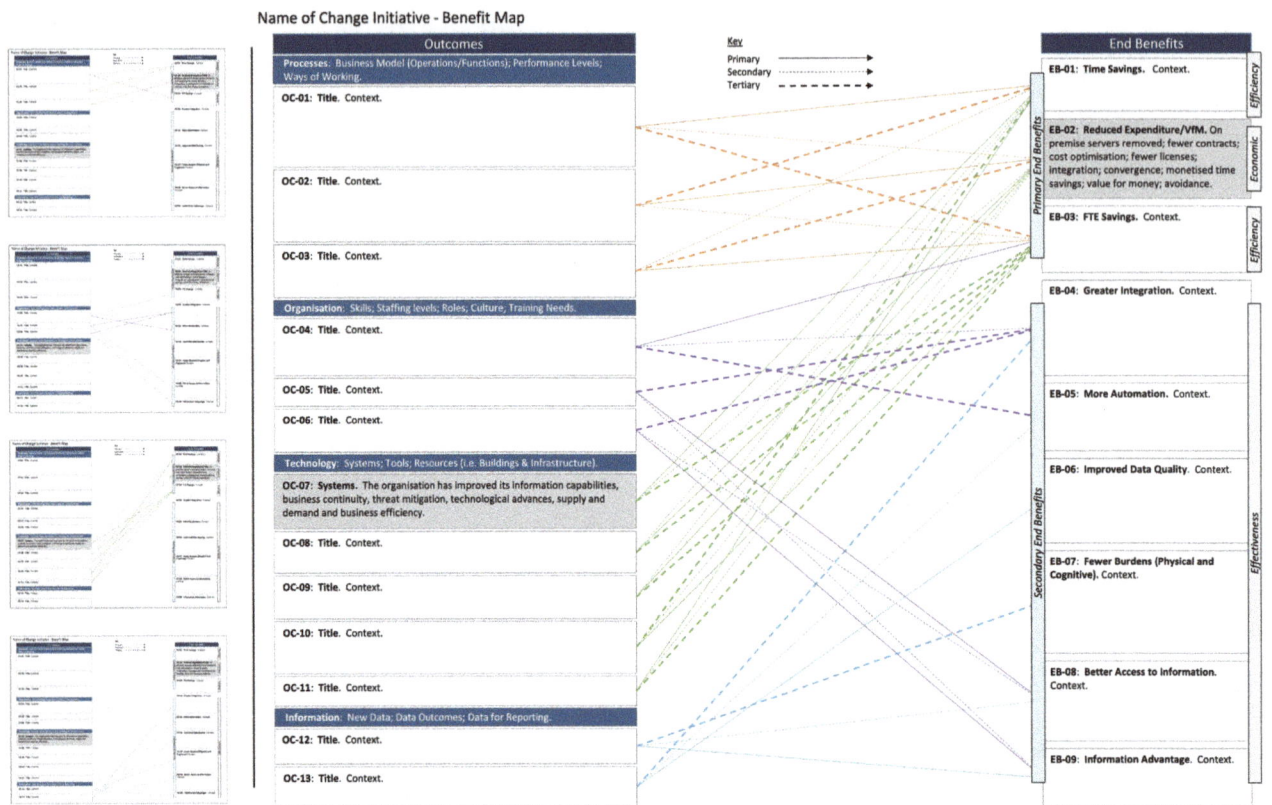

IMAGE 17 *Example – using the software to better communicate the logical thread.*

3.8.2 In the above example you can see the End Benefits have been labelled with 3E Categorisations, 'Economic, Efficiency and Effectiveness'. This helps to ensure the context of the End Benefits is understood and avoids overlap or duplication with other End Benefits. The same also applies to the low level Intermediate, and Emergent and Dis-Benefits. The Economic Benefit is concerning money so the associated values will be monetised; the Efficiency Benefits are concerning numeric values that are not monetised (i.e. time, percentage, scale, other); the Effectiveness Benefits are concerning the capabilities themselves. Effectiveness Benefits can have (a) numeric values[43], (b) objective descriptors that are 'matter of fact', or (c) qualitative descriptors that are subjective and should be kept to a minimum.

3.8.3 The End Benefits can be grouped under primary, secondary and, if necessary, tertiary End Benefits to help prioritise work and keep focus on 'the main thing'. For example, it would be nice to have x but later; y is more important and can be addressed soon; z is an absolute imperative and needs to be addressed now. If this approach is agreed at the outset, the CI and BM can better prioritise their work and provide a structured approach and timely contribution to all of the End Benefits.

---

43 Ideally, Effectiveness Benefits are to contain numeric values as far as possible to avoid the subjectivity that may arise from them.

3.8.4 It is recommended that the lower-level Intermediate and Emergent Benefits and Dis-Benefits have a primary association with an End Benefit and up to 2 more associations where appropriate; see para 1.9 and Image 3).

Benefit Profile Categorisations

4.1 Introduction

4.1.1 The lower-level Benefits are recorded in the Benefit Register. Full/completed Benefit Profiles contain a number of populated fields and categorisations that include drop-down data validations[44]; they help the BM to (a) mature each Benefit Profile, (b) improve understanding of the Benefits themselves; 'categorising the Benefits provides a deeper understanding of Benefit Management with significant learning opportunities/outcomes for the BM and stakeholders involved[45]', (c) use the information to develop PivotTables and visualisations to inform and assist reporting requirements.

4.1.2 Benefit Profile categorisations can be seen in Table 4. Each categorisation is explained with examples at the bottom of the table. The categorisations can be adapted, if required, to incorporate additional data but these are commonly used and have been defined/structured from experience and engagements across the organisations listed in the second introductory paragraph on page 1.

---

44 How to create a Data Validation is shown at para 5.5.2. Data validations are important because they provide consistency when categorising the Benefit Profiles.

45 Experience shows BMs are best placed to inform the development of an organisation's software capability used to store Benefits data, when they understand and have successfully implemented E2E Benefits Management (i.e. identify, quantify, measure, report). In other words, Excel is a good platform to support the BM in his/her development; it enables them to better inform the development of other software capabilities (not the other way round).

Type	Categorisations	Remarks
(a)	**(b)**	**(c)**
Core Data Set	Benefit ID	Explained below (para 4.2)
	Owner of the Benefit Profile	Explained below (para 4.3)
	Benefit Category	See 'drop-down' data validations below (para 4.4)
	Benefit Name	Explained below (para 4.5)
	Benefit Description/ Formula	Explained below (para 4.6)
	Baseline Value/ Description	Field may require formatting; Explained below (para 4.7)
	Target Value/ Description	Field may require formatting; Explained below (para 4.8)
	Benefit (i.e. difference) Value/Description	Field may require formatting; Explained below (para 4.9)
Mature the Benefit Profile	Benefit Type	See 'drop-down' data validations below (para 4.10)
	3E Value	See 'drop-down' data validations below (para 4.11)
	Assessment Type	See 'drop-down' data validations below (para 4.12)
	Reinvestment	See 'drop-down' data validations below (para 4.13)
	Method of Approach	Explained below (para 4.14)
	Benefit Report Status	See 'drop-down' data validations below (para 4.15)
	Current Value	Field may require formatting; Explained below (para 4.16)
	Beneficiary	Explained below (para 4.17)
	Business Function	See example of 'drop-down' data validations below (para 4.18)
	Benefit Champion (i.e. BaU Directorate)	See example of 'drop-down' data validations below (para 4.19)
	Benefit State/Maturity	See 'drop-down' data validations below (para 4.20)

Type	Categorisations	Remarks
(a)	(b)	(c)
Strategic Alignment	Primary End Benefit	Explained below; requires 'drop-down' data validation (para 4.21)
	Secondary End Benefit (if required)	Explained below; requires 'drop-down' data validation (para 4.22)
	Tertiary End Benefit (if required)	Explained below; requires 'drop-down' data validation (para 4.23)
	Primary Strategic Objective	Explained below; requires 'drop-down' data validation (para 4.24)
	Secondary Strategic Objective (if required)	Explained below; requires 'drop-down' data validation (para 4.25)
	Tertiary Strategic Objective (if required)	Explained below; requires 'drop-down' data validation (para 4.26)
Dates	Benefit Realisation Report Date	Explained below (para 4.27)
	Date of Last Review	Explained below (para 4.28)
	Date of Next Review	Explained below (para 4.29)
	Remarks/Comments	Explained below (para 4.30)

TABLE 4 *Elements of the Benefit Profile.*

4.2 Benefit ID:

4.2.1 A unique reference number is used to identify the Benefit. For example, CI name followed by a numeric value 'Name-001'. The portfolio office may direct the structure of the Benefit ID so they can recognise them (there could be thousands of Benefits across a portfolio). The BM is advised to check first before adopting their own approach.

4.3 Owner of the Benefit Profile:

4.3.1 Are usually those individuals who are experiencing advantages (Benefits) and disadvantages (Dis-Benefits) of change and best placed to assist the BM to quantify them. The 'role' of the owner of the Benefit Profile should be included.

4.4 Benefit Category:

4.4.1 Direct Benefit: Savings from as-is costs.

4.4.2 Avoidance (Time): Time that could have been consumed in the future to achieve something not yet started has been prevented.

4.4.3 Avoidance (£): Money that could have been spent in the future on activities that have not yet started is no longer required.

4.4.4 Avoidance (FTE): A user that could have been scheduled to work in the future on something not yet started is no longer required to do it.

4.4.5 Efficiency (Time): Time being consumed doing something now has been reduced or removed.

4.4.6 Efficiency (£): Money that is spent on something now has been reduced or removed.

4.4.7 Efficiency (FTE): An aspect of a user's work has been automated; the user has been given other value-added tasks.

4.4.8 Dis-Benefit (Time): A new business process brought complexity; it now takes the End Users more of their time to complete an action.

4.4.9 Dis-Benefit (£): The organisation is now spending more on salary to complete additional unnecessary work. The organisation is not getting VfM.

4.4.10 Dis-Benefit (FTE): More human resource(s) are required to complete an activity that is more complicated than before.

4.4.11 Other/Descriptive: Use for descriptive Benefits that are either objective (i.e. matter of fact) or qualitative (i.e. subjective).

4.5 Benefit Name:

4.5.1 Keep the Benefit Name short and to the point.

4.6 Benefit Description/Formula:

4.6.1 Description: Avoid technical jargon. Keep it simple with good context and reasoning. Avoid acronyms. Assume the reader has no knowledge of the subject and your aim is to enable them to understand it (see example at para 1.3.1 b).

4.6.2 Formula: Use the formulas provided. Lay it out as shown previously so the reader can see and understand the logic behind it (see examples at para 1.3.1 d, e and f).

4.7 Baseline Value/Description[46]:

4.7.1 What is the as-is value (or description) prior to change (i.e. how long does it take to complete x using the legacy system). If the baseline value is numeric, format the field on 'numeric', use 1000 separator & 3 decimals. If the baseline value is expressed in £, format the field on 'currency', use the £ symbol & 3 decimals. If the baseline value is expressed in descriptive terms, do not format the field.

4.8 Target Value/Description:

4.8.1 What is the to-be value (or description) post change (i.e. how long does it take to complete x using the new system). If the target value is numeric, format the field on 'numeric', use 1000 separator & 3 decimals. If the target value is expressed in £, format the field on 'currency', use the £ symbol & 3 decimals. If the target value is expressed in descriptive terms, do not format the field.

4.9 Benefit (i.e. difference) Value/Description:

4.9.1 Difference between as-is and to-be values (or descriptions). If the Benefit value is numeric, format the field on 'numeric', use 1000 separator & 3 decimals. If the Benefit is expressed in £, format the field on 'currency', use the £ symbol & 3 decimals. If the Benefit is expressed in descriptive terms, do not format the field.

4.10 Benefit Type:

4.10.1 Intermediate Benefit: These are expected Benefits that combine to quantify the End Benefits of the CI.

4.10.2 Emergent Benefit: These are unexpected or new Benefits that combine to quantify the End Benefits of the CI.

---

46 'Value' in this context means numeric or monetised (i.e. quantitative). 'Description' refers to the use of 'words' to explain something (i.e. objective or qualitative).

4.11 3E Value:

4.11.1 Economic (Cash Releasing). A financial improvement that is cash releasing (i.e. reducing expenditure; increasing income). Departmental CTs will be adjusted as a result.

4.11.2 Economic (Non-Cash Releasing). A financial improvement that is monetised but is not cash releasing. Departmental CTs will not be adjusted as a result.

4.11.3 Efficiency. Doing more for the same or the same with less (i.e. processing more enquiries but with the same number of people).

4.11.4 Effectiveness. Doing things better or to a higher standard.

4.11.5 N/A. Used for Dis-Benefits.

4.12 Assessment Type:

4.12.1 Quantitative. The Benefit is expressed in numeric terms (i.e. time, £, percentage).

4.12.2 Objective. The Benefit is expressed in descriptive terms that are not subjective (i.e. matter of fact).

4.12.3 Qualitative. The Benefit is expressed in descriptive terms that are subjective. The description should be as objective as possible to avoid the uncertainty that could arise from it.

4.13 Reinvestment[47]:

4.13.1 Yes. The Benefit can be reinvested.

4.13.2 No. The Benefit cannot be reinvested.

---

47 See 'Reinvestment' para 1.8.

4.14 Method of Approach (MoA)[48]:

4.14.1 The BM is to assist the owner of the Benefit Profile to identify the MoA. There could be many different MoAs. For example: UAT, Test Witnessing, Survey, Judgement Panel, User Experience, other.

4.15 Benefit Report Status:

4.15.1 Open Reporting:

a. Not Yet Reported. The first Benefit Realisation Report Date has not been reached.

b. Under Delivering. Evidence exists that confirms the Benefit is performing less well than expected or promised (i.e. a milestone has slipped causing a delay; the Benefit had been overstated). Benefits under delivering will be tagged with either *performance issue, cost issue or time issue* to enable the CI to understand underperformance and the steps necessary for improvement.

c. On Track. Evidence exists that confirms the Benefit is on track and is likely to be reached.

d. Over Delivering. Evidence exists that confirms the Benefit is likely to be exceeded.

4.15.2 Closed Reported:

a. Under Delivered. Evidence exists that confirms some of the Benefit has been delivered; the Benefit has been closed.

b. Delivered. Evidence exists that confirms the Benefit has been fully delivered; the Benefit has been closed.

c. Over Delivered. Evidence exists that confirms the Benefit has been exceeded and performance was greater than expected; the Benefit has been closed.

d. Not Delivered. The Benefit is cancelled; or was not approved; or none of the Benefit was delivered. Reasons have been recorded in the Benefit Register.

---

48 Also referred to as a 'Performance Management System' (PMS).

4.16 Current Value:

4.16.1 Measure recorded in the Benefit Realisation Report. If the current value is expressed in time, format the field on 'numeric' & 3 decimals. If the current value is expressed in £, format the field on 'currency' & 3 decimals. If the current value is expressed in descriptive terms, do not format the field.

4.17 Beneficiary:

4.17.1 The organisation, cohort of people, team or area that is advantaged (or disadvantaged) by change. The owner of the Benefit Profile usually works within or directly for the beneficiary.

4.18 Business Function:

4.18.1 The functions across the business area advantaged (or disadvantaged) by change (i.e. Payroll, ERP, Enterprise Performance Management (EPM), Project/Programme Management (PPM), Role Based Access Control (RBAC), Data, other).

4.19 Benefit Champion (i.e. Associated BaU Directorates):

4.19.1 See para 7.1.1 e.

4.20 Benefit State/Maturity[49]:

4.20.1 Open Benefit:

   a. Being Drafted. Benefit Indicators are being identified/articulated.

   b. Being Defined. Benefit Indicators are being defined and aligned to SOs.

   c. Being Quantified. Benefit Indicators are being quantified and metricised; baselines, targets and measurements are informing the Benefit Profile.

   d. Being Planned. The full Benefit Profile has been evaluated and matured by the stakeholders.

---

49 See also, para 1.11 'Benefit Process Model'.

e. In Delivery. New products and services are being contracted for delivery, transitioned into BaU structures and being used. Benefits are being released and reported.

4.20.2 Closed Benefit:

a. Realised. There is evidence to confirm the Benefit has been realised. The Benefit Report Status (para 4.15.2) will confirm to what extent.

b. Cancelled. The Benefit was not delivered (applies to Benefits that were either cancelled or not approved/rejected).

4.21 Primary End Benefit:

4.21.1 Select the Primary End Benefit (see Benefit Map) this Benefit contributes to. How: 'this is a drop-down data validation field; the BM copies the End Benefits from the Benefit Map into the "Look-Up" worksheet in the Benefit Register to incorporate a data validation'.

4.22 Secondary End Benefit:

4.22.1 Select the Secondary End Benefit (see Benefit Map) this Benefit contributes to. How: 'this is a drop-down data validation field; the BM copies the End Benefits from the Benefit Map into the "Look-Up" worksheet in the Benefit Register to incorporate a data validation'. Select N/A if a Secondary End Benefit does not apply (i.e. too tenuous a link).

4.23 Tertiary End Benefit:

4.23.1 Select the Tertiary End Benefit (see Benefit Map) this Benefit contributes to. How: 'this is a drop-down data validation field; the BM copies the End Benefits from the Benefit Map into the "Look-Up" worksheet in the Benefit Register to incorporate a data validation'. Select N/A if a Tertiary End Benefit does not apply (i.e. too tenuous a link).

4.24 Primary Strategic Objective:

4.24.1 Select the Primary Strategic Objective this Benefit contributes to. How: 'this is a drop-down data validation field; the BM copies the SOs from the Benefit Map into the "Look-Up" worksheet in the Benefit Register to incorporate a data validation'.

4.25 Secondary Strategic Objective:

4.25.1 Select the Secondary Strategic Objective this Benefit contributes to. How: 'this is a drop-down data validation field; the BM copies the SOs from the Benefit Map into the "Look-Up" worksheet in the Benefit Register to incorporate a data validation'. Select N/A if a Secondary Strategic Objective does not apply (i.e. too tenuous a link).

4.26 Tertiary Strategic Objective:

4.26.1 Select the Tertiary Strategic Objective this Benefit contributes to. How: 'this is a drop-down data validation field; the BM copies the SOs from the Benefit Map into the "Look-Up" worksheet in the Benefit Register to incorporate a data validation'. Select N/A if a Tertiary Strategic Objective does not apply (i.e. too tenuous a link).

4.27 Benefit Realisation Report Date:

4.27.1 The Benefit Realisation Report Date (BRRD) is confirmed by the owner of the Benefit Profile with assistance from the BM. On this date, the owner of the Benefit Profile submits a Benefit Realisation Report to the BM[50]. The BM monitors this date using the Benefit Tracker in the Benefit Register[51].

4.28 Date of Last Review:

4.28.1 Date when the Benefit Profile was last reviewed by the BM and owner of the Benefit Profile.

4.29 Date of Next Review:

4.29.1 The next review date is agreed between the BM and the owner of the Benefit Profile. The BM monitors this date using a tracker in the Benefit Register.

4.30 Remarks/Comments:

4.30.1 Record useful/pertinent information in this field if required. Include the name/date of those commenting.

---

50 See para 6.3.

51 See para 5.7.

SECTION 5

Benefit Register

5.1 Introduction[52]

5.1.1 P3Os have different software options available to them to record the Benefit Profiles and Benefits data. Whatever software is used, the approach, structure and categorisations in *The Benefit Manager's Desktop Step-by-Step Guide* can be used to develop and inform the various options available.

5.1.2 Aggregated reporting of Benefits data up/down the portfolio (i.e. between the portfolio office and subsidiary work packages, projects and programmes both ways) is difficult and trust in the information is reduced if different applications, systems, and approaches are used with little coherence and/or standardisation. This is a significant problem, particularly for the portfolio offices; standardisation is key[53].

5.1.3 Let us begin by developing a Benefit Register using the Excel application in Office 365[54]. The Benefit Register can have numerous worksheets to suit different purposes. You will see 6 worksheets in Image 18 to get you started; each is then explained in turn. More worksheets will be added later; the additional worksheets consist of PivotTables and visualisations drawn from data in the EBP and Benefit Profiles worksheets[55] to enable reporting of the data. If the

52 The Benefit Register is more useful when it contains the BM's schedule of work, the EBP, a Benefit Tracker to be able to monitor reporting and, of course, the Benefit Profiles themselves. Other useful information provides the ability to aggregate and extract information using PivotTables and charts to assist reporting requirements and inform the development of the BRP.

53 A well-structured portfolio BRP with direction to the work packages, projects, and programmes beneath them on the use of software applications, systems, approach to Benefit Management, formulas, structure of the EBP, reporting requirements and formats, size and structure of the organisation etc. will bring standardisation and coherence.

54 Excel is relatively straightforward to use; significant self-learning resources are available on the www/ YouTube.

55 PivotTables and visualisations/charts generated from the EBP and Benefit Profiles worksheets are to be 'refreshed' when the EBP and Benefit Profiles worksheets have been updated.

information/visuals do not suit the organisation's information or reporting requirements, the examples can be used to stimulate thinking.[56]

Look-Up	BM Work Schedule	EBP	Benefit Profiles	Benefit Tracker	Outputs

IMAGE 18 *Benefit Register – 1st 6 worksheets.*

5.2 Look-Up

5.2.1 The drop-down data validations required for use in the Benefit Profiles worksheet (or any other worksheet in the Benefit Register) are populated into the 'Look-Up' worksheet. You can find the Benefit Profiles data validations listed at paras 4.4; 4.10; 4.11; 4.12; 4.13; 4.15; 4.18; 4.19; 4.20–4.26. Image 19 shows the Look-Up worksheet being populated with the information.

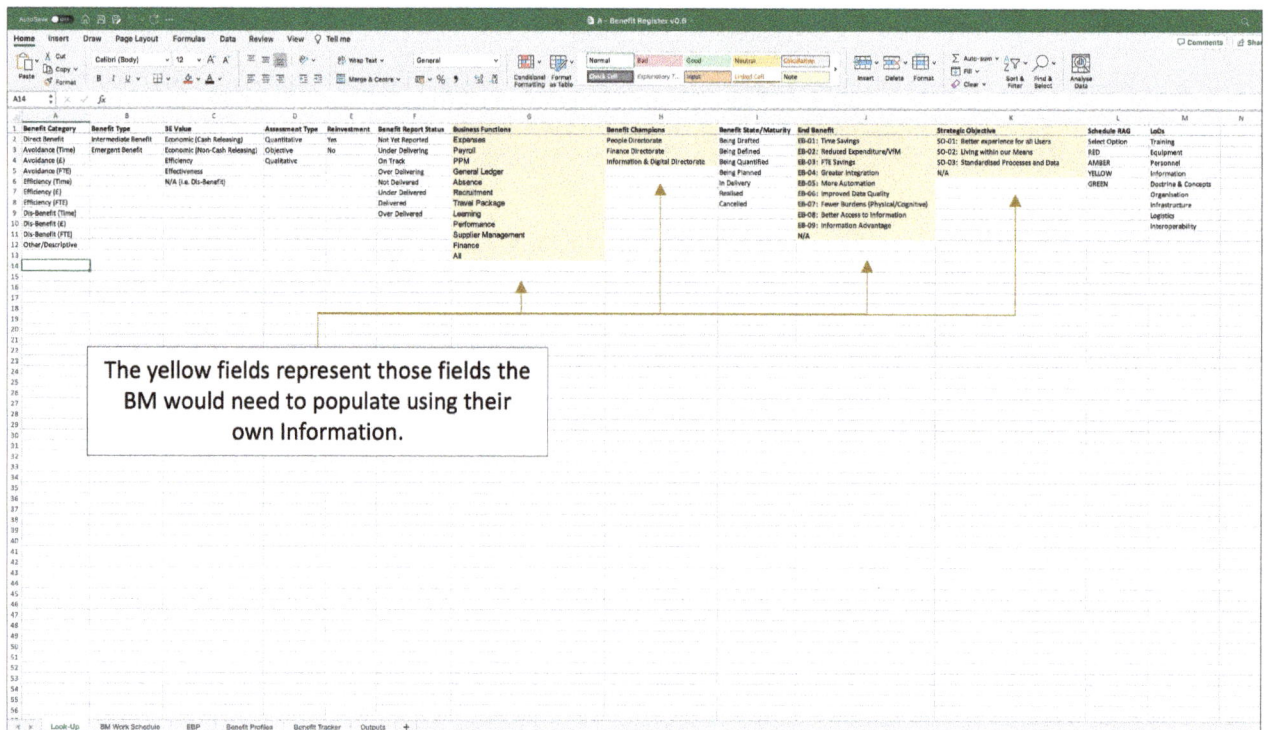

IMAGE 19 *Populating the 'Look-Up' worksheet.*

5.2.2 When reviewing Image 19, note the following points:

---

56 It can be difficult for organisations to know how to best structure the information it is using for reporting purposes so that it becomes useful/insightful. Being presented with information pictorially to start with stimulates further ideas that result in accepted reporting formats; they continue to improve with imaginative thinking. There are positive learning outcomes for all involved in the process. More on this later at section 9.

a. Business Functions[57]. The BM can identify the business functions through engagements inside the organisation. Examples have been populated into Column G.

b. Benefit Champions[58]. The BM can identify the Directorates belonging to the Benefit Champions through engagements inside the organisation. Examples have been populated into Column H.

c. End Benefits. The End Benefit 'names' are copied into Column J from Image 16 and used as an example for the purpose of this exercise. The BM should use the CI's End Benefits upon the agreed Benefit Map in reality.

d. SOs. A few simple examples of SOs have been copied into Column K. They can consist of (a) internal, low level departmental objectives (b) portfolio office objectives (c) other – for example: the missions in the Government Digital Strategy; the objectives in the Shared Services Strategy for Government; and the principles in the Government Functional Standards. The information is accessible via the WWW. The BM is to identify the appropriate missions, objectives, and principles when developing the Benefit Map.

5.3 BM Work Schedule

5.3.1 The author has seen several CIs positioning the role of the BM in the Business Change (BCHG) team; see para 7.2. The BCHG team leader is responsible for the management of a schedule of work (i.e. the BCHG plan)[59].

5.3.2 The BCHG plan usually sits in MS Project and is managed by a scheduler. The scheduler requires updates to the plan from each work pillar within the BCHG team. BRM is one of the work pillars. This means the BM is required to develop a schedule of work; when agreed it will be incorporated into the master BCHG plan for management control and oversight.

5.3.3 The BM's working copy of the schedule can be recorded/managed from the Benefit Register. The BM uses the schedule to keep track of time and monitor/report performance (i.e. update the BCHG leader during weekly progress reviews), using the information to provide dynamic updates into the master BCHG plan.

---

57 See para 4.18.

58 See para 7.1.1 e.

59 The BCHG Plan consists of PBS and WBS incorporating milestones and assigned ownership. See image 20, column D.

5.3.4 An example of the BM's schedule of work can be seen at Image 20[60].

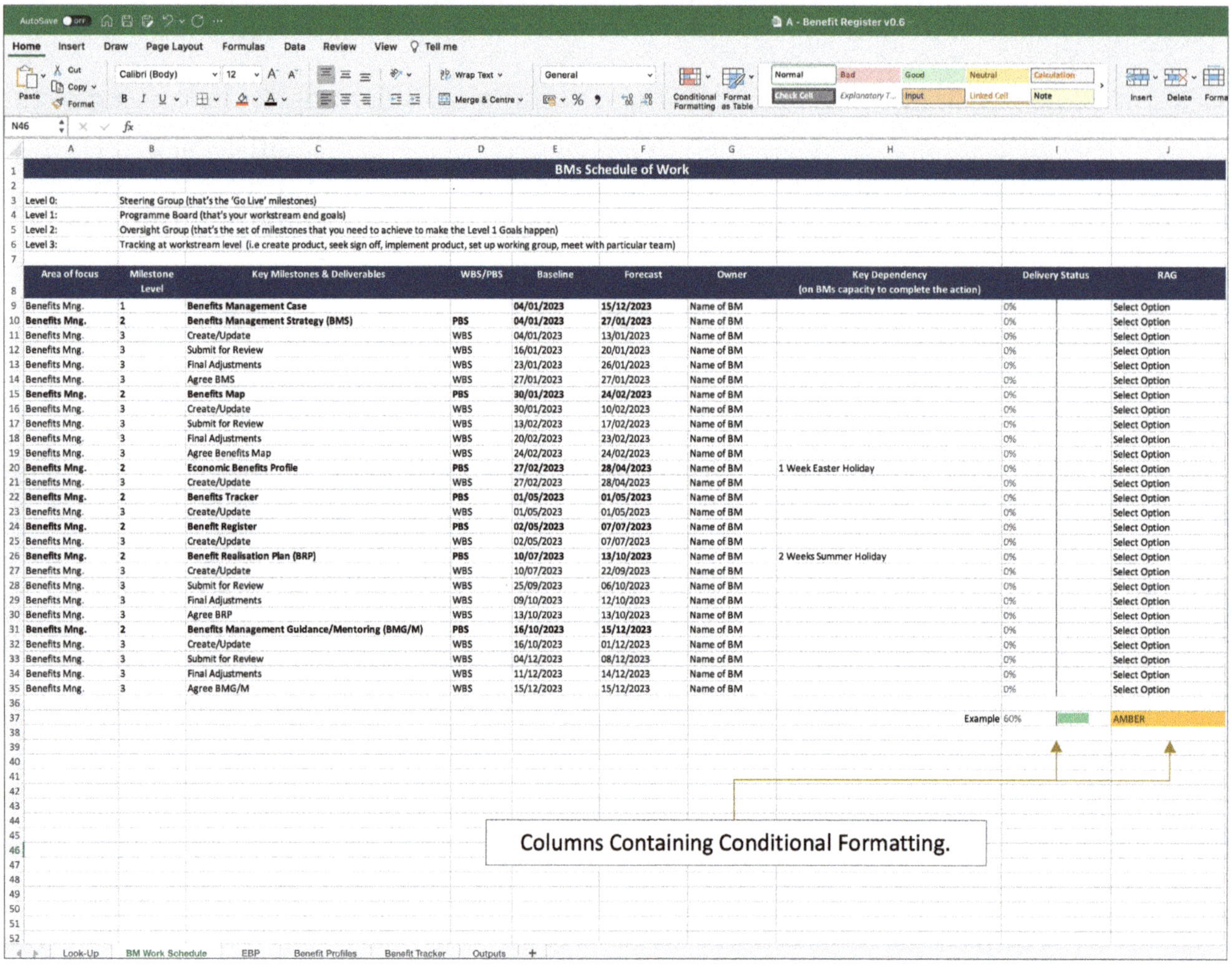

BMs Schedule of Work

Level 0: Steering Group (that's the 'Go Live' milestones)
Level 1: Programme Board (that's your workstream end goals)
Level 2: Oversight Group (that's the set of milestones that you need to achieve to make the Level 1 Goals happen)
Level 3: Tracking at workstream level (i.e create product, seek sign off, implement product, set up working group, meet with particular team)

Area of focus	Milestone Level	Key Milestones & Deliverables	WBS/PBS	Baseline	Forecast	Owner	Key Dependency (on BMs capacity to complete the action)	Delivery Status	RAG
Benefits Mng.	1	**Benefits Management Case**		**04/01/2023**	**15/12/2023**	Name of BM		0%	Select Option
Benefits Mng.	**2**	**Benefits Management Strategy (BMS)**	**PBS**	**04/01/2023**	**27/01/2023**	Name of BM		0%	Select Option
Benefits Mng.	3	Create/Update	WBS	04/01/2023	13/01/2023	Name of BM		0%	Select Option
Benefits Mng.	3	Submit for Review	WBS	16/01/2023	20/01/2023	Name of BM		0%	Select Option
Benefits Mng.	3	Final Adjustments	WBS	23/01/2023	26/01/2023	Name of BM		0%	Select Option
Benefits Mng.	3	Agree BMS	WBS	27/01/2023	27/01/2023	Name of BM		0%	Select Option
Benefits Mng.	**2**	**Benefits Map**	**PBS**	**30/01/2023**	**24/02/2023**	Name of BM		0%	Select Option
Benefits Mng.	3	Create/Update	WBS	30/01/2023	10/02/2023	Name of BM		0%	Select Option
Benefits Mng.	3	Submit for Review	WBS	13/02/2023	17/02/2023	Name of BM		0%	Select Option
Benefits Mng.	3	Final Adjustments	WBS	20/02/2023	23/02/2023	Name of BM		0%	Select Option
Benefits Mng.	3	Agree Benefits Map	WBS	24/02/2023	24/02/2023	Name of BM		0%	Select Option
Benefits Mng.	**2**	**Economic Benefits Profile**	**PBS**	**27/02/2023**	**28/04/2023**	Name of BM	1 Week Easter Holiday	0%	Select Option
Benefits Mng.	3	Create/Update	WBS	27/02/2023	28/04/2023	Name of BM		0%	Select Option
Benefits Mng.	**2**	**Benefits Tracker**	**PBS**	**01/05/2023**	**01/05/2023**	Name of BM		0%	Select Option
Benefits Mng.	3	Create/Update	WBS	01/05/2023	01/05/2023	Name of BM		0%	Select Option
Benefits Mng.	**2**	**Benefit Register**	**PBS**	**02/05/2023**	**07/07/2023**	Name of BM		0%	Select Option
Benefits Mng.	3	Create/Update	WBS	02/05/2023	07/07/2023	Name of BM		0%	Select Option
Benefits Mng.	**2**	**Benefit Realisation Plan (BRP)**	**PBS**	**10/07/2023**	**13/10/2023**	Name of BM	2 Weeks Summer Holiday	0%	Select Option
Benefits Mng.	3	Create/Update	WBS	10/07/2023	22/09/2023	Name of BM		0%	Select Option
Benefits Mng.	3	Submit for Review	WBS	25/09/2023	06/10/2023	Name of BM		0%	Select Option
Benefits Mng.	3	Final Adjustments	WBS	09/10/2023	12/10/2023	Name of BM		0%	Select Option
Benefits Mng.	3	Agree BRP	WBS	13/10/2023	13/10/2023	Name of BM		0%	Select Option
Benefits Mng.	**2**	**Benefits Management Guidance/Mentoring (BMG/M)**	**PBS**	**16/10/2023**	**15/12/2023**	Name of BM		0%	Select Option
Benefits Mng.	3	Create/Update	WBS	16/10/2023	01/12/2023	Name of BM		0%	Select Option
Benefits Mng.	3	Submit for Review	WBS	04/12/2023	08/12/2023	Name of BM		0%	Select Option
Benefits Mng.	3	Final Adjustments	WBS	11/12/2023	14/12/2023	Name of BM		0%	Select Option
Benefits Mng.	3	Agree BMG/M	WBS	15/12/2023	15/12/2023	Name of BM		0%	Select Option
							Example	60%	AMBER

IMAGE 20 *Example – BM's Schedule of Work.*

5.3.5 Image 20 shows Conditional Formatting (CF) in Columns I and J; see example row 37. The CF can be achieved for Columns I and J by following these steps[61]:

a. Column I (Delivery Status):

60 The example shows how an experienced BM can deliver a Benefit Management capability in 12 months and is drawn from experience when working with the organisations listed in the second introductory paragraph on page 1.

61 These visuals/steps will help the BM to become more competent with Excel.

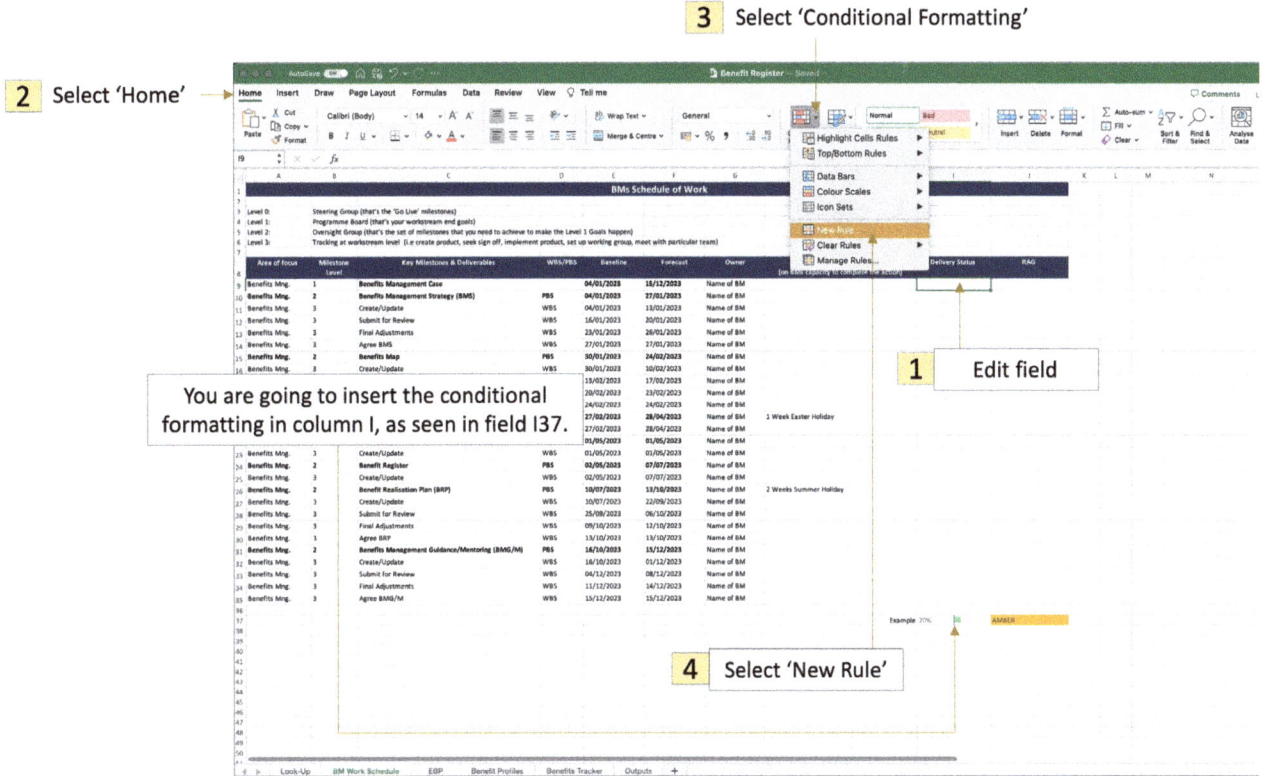

IMAGE 21 *Create New Rule.*

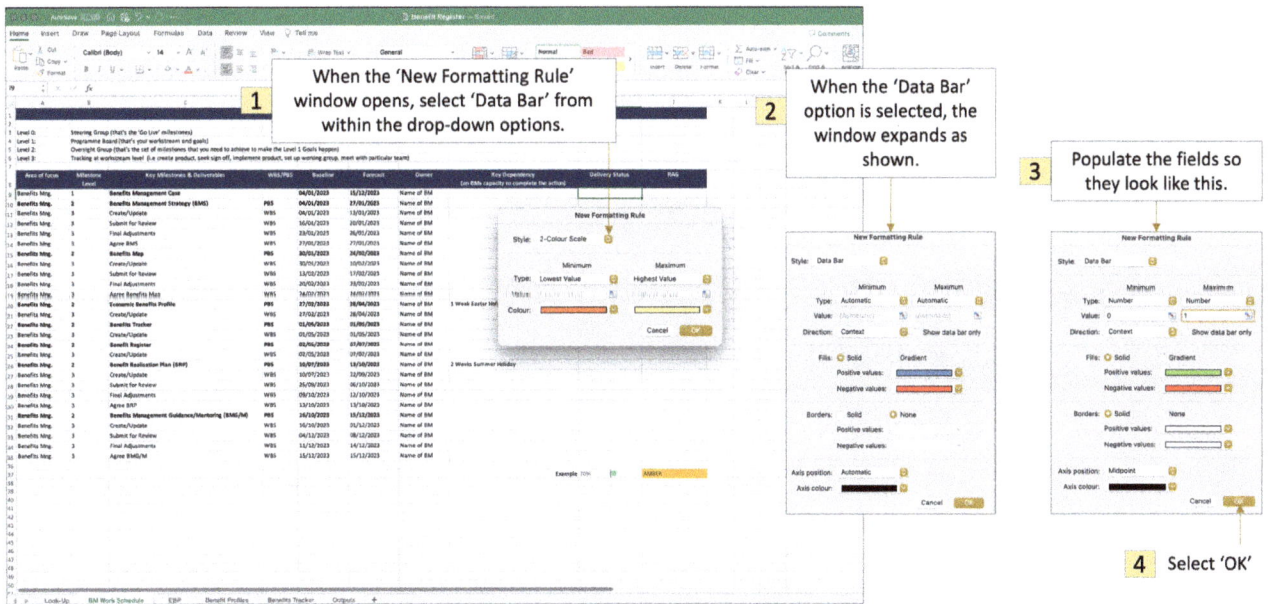

IMAGE 22 *Format New Rule.*

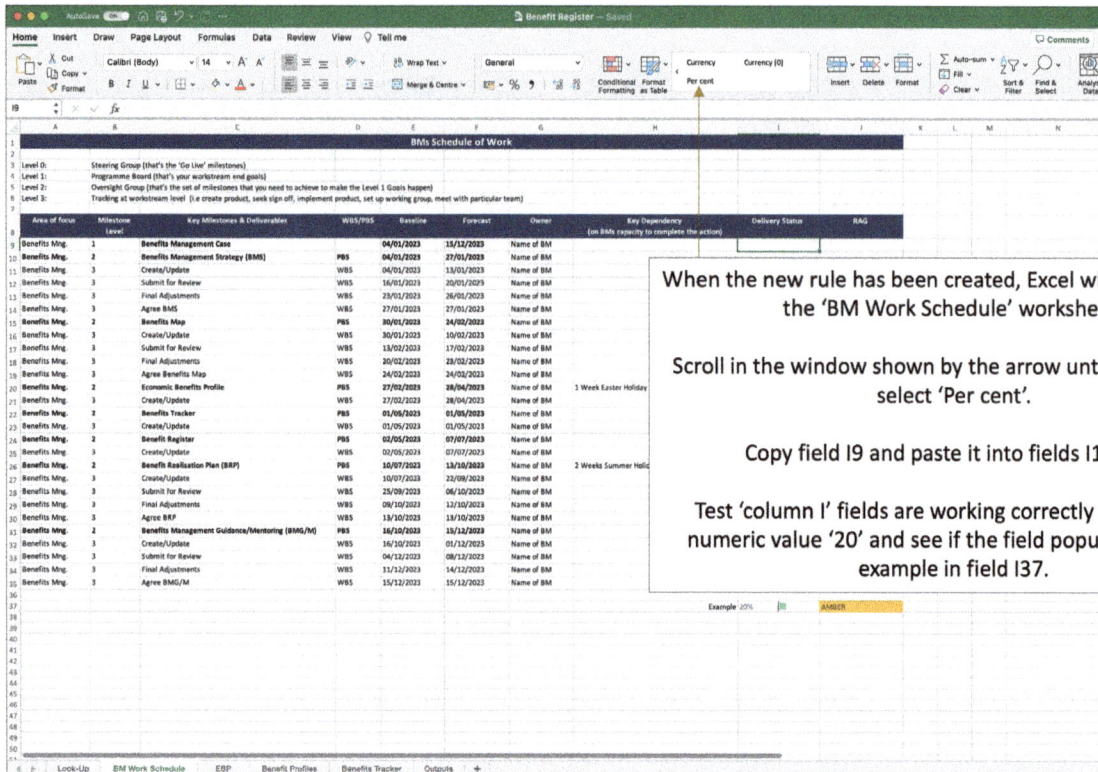

IMAGE 23 *Use the 'Per Cent' Value.*

b. Column J (RAG):

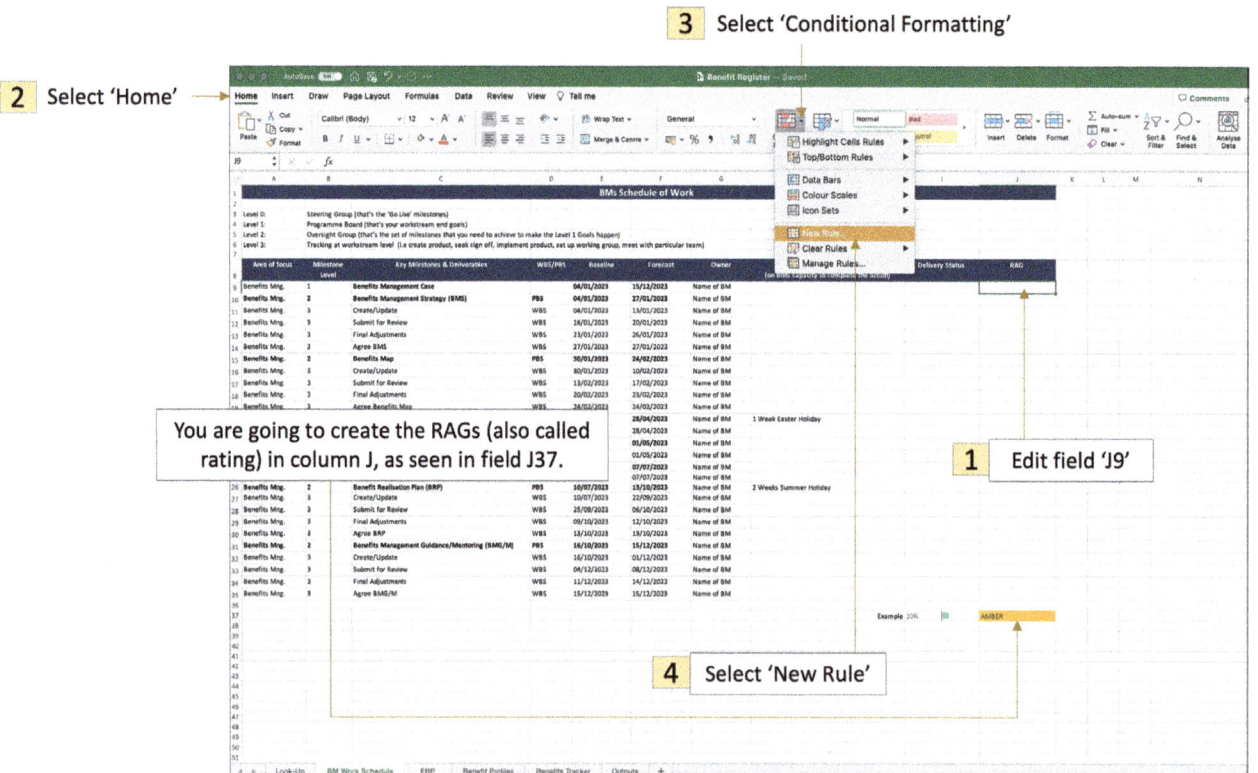

IMAGE 24 *Create New Rule.*

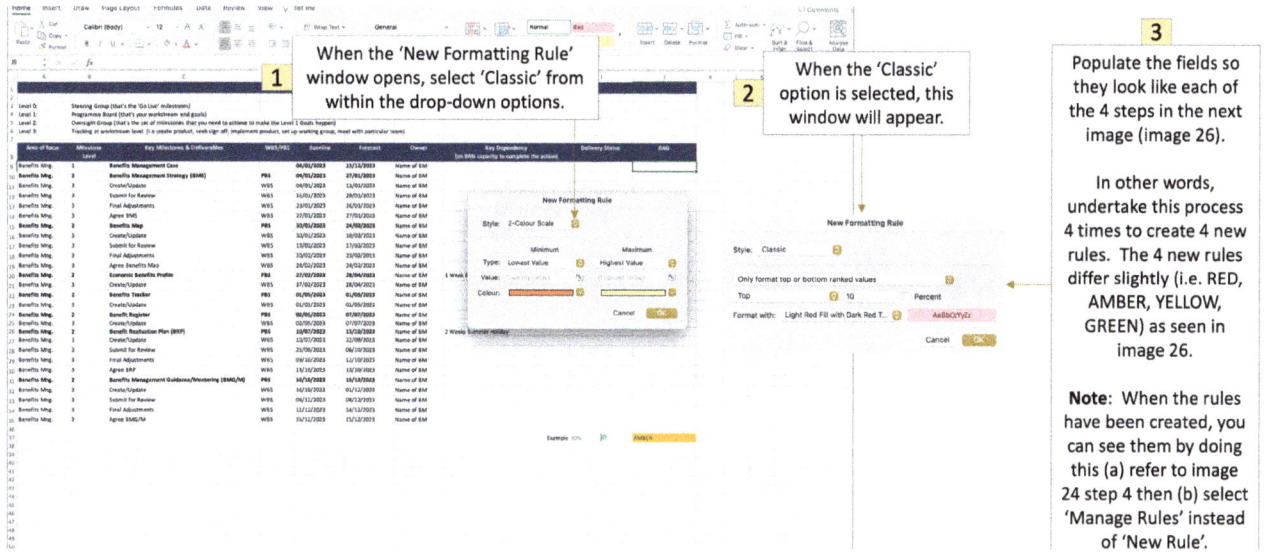

IMAGE 25 *Format New Rule.*

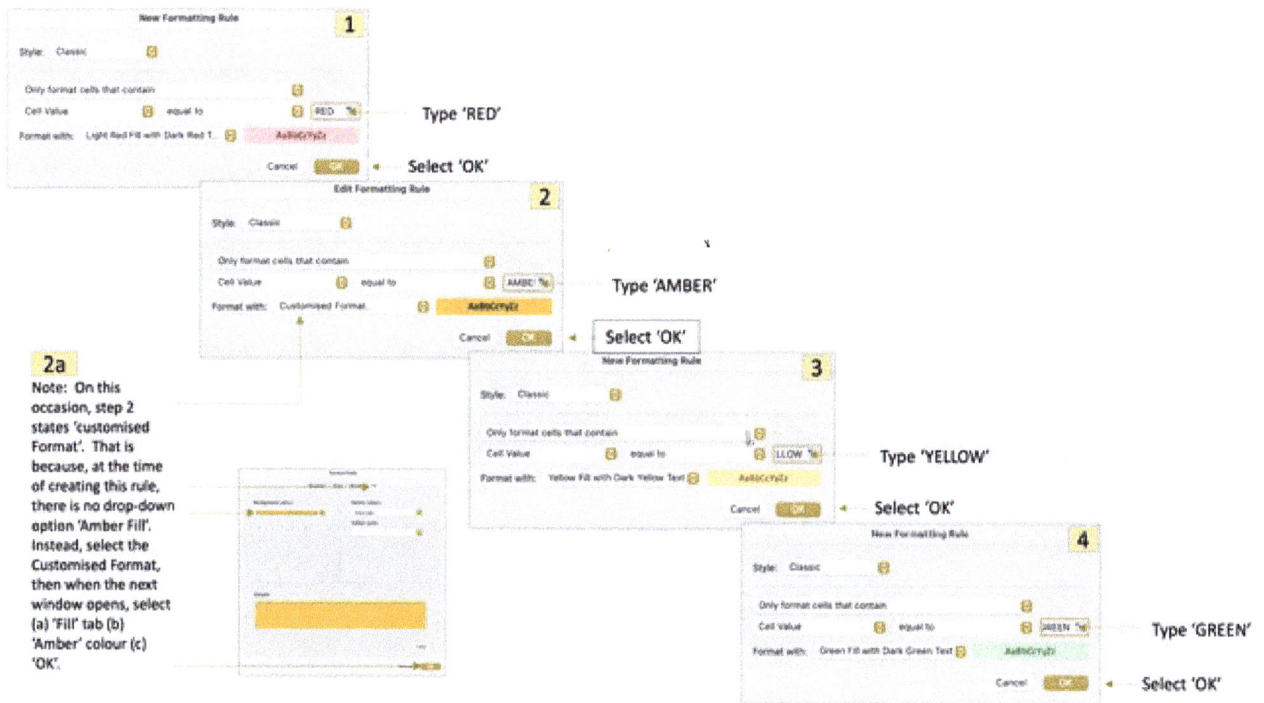

IMAGE 26 *The 4 New Rules.*

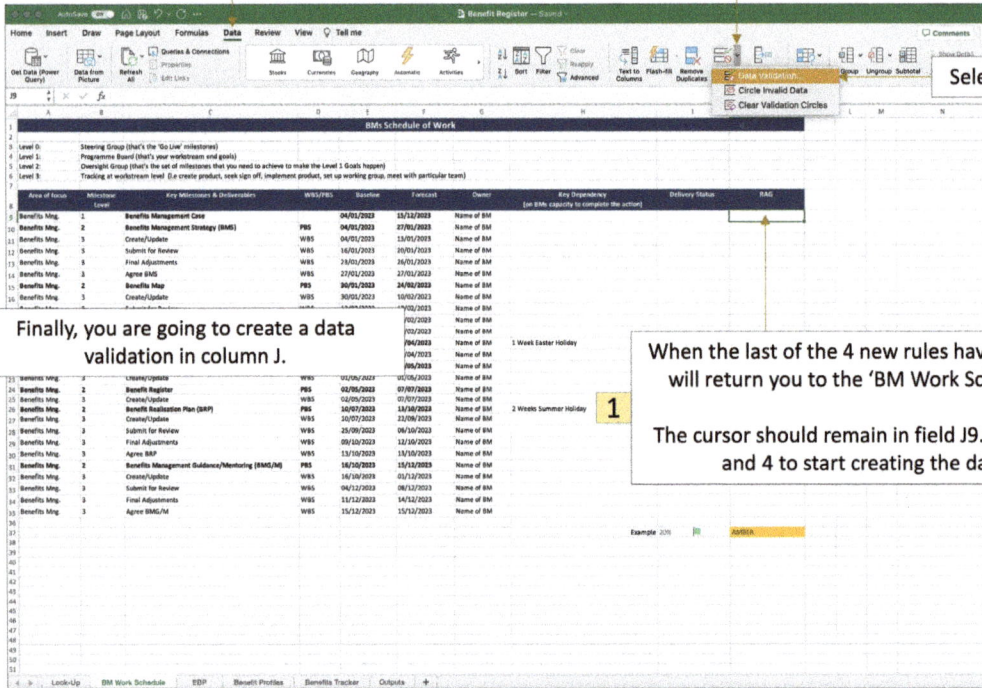

IMAGE 27 *Create Data Validation.*

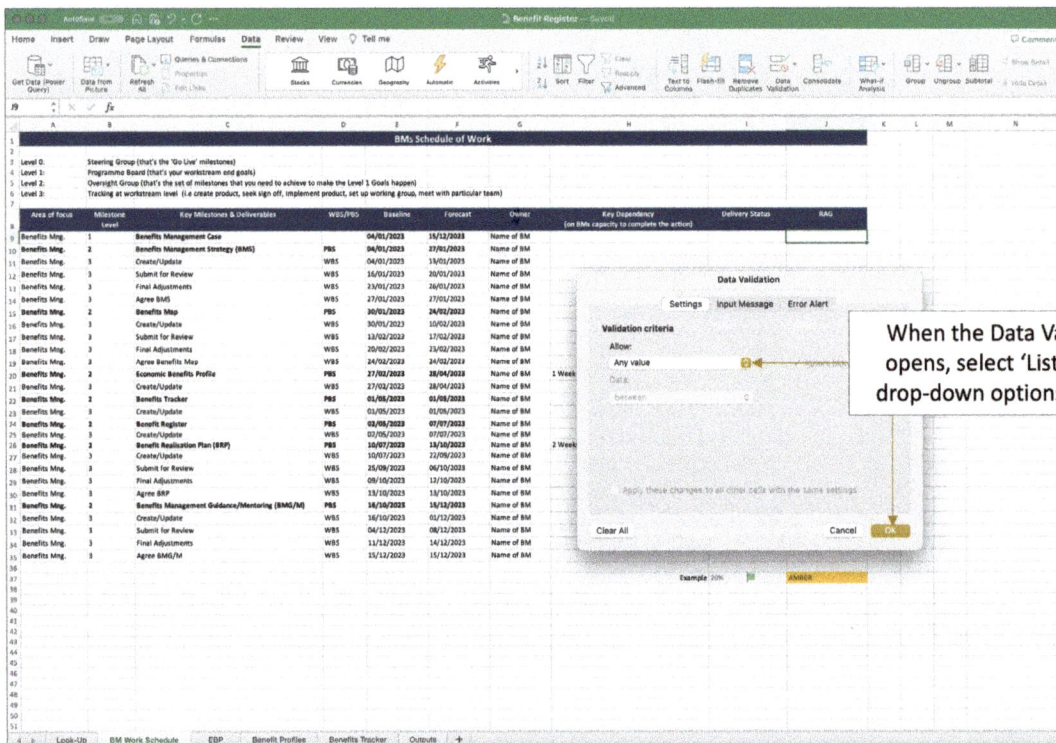

IMAGE 28 *Select 'List'.*

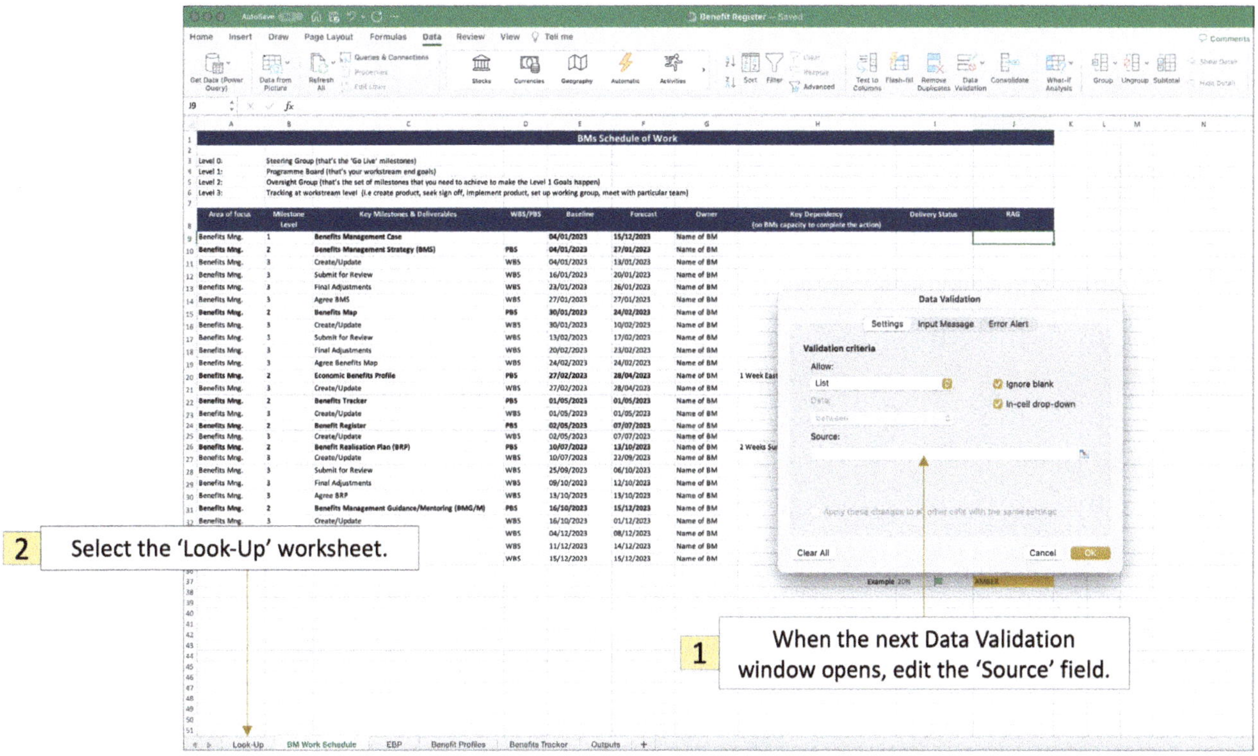

IMAGE 29 *Edit Source Field.*

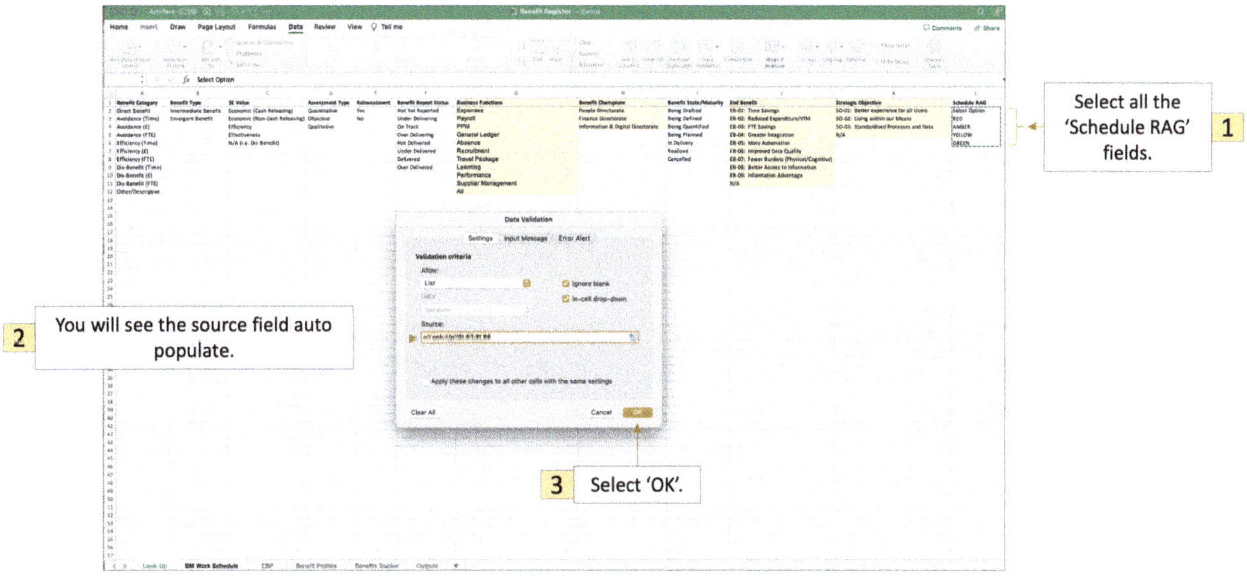

2 — Select the 'Look-Up' worksheet.

1 — When the next Data Validation window opens, edit the 'Source' field.

IMAGE 30 *Select Source Information.*

1 — Select all the 'Schedule RAG' fields.

2 — You will see the source field auto populate.

3 — Select 'OK'.

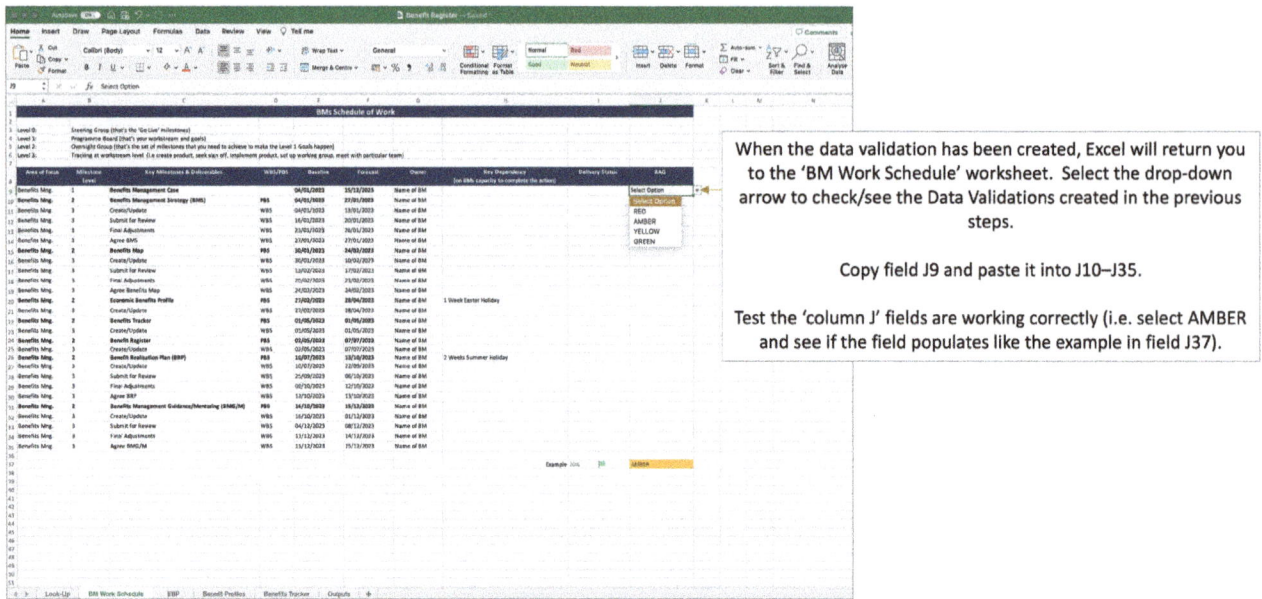

IMAGE 31 *Review.*

5.4 Economic Benefit Profile

5.4.1 Refer to Section 2 'The Economic Benefit Profile (EBP)'.

5.5 Benefit Profiles (Create Template)

5.5.1 Each 'row' in the Benefit Profiles worksheet consists of a single Benefit Profile with its attributes and dependencies. Each Benefit Profile is constructed from the 29 data fields in Table 4 (i.e. the 29 'categorisations' in Column (b) are the headings in each of the 29 columns in the Benefit Profiles worksheet in the Benefit Register). Image 32 consists of 4 screenshots comprising the 29 data fields populated into the Benefit Profiles worksheet; when connected or continuous, they consist of the full Benefit Profiles[62].

---

62 The Benefit Profiles can be adapted or include additional data fields (i.e. columns) if necessary. For example, the portfolio office adds a new column with common taxonomy and/or drop-down data validation, to capture spend on 'back office' technology and services so Benefits capture can be grouped into buckets of a particular nature of interest to the portfolio office (i.e. IT Software/Hardware; Licences; Internal FTE Support/Resource Salary, NI/Pension, Training, Location Allowances; External FTE Support/Resource Salary, other).

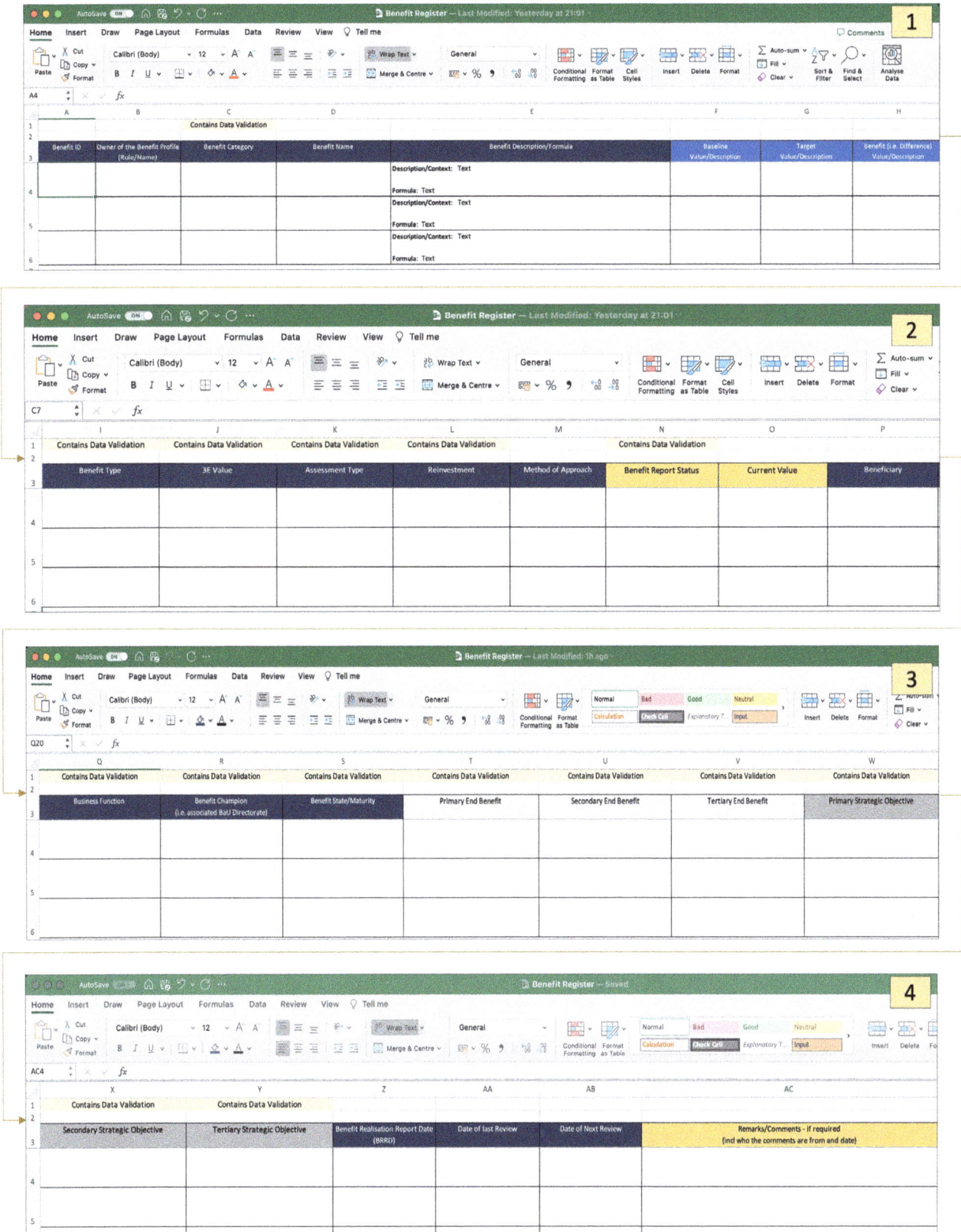

IMAGE 32 *Create the Benefit Profiles Worksheet.*

5.5.2 The 1st row of each screenshot confirms which columns have an associated drop-down data validation/field. Data validations are achieved via the 'Look-Up' worksheet explained at para 5.2. Images 33–37 show the BM how to create the data validation fields in the Benefit Profiles worksheet.

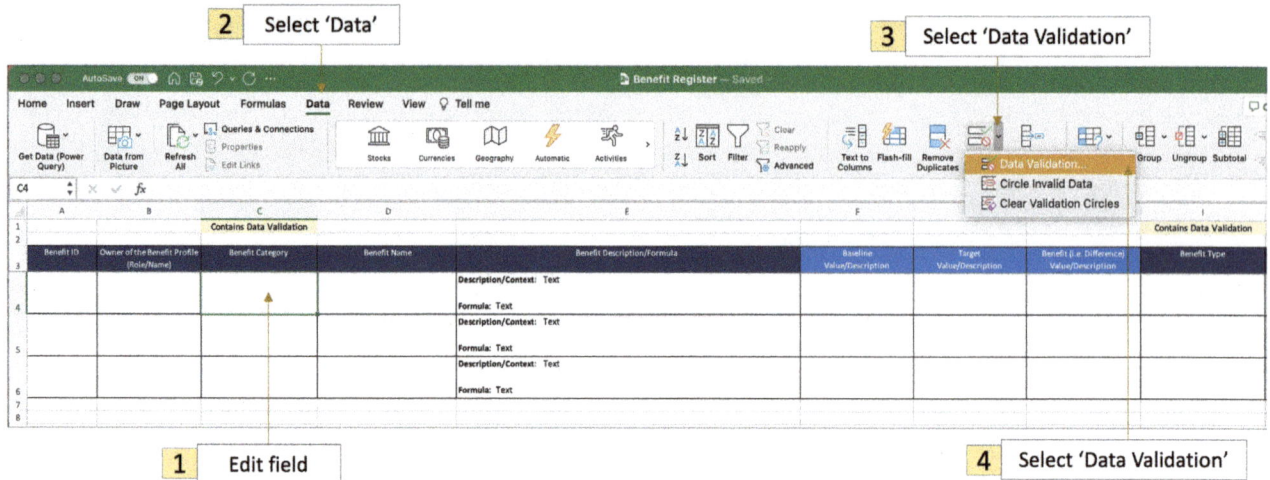

IMAGE 33 *Create Data Validation.*

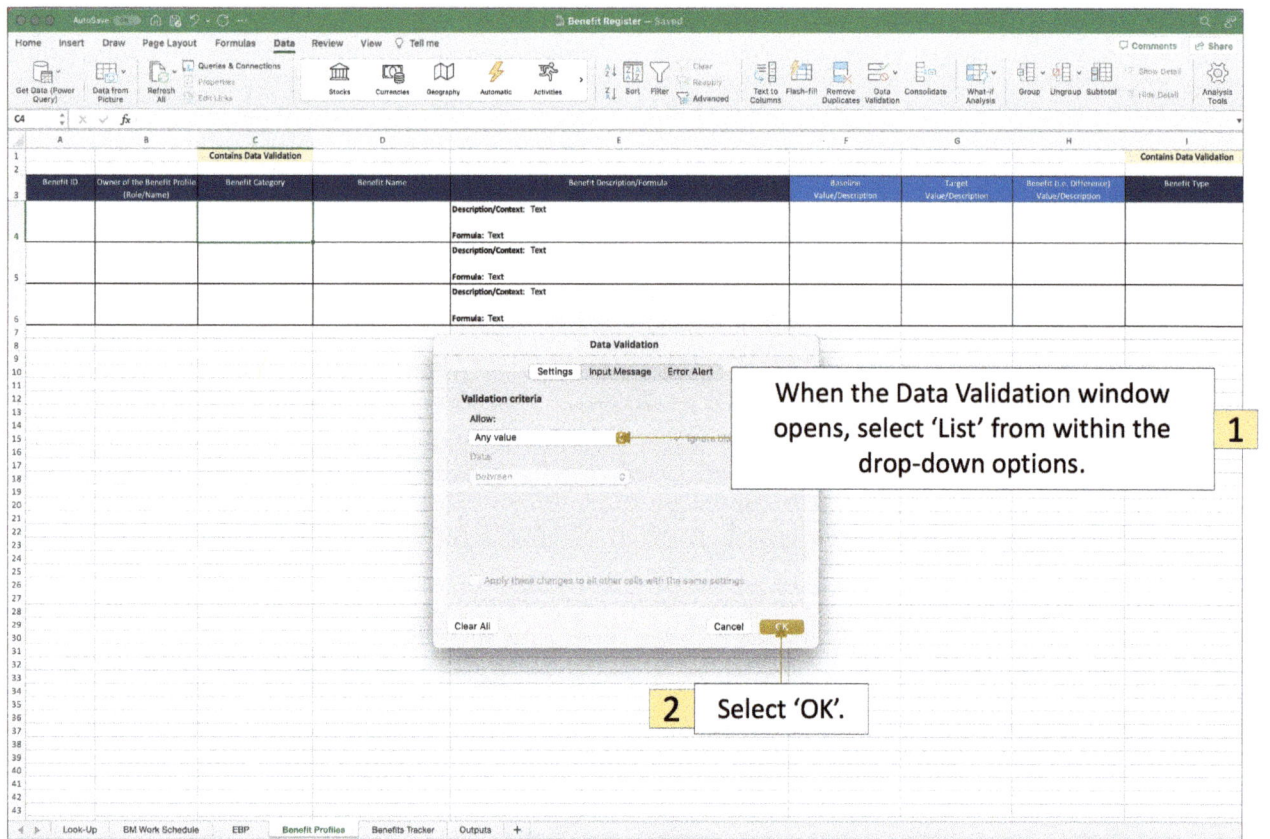

IMAGE 34 *Select List.*

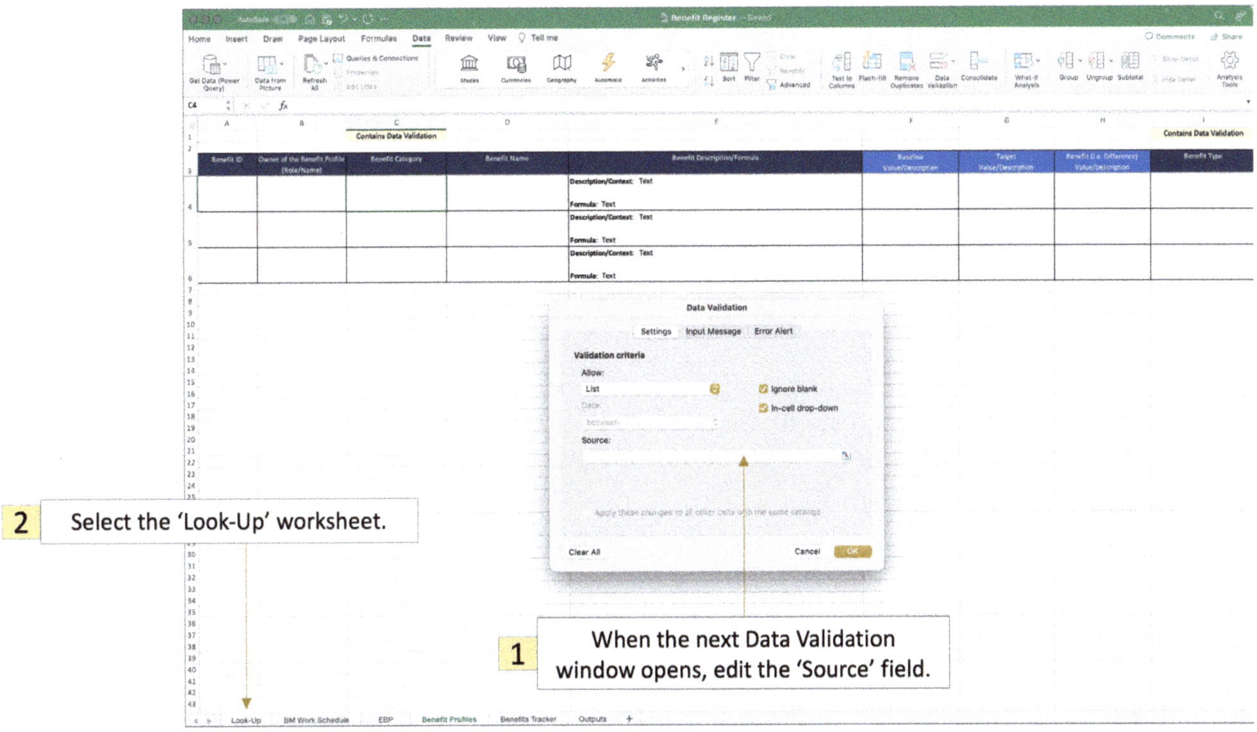

IMAGE 35 *Edit Source Field.*

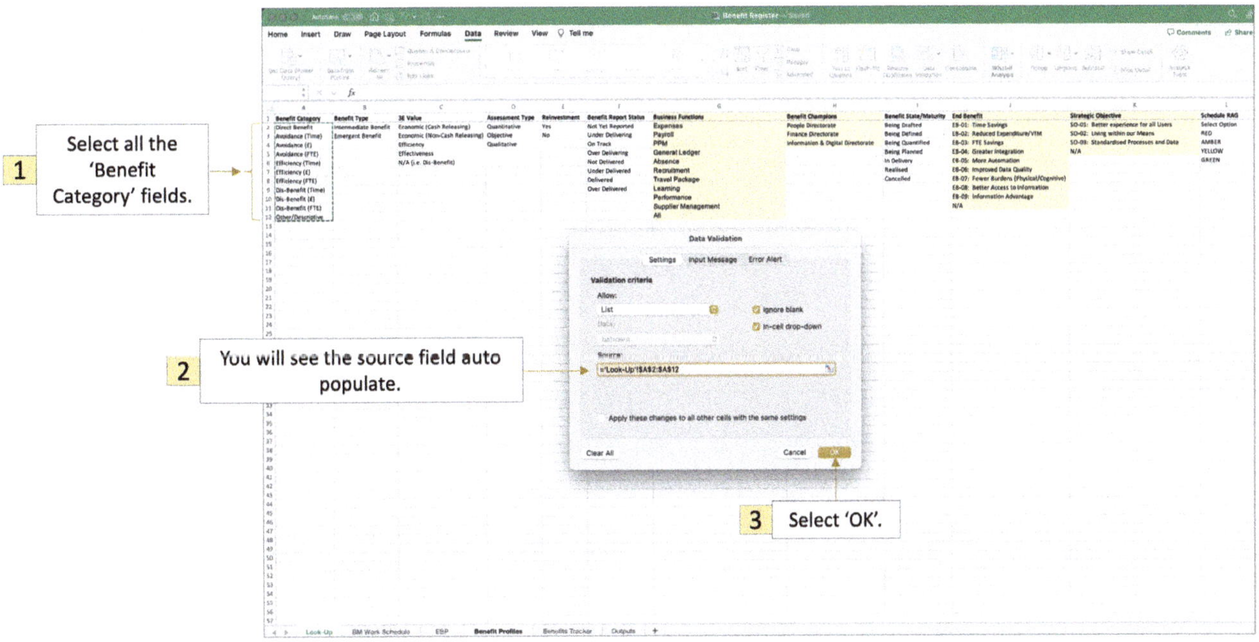

IMAGE 36 *Select Source Information.*

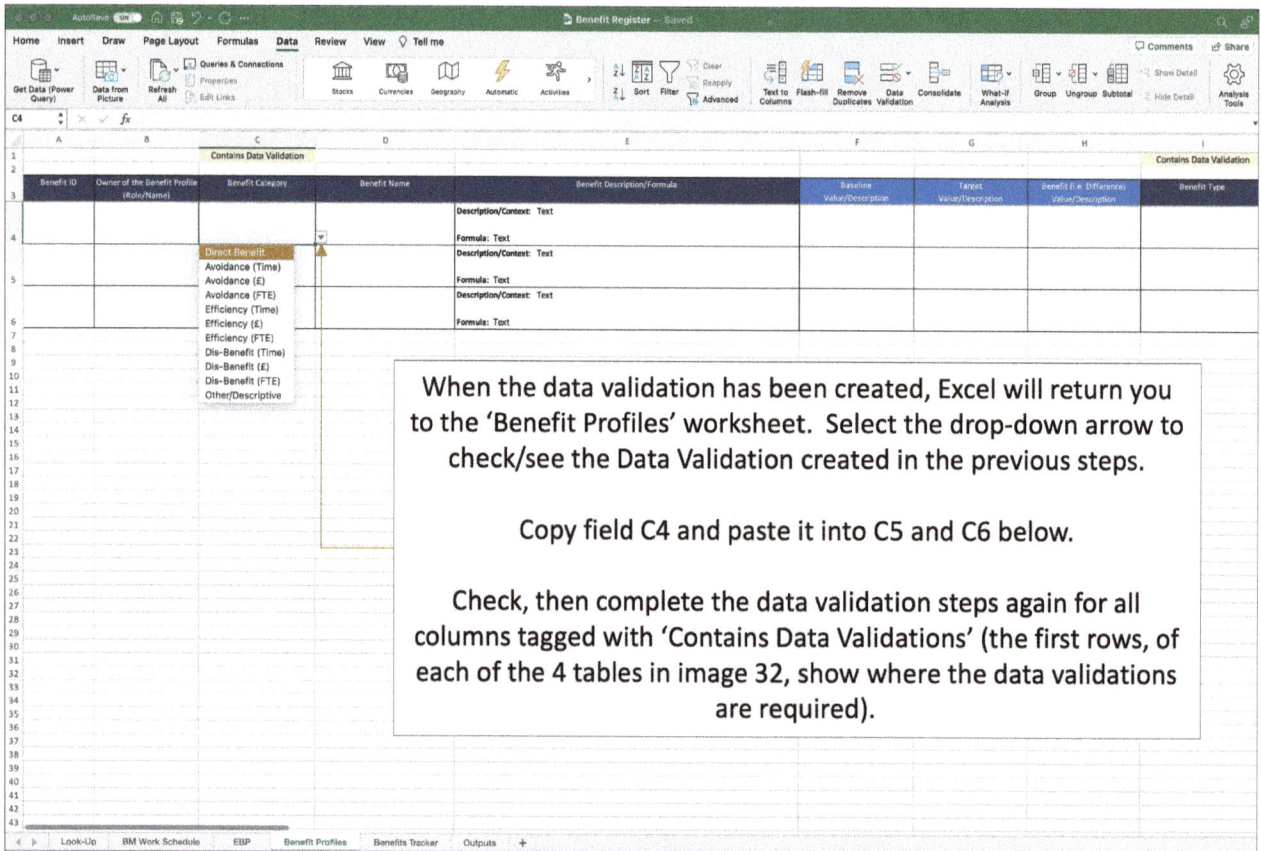

When the data validation has been created, Excel will return you to the 'Benefit Profiles' worksheet. Select the drop-down arrow to check/see the Data Validation created in the previous steps.

Copy field C4 and paste it into C5 and C6 below.

Check, then complete the data validation steps again for all columns tagged with 'Contains Data Validations' (the first rows, of each of the 4 tables in image 32, show where the data validations are required).

IMAGE 37 *Review.*

5.6 Benefit Profiles (Populate Template)

5.6.1 At Images 38 and 39, you will find the 3 Benefit Profiles captured under para 1.3.1, sub paras d, e and f, underline starting to be populated into the Benefit Profiles worksheet in the Benefit Register; both of these images incorporate guidance to help you. Review para 1.3.1 and see how the information has been transferred into the 'grey' fields below. Image 38 consists of the first 17 columns of the Benefit Profiles. When populating the fields, refer to the logic to remind you (Table 1) and the Benefit Profiles Categorisations between para 4.2–4.30 until you are comfortable.

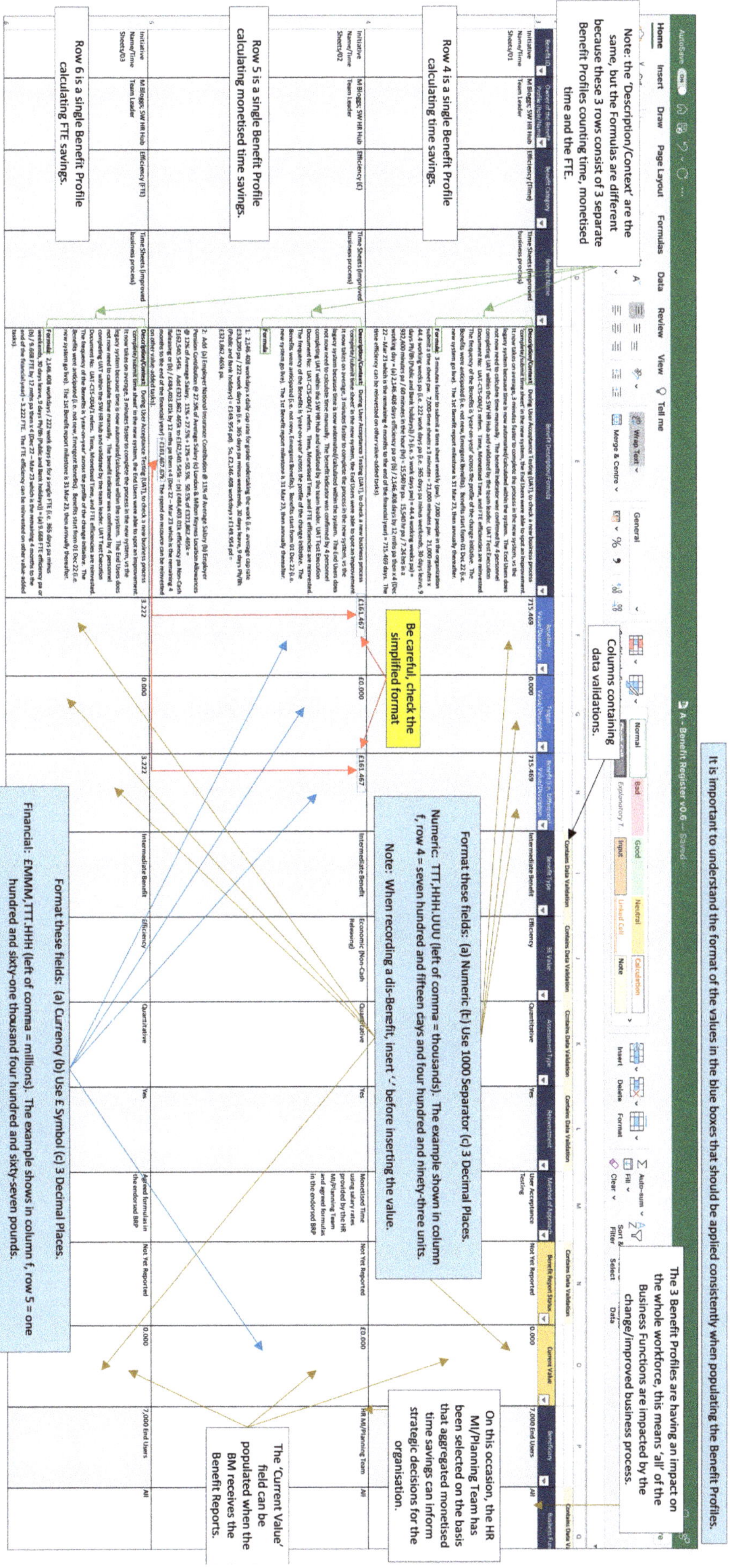

IMAGE 38 *Populating the Benefit Profiles in the Benefit Profiles Worksheet – First 17 Columns.*

5.6.2 Image 39 captures the final 12 columns of the first 3 Benefit Profiles.

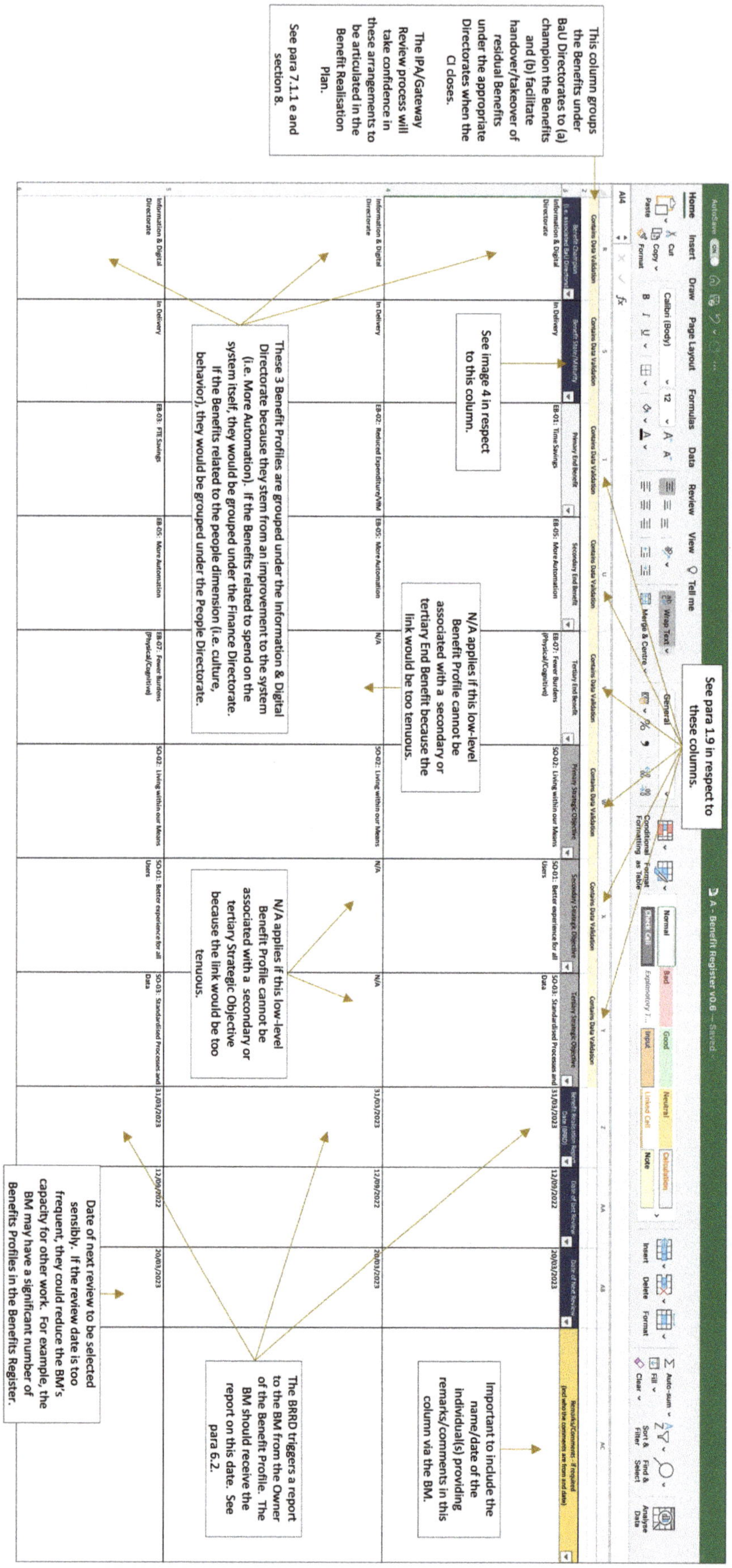

IMAGE 39 *Populating the Benefit Profiles in the Benefit Profiles Worksheet – Final 12 Columns.*

5.6.3 Having <u>initially</u> created the 3 Benefit Profiles, the BM is aware they are not one off, they are recurring year-on-year efficiencies. Para 1.4.3 a, b and c shows the 3 Benefit Profiles result in 24 Benefit Profiles (i.e. 8 x time, 8 x monetised time and 8 x FTE efficiencies across the life of the CI).

5.6.4 The following steps show the BM how to generate the 24 Benefit Profiles from the initial 3 shown in Images 38 and 39.

a. Colour the 3 Benefit Profiles (Column A 'Benefit ID') as follows or use your own choice of colour; this will help you in the subsequent steps:

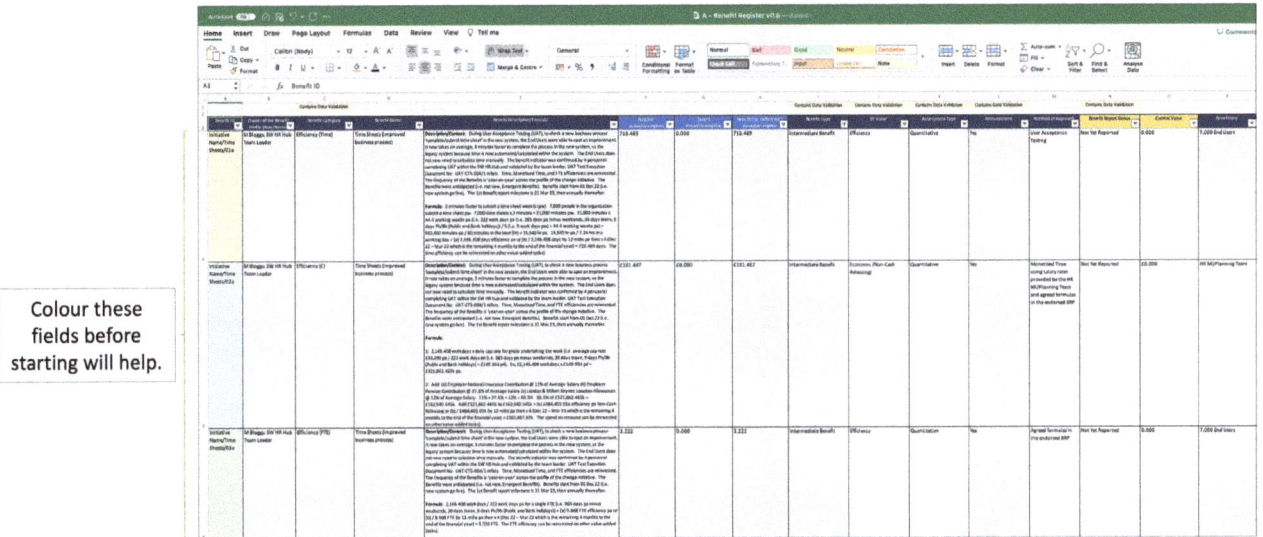

Colour these fields before starting will help.

IMAGE 40 *Prepare to Generate 24 Benefit Profiles from 3.*

b. Copy the yellow, blue and green rows 7 more times each so you have 8 of each[63]. When copying the profiles, highlight the entire row (i.e. row 4), right click and select 'copy'; then move/highlight the next row down and select '**insert copied cells**', then carry on with this process until you have 8 yellow, 8 blue and 8 green rows. They should look like this (it is easy to make a mistake – be careful to ensure you have 8 of each):

---

63 Inserting a colour before copying the Benefit Profiles reduces risk of error (i.e. the BM can see which 8 profiles relate to time, which 8 profiles relate to monetised time, and which 8 profiles relate to the FTE).

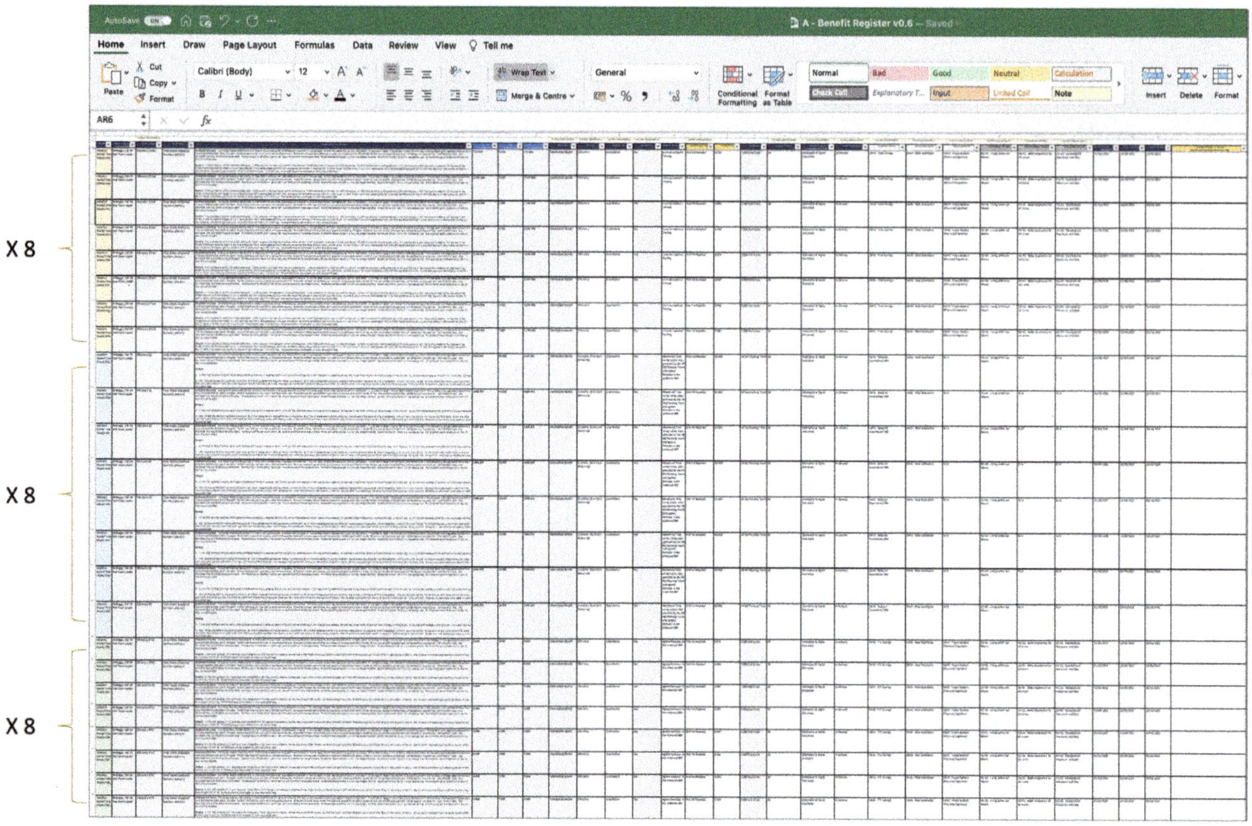

IMAGE 41 *Generating 24 Benefit Profiles from 3.*

c. Complete the 3 steps/actions demonstrated in Image 42.

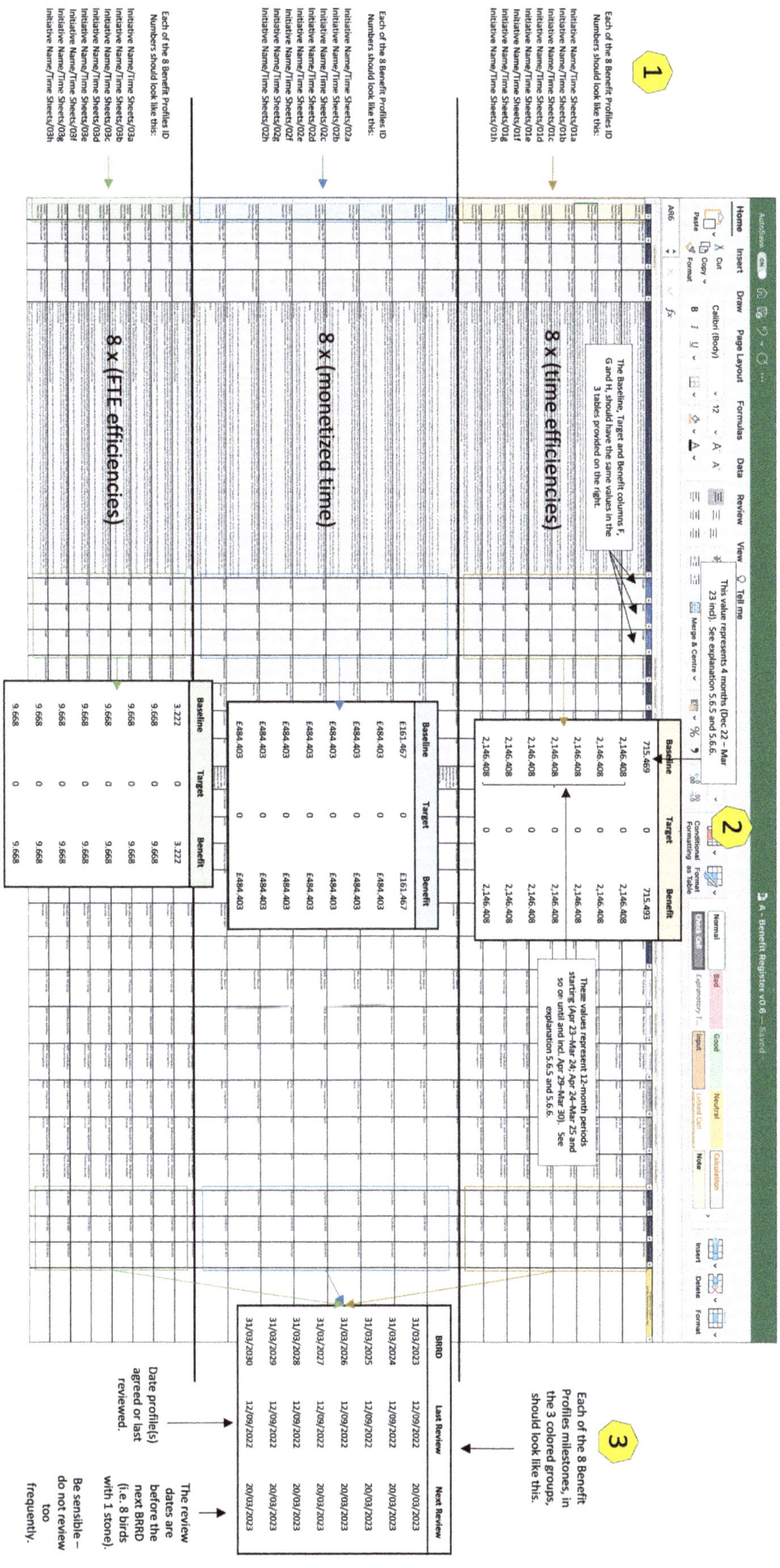

IMAGE 42 *Complete the 24 Benefit Profiles.*

5.6.5 There are 3 tables at step 2, Image 42. The values came from the Benefit Profiles explained in para 1.4.3 a, b and c. Remember, 'the new business process was implemented Nov 22; the Benefits are calculated from 01 Dec 22 (01 Dec 22 is year 3 in the life of the CI); each year calculation is 01 Apr–31 Mar'. That means the 3 groups of 8 Benefit Profiles (i.e. time, monetised time and FTE) are structured as follows.

Period	Year	Duration
(a)	(b)	(c)
01 Dec 22–31 Mar 23	This is year 3	4 months
01 Apr 23–31 Mar 24	This is year 4	1 year
01 Apr 24–31 Mar 25	This is year 5	1 year
01 Apr 25–31 Mar 26	This is year 6	1 year
01 Apr 26–31 Mar 27	This is year 7	1 year
01 Apr 27–31 Mar 28	This is year 8	1 year
01 Apr 28–31 Mar 29	This is year 9	1 year
01 Apr 29–31 Mar 30	This is year 10	1 year

TABLE 5 *Structure of the 8 Benefit Profiles, in each of the 3 groups shown in Image 42.*

5.6.6 Table 6 consists of a cut/paste of the 'Formula' from Column E, Image 42: The 4 months value can be seen in GREEN; the annual value can be seen in BLUE.

Type	Benefit Description/Formula
(a)	(b)
Time	3 minutes faster to submit a time sheet weekly (pw). 7,000 people in the organisation submit a time sheet pw. 7,000-time sheets x 3 minutes = 21,000 minutes pw. 21,000 minutes x 44.4 working weeks pa (i.e. 222 work days pa (i.e. 365 days pa minus weekends, 30 days leave, 9 days Ph/Bh / 5 (i.e. 5 work days pw) = 44.4 working weeks pa) = 932,400 minutes pa / 60 minutes in the hour (hr) = 15,540 hr pa. 15,540 hr pa / 7.24 hrs in a working day = (a) 2,146.408 days efficiency pa or (b) / 2,146.408 days by 12 mths pa then x 4 (Dec 22–Mar 23 which is the remaining 4 months to the end of the financial year) = 715.469 days. The time efficiency can be reinvested on other value-added tasks).

Type	Benefit Description/Formula
(a)	(b)
Monetised Time	1: 2,146.408 workdays x daily cap rate for grade undertaking the work (i.e. average cap rate £33,290 pa) / 222 work days pa (i.e. 365 days pa minus weekends, 30 days leave, 9 days Ph/Bh = £149.954 pd). So, £2,146.408 workdays x £149.954 pd = £321,862.465k pa. 2: Add (a) Employer National Insurance Contribution @ 11% of Average Salary (b) Employer Pension Contribution @ 27.5% of Average Salary (c) London & Milton Keynes Location Allowances @ 12% of Average Salary. 11% + 27.5% + 12% = 50.5%. 50.5% of £321,862.465k = £162,540.545k. Add £321,862.465k to £162,540.545k = (a) £484,403.01k efficiency pa Non-Cash Releasing or (b) / £484,403.01k by 12 mths pa then x 4 (Dec 22–Mar 23 which is the remaining 4 months to the end of the financial year) = £161,467.67k. The spend on resources can be reinvested on other value-added tasks).
FTE	Formula: 2,146.408 workdays / 222 work days pa for a single FTE (i.e. 365 days pa minus weekends, 30 days leave, 9 days Ph/Bh) = (a) 9.668 FTE efficiency pa or (b) / 9.668 FTE by 12 mths pa then x 4 (Dec 22–Mar 23 which is the remaining 4 months to the end of the financial year) = 3.222 FTE. The FTE efficiency can be reinvested on other value-added tasks).

TABLE 6 *Cut/paste of the 'Formula' from Column E, Image 42.*

5.6.7 When all steps/actions to generate the 24 Benefit Profiles from 3 are complete, calculate the totals to check you have populated the values correctly. For example (a) total time efficiency: 15,740.325k (b) total monetised time: circ. £3.552M (c) total FTE efficiencies: 70.898 FTE. Check these values with what has been articulated in para 1.4.3 a, b and c.

5.6.8 Remember, the monetised values in the Benefit Profiles worksheet, are to be like-for-like with the monetised values in the EBP worksheet. Both worksheets are updated concurrently. Image 43 shows the values being incorporated into the EBP worksheet under the 'Other Benefits':

Here are the 8 x monetised time, year-on-year efficiencies (also called (a) Non-Cash Releasing Benefits (b) year-on-year targets) in the EBP.

Total = same monetised value specified in para 5.6.7 above.

Previous Years
Current Year (also called 'in-year')
Future Forecast

		FY 20/21 Year 1	FY 21/22 Year 2	FY 22/23 Year 3	FY 23/24 Year 4	FY 24/25 Year 5	FY 25/26 Year 6	FY 26/27 Year 7	FY 27/28 Year 8	FY 28/29 Year 9	FY 29/30 Year 10	Total	Owner of the Profile
Other Benefit	New Business Process	£0.000	£0.000	£161.467	£484.403	£484.403	£484.403	£484.403	£484.403	£484.403	£484.403	£3,552.288	Role/Name
Other Benefit	Licenses (PaaS/IaaS) - Forecast Reduced	£0.000	£0.000	£0.000	£50.000	£50.000	£50.000	£50.000	£50.000	£50.000	£50.000	£350.000	Role/Name
Other Benefit	FBC Final Options 4 vs Option 5 Difference	£0.000	£17,365.222	£0.000	£0.000	£0.000	£0.000	£0.000	£0.000	£0.000	£0.000	£17,365.222	Role/Name
Other Benefit	Increased preventative Fruad/Misuse of Funds	£0.000	£0.000	£1,534.000	£1,534.000	£1,534.000	£1,534.000	£1,534.000	£1,534.000	£1,534.000	£1,534.000	£12,272.000	Role/Name
Other Benefit	Platform Security Assurance (Initial)	£0.000	£0.000	£31.500	£0.000	£0.000	£0.000	£0.000	£31.500	£0.000	£0.000	£63.000	Role/Name
Other Benefit	Platform Security Assurance (Annual)	£0.000	£0.000	£0.000	£4.500	£4.500	£4.500	£4.500	£4.500	£4.500	£4.500	£31.500	Role/Name
Other Benefit	Procure a New Platform	£0.000	£0.000	£28.728	£0.000	£0.000	£0.000	£0.000	£28.728	£0.000	£0.000	£57.456	Role/Name
Other Benefit	Other	£0.000	£0.000	£0.000	£0.000	£0.000	£0.000	£0.000	£0.000	£0.000	£0.000	£0.000	
	Total (£)	£0.000	£17,365.222	£1,755.695	£2,072.903	£2,072.903	£2,072.903	£2,072.903	£2,133.131	£2,072.903	£2,072.903	£33,691.466	

IMAGE 43 *Reconciling EBP and Benefit Profiles Worksheets With Monetised Values.*

5.6.9 PivotTables/charts in the Benefit Register are to be refreshed when the EBP or Benefit Profiles worksheets have been updated.

5.6.10 In the context of numeric or monetised values, the format of the Baseline, Target and Benefit fields (columns F, G and H, Image 38), can be constructed in 2 different ways. Using monetised values as an example, both formats can be seen in Table 7.

Baseline	**Target**	**Benefit**	**Explanation**
(a)	**(b)**	**(c)**	**(d)**
£17.234k	£0	£17.234k	The owner of this Benefit Profile is content that the scale of the saving has been quantified correctly, but the owner does not know the full extent of the budget in which the £17.234k saving belongs.
£15,067.234M	£15,050.000M	£17.234k	The owner of this Benefit Profile is content that the scale of the saving has been quantified correctly, and the owner has access to and knows the full extent of the budget in which the £17.234k saving belongs.

TABLE 7 *Format of the Baseline, Target and Benefit Monetised Values with Explanation.*

5.7 Benefit Tracker

5.7.1 The BM requires a Benefit Tracker (BT) to be able to track milestones such as the BRRDs and Benefit Review Dates. This enables the BM to plan and initiate Benefit reporting activity and, reviews of Benefit Profiles with their owners, so they remain accurate, supported, and validated. In addition, the CI will take confidence in the knowledge that a Benefit Monitoring and Reporting regime is being undertaken by the BM.

5.7.2 The BT is straight forward to create in Excel. It consists of a Line Chart that has been generated from a PivotTable that draws information from the Benefit Profiles worksheet. How to create the BT is shown at Images 44–53. The BT is drawing from 74 Benefit Profiles comprising (a) the 24 Benefit Profiles created at Image 42, and (b) the 50 Direct Benefits referred to at para 2.4.6.

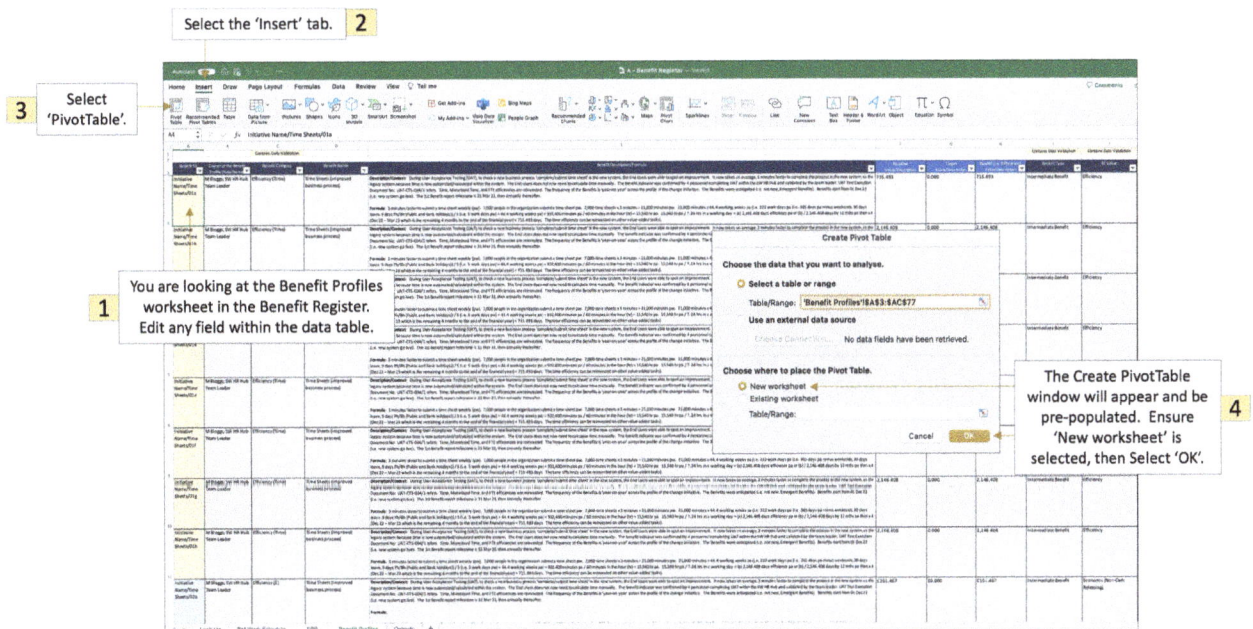

IMAGE 44 *Create a PivotTable from the Benefit Profiles Worksheet.*

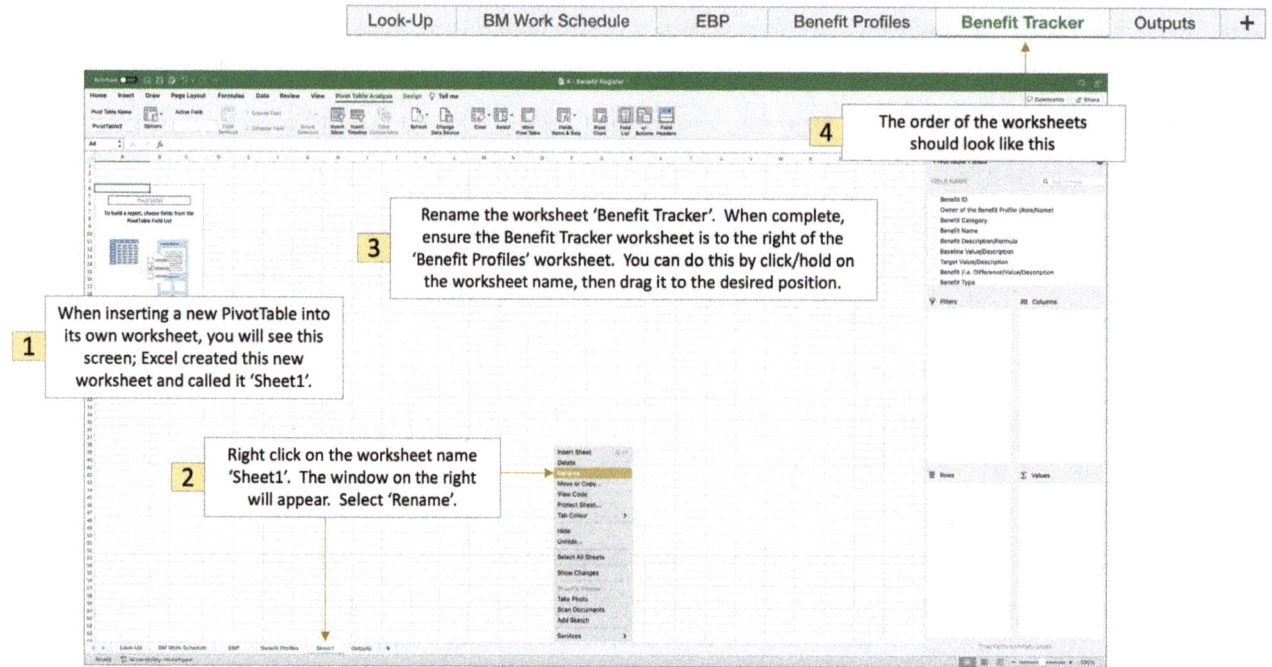

IMAGE 45 *Name and Position the PivotTable.*

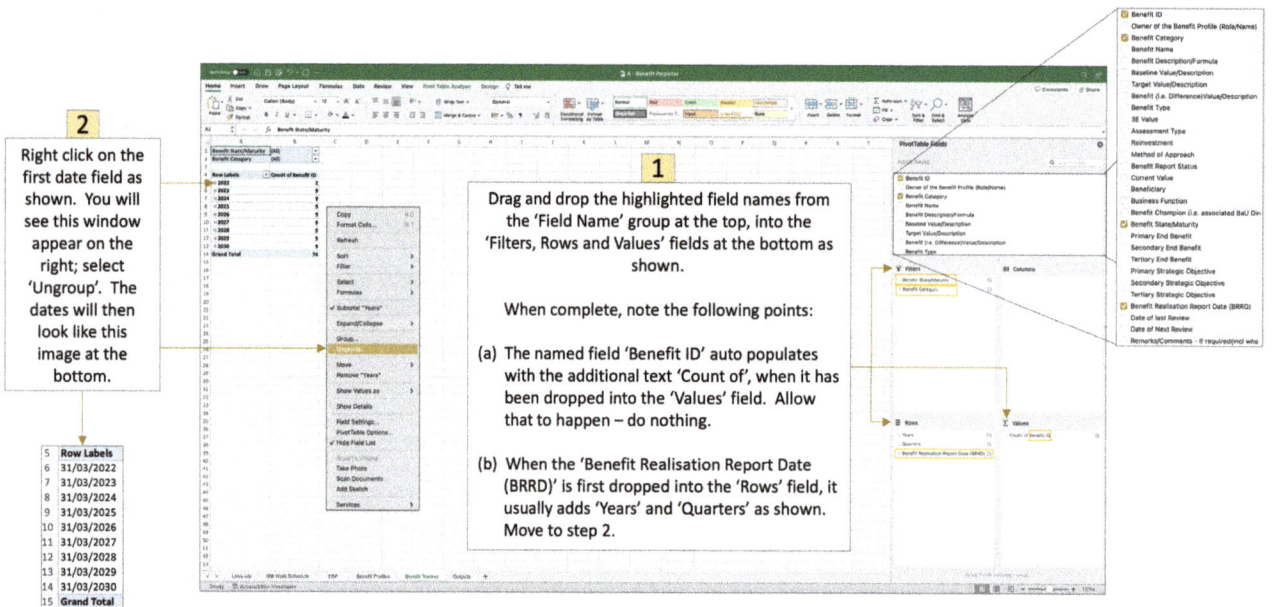

IMAGE 46 **Populate the PivotTable.**

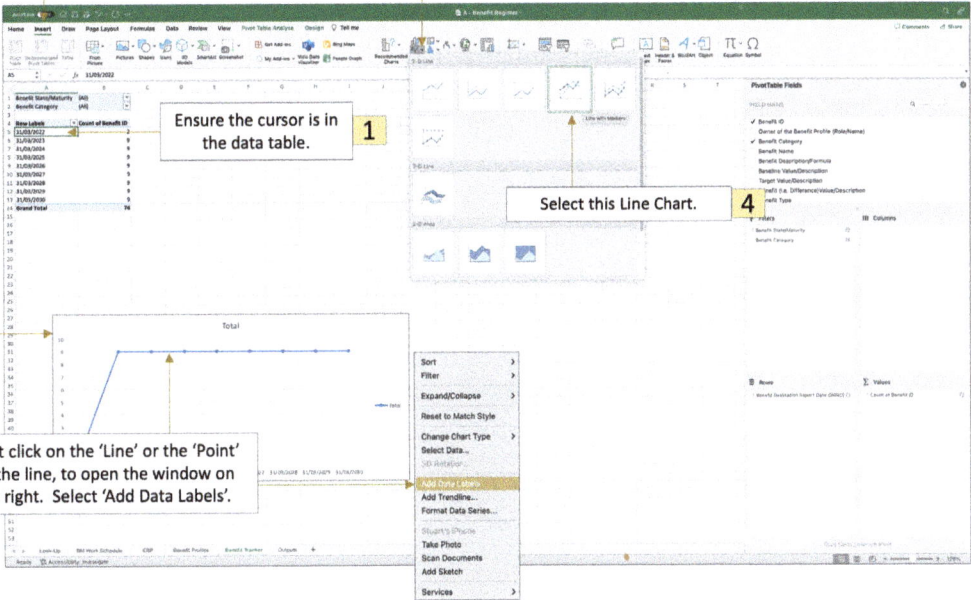

2 Select the 'Insert' tab.

3 Select the Line Chart field.

1 Ensure the cursor is in the data table.

4 Select this Line Chart.

5 After selecting the specified Line Chart in step 4, it will drop into the middle of your screen and look like this. You can click onto the chart then 'drag' one of the 4 corners to increase its size so you can see what you are doing.

6 Right click on the 'Line' or the 'Point' on the line, to open the window on the right. Select 'Add Data Labels'.

IMAGE 47 *Insert the Line Chart.*

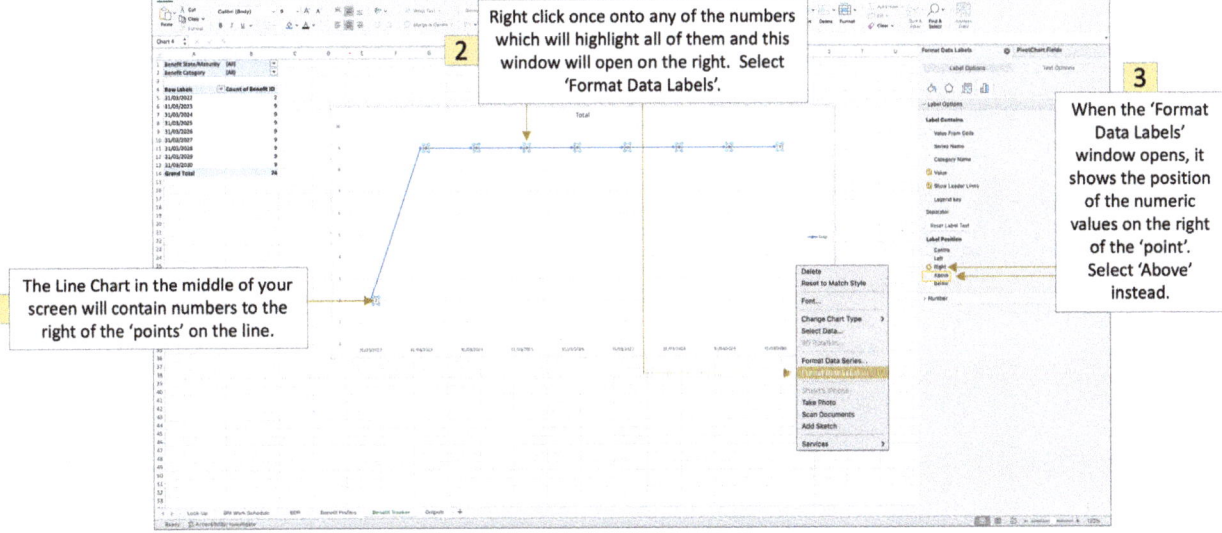

2 Right click once onto any of the numbers which will highlight all of them and this window will open on the right. Select 'Format Data Labels'.

3 When the 'Format Data Labels' window opens, it shows the position of the numeric values on the right of the 'point'. Select 'Above' instead.

1 The Line Chart in the middle of your screen will contain numbers to the right of the 'points' on the line.

IMAGE 48 *Format the Line Chart.*

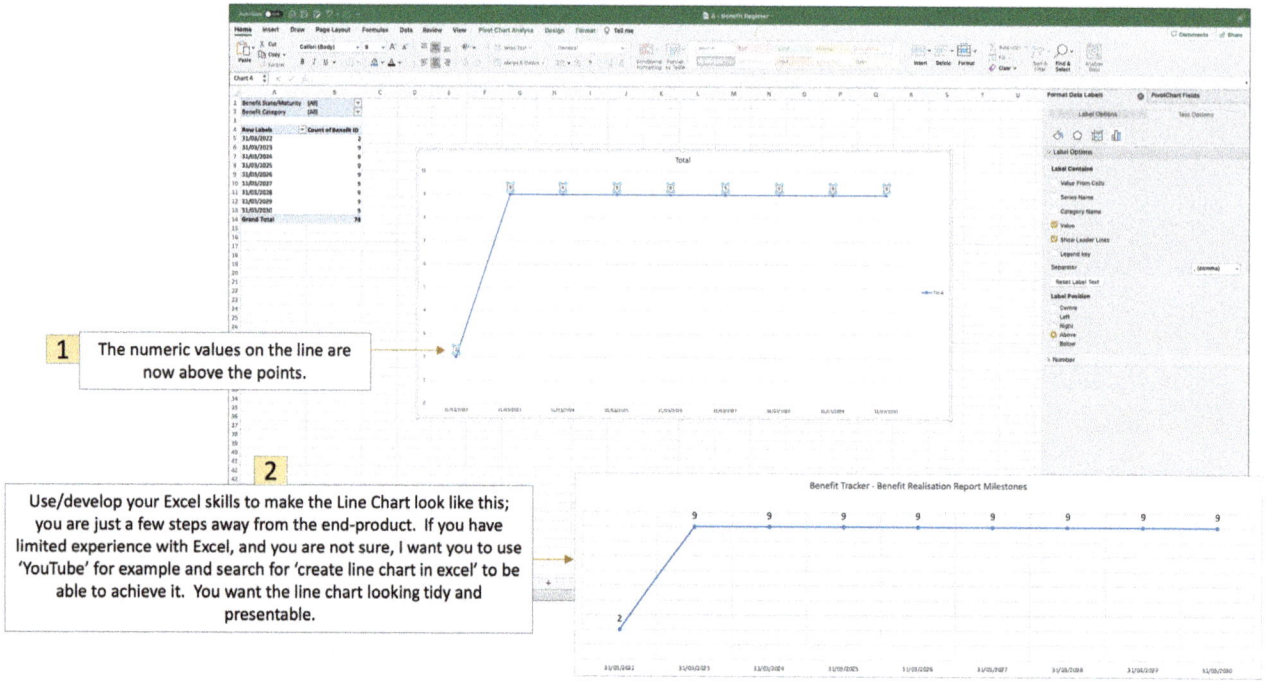

1 The numeric values on the line are now above the points.

2 Use/develop your Excel skills to make the Line Chart look like this; you are just a few steps away from the end-product. If you have limited experience with Excel, and you are not sure, I want you to use 'YouTube' for example and search for 'create line chart in excel' to be able to achieve it. You want the line chart looking tidy and presentable.

IMAGE 49 *Final Steps/Formatting.*

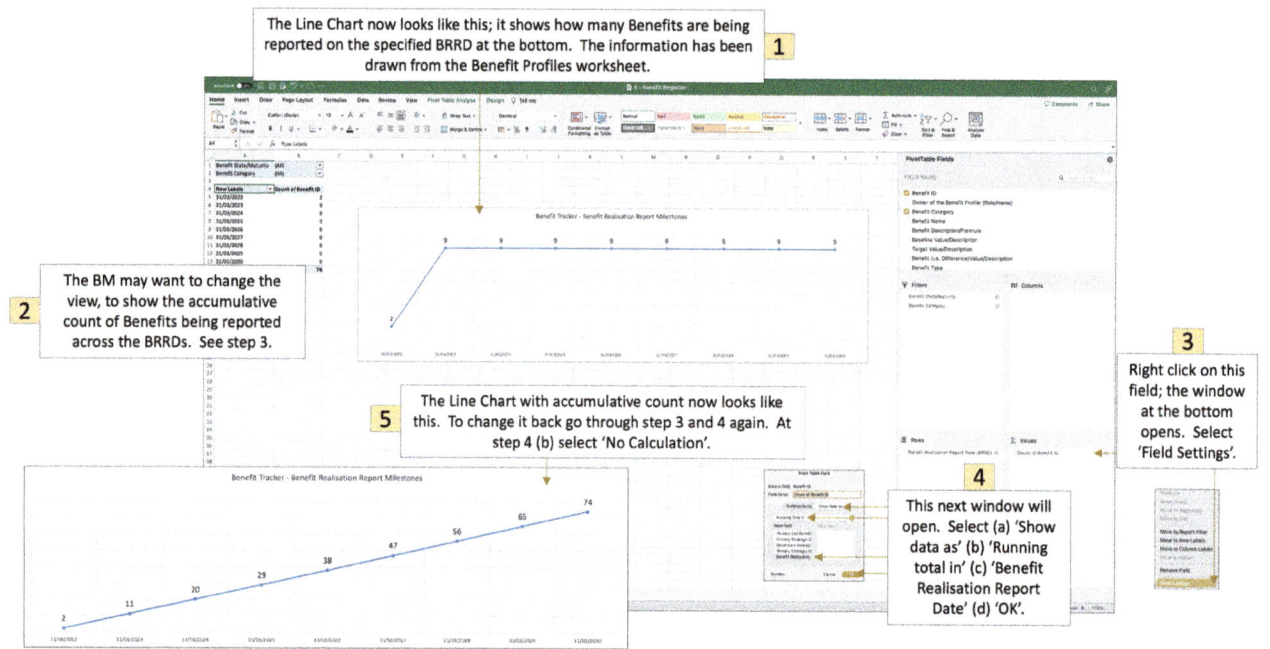

1 The Line Chart now looks like this; it shows how many Benefits are being reported on the specified BRRD at the bottom. The information has been drawn from the Benefit Profiles worksheet.

2 The BM may want to change the view, to show the accumulative count of Benefits being reported across the BRRDs. See step 3.

3 Right click on this field; the window at the bottom opens. Select 'Field Settings'.

4 This next window will open. Select (a) 'Show data as' (b) 'Running total in' (c) 'Benefit Realisation Report Date' (d) 'OK'.

5 The Line Chart with accumulative count now looks like this. To change it back go through step 3 and 4 again. At step 4 (b) select 'No Calculation'.

IMAGE 50 *Exploit the software.*

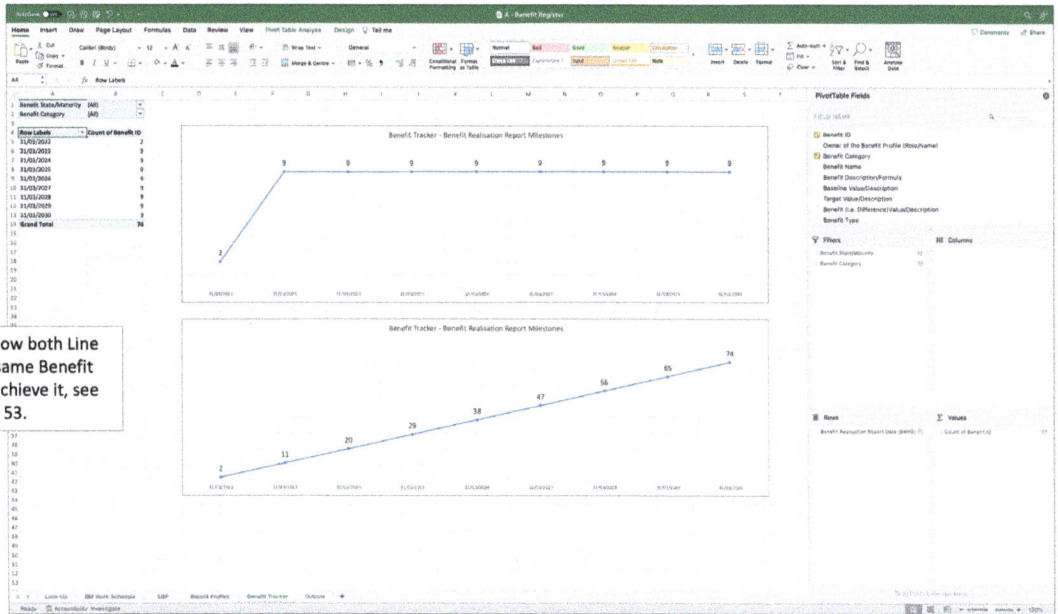

The author prefers to show both Line Charts together in the same Benefit Tracker worksheet. To achieve it, see images 52 and 53.

IMAGE 51 *Both Benefit Trackers side-by-side.*

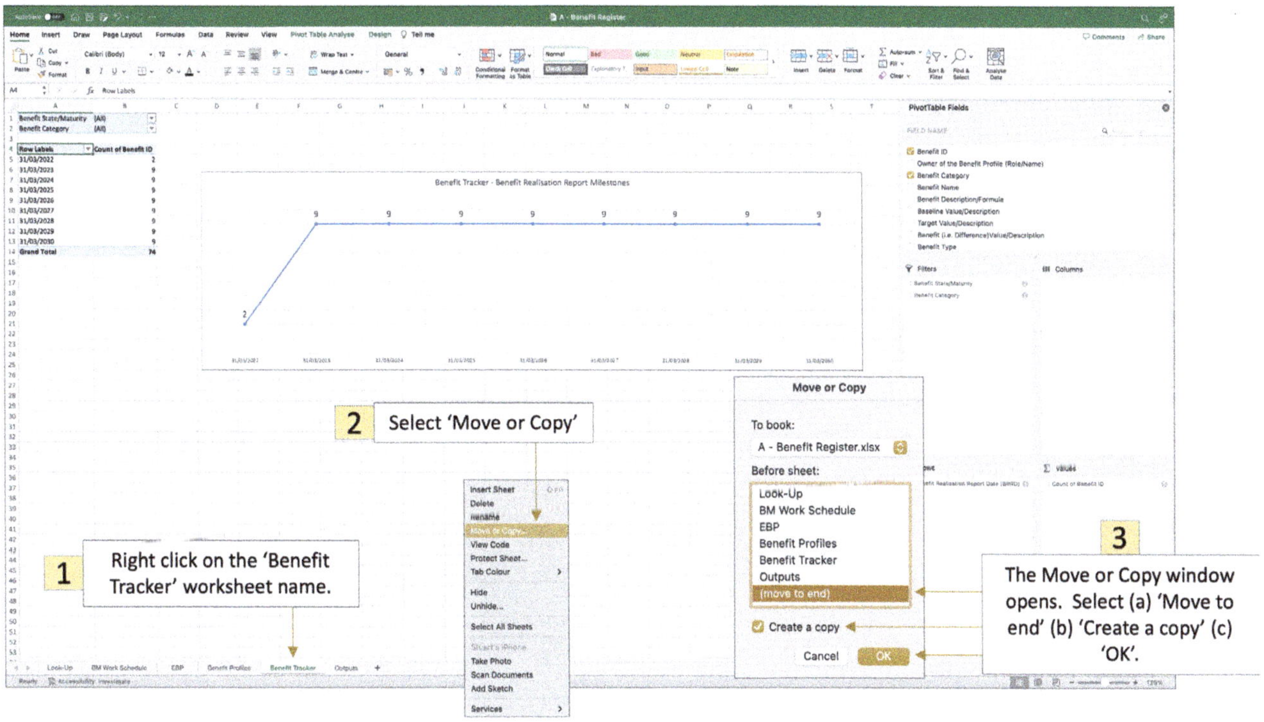

2 Select 'Move or Copy'

1 Right click on the 'Benefit Tracker' worksheet name.

3 The Move or Copy window opens. Select (a) 'Move to end' (b) 'Create a copy' (c) 'OK'.

IMAGE 52 *Copy the Benefit Tracker Worksheet.*

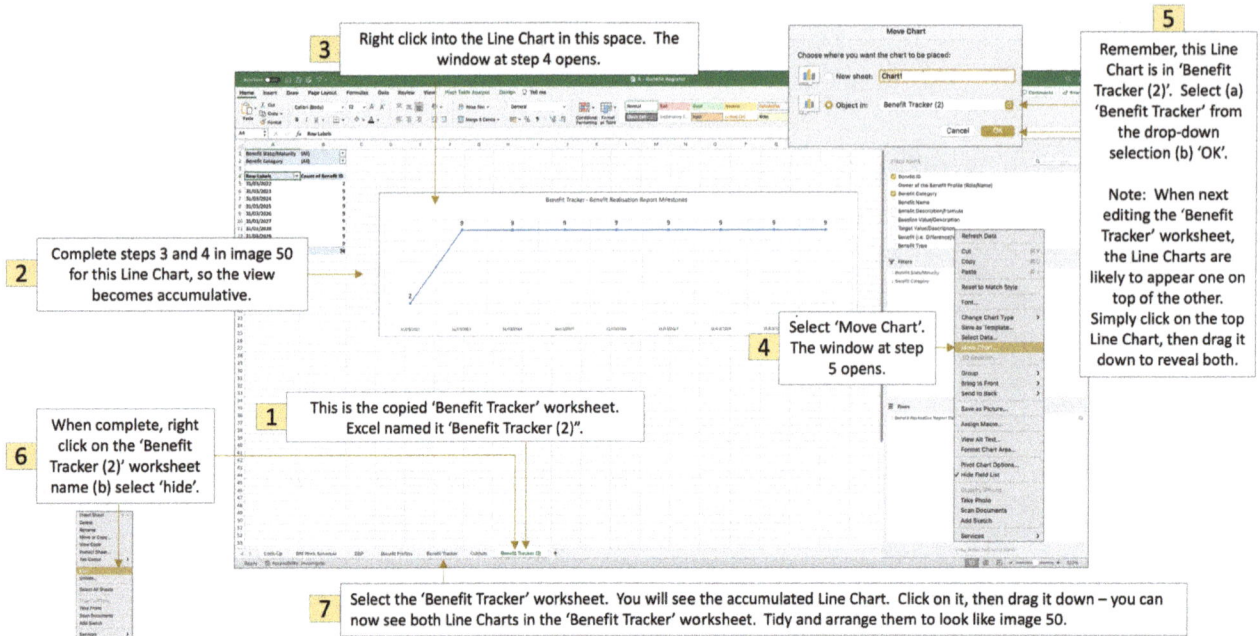

3 Right click into the Line Chart in this space. The window at step 4 opens.

5 Remember, this Line Chart is in 'Benefit Tracker (2)'. Select (a) 'Benefit Tracker' from the drop-down selection (b) 'OK'.

Note: When next editing the 'Benefit Tracker' worksheet, the Line Charts are likely to appear one on top of the other. Simply click on the top Line Chart, then drag it down to reveal both.

2 Complete steps 3 and 4 in image 50 for this Line Chart, so the view becomes accumulative.

4 Select 'Move Chart'. The window at step 5 opens.

1 This is the copied 'Benefit Tracker' worksheet. Excel named it 'Benefit Tracker (2)'.

6 When complete, right click on the 'Benefit Tracker (2)' worksheet name (b) select 'hide'.

7 Select the 'Benefit Tracker' worksheet. You will see the accumulated Line Chart. Click on it, then drag it down – you can now see both Line Charts in the 'Benefit Tracker' worksheet. Tidy and arrange them to look like image 50.

IMAGE 53 *Prepare/Move Line Chart from 'Benefit Tracker (2)' Worksheet to the 'Benefit Tracker' Worksheet.*

5.7.3 The BT in this section of the guide is used to monitor the BRRD. The BM uses it to chase Benefit Reports that have not been submitted and plan for subsequent Benefit Reports to be sent to the owner of the Benefit Profile for their completion.

5.7.4 If the BM wants to create a similar Line Chart to visualise the 'Date of Next Review' so they can be monitored for planning purposes, follow the seps in Images 44–53 but this time, in Image 46 step 1, insert the 'Date of Next Review' into the 'Rows' field, not the BRRD.

5.7.5 When the Benefit State/Maturity categorisations, in the Benefit Profiles worksheet, have been populated with 'Realised' or 'Cancelled', these 2 categorisations are to be de-selected from inside the BT; otherwise, the BM will be planning BRRDs and Date of Next Reviews for Benefit Profiles that have either been Delivered or Cancelled. Image 54 is a screen grab of the BT showing where to de-select the specified fields when they appear.

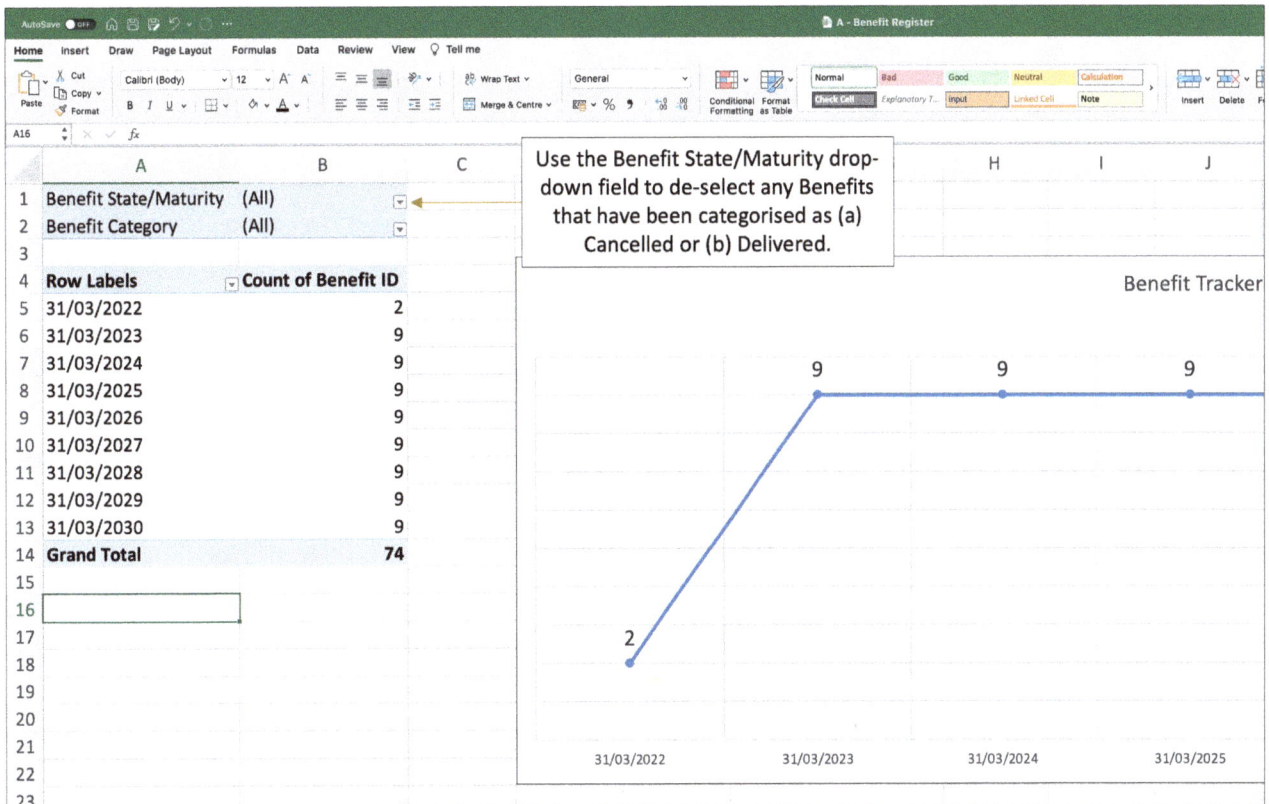

IMAGE 54 *Deselect 'Delivered' and 'Cancelled' Benefits from the Tracker.*

5.7.6 Tip. After a PivotTable has been created from the Benefit Profiles worksheet, and in the event more Benefit Profiles are added into the Benefit Profiles worksheet after the last entry, the PivotTable does not always pick them up. You can get around this by adding new profiles 'before' the last entry.

5.8 Outputs

5.8.1 Para 3.4 explains what an output is; para 3.3 explains the associated LoDs; para 6.6 explains output reporting and an associated report/template that has been used in the MOD/HO.

5.8.2 Why is it useful to record the outputs in the Benefit Register? To enable a reporting regime, if that is required. Most organisations who have captured and recorded the high-level outputs on the left-hand side of the Benefit Map do not appear to be reporting the 'Delivery Confidence' of those outputs because governance is not asking for it. An old saying: *'take care of the pennies and the pounds will take care of themselves'*. In other words, take care of the outputs and the outcomes will take care of themselves. However, not entirely true but, the point is that outputs are of significant importance and enablers of the 'new state' (i.e. the outcomes). Underperformance will require coordinated, corrective action to shore up the Outcomes, Benefits and Objectives.

5.8.3 Post endorsement of the CI's Benefit Map, the outputs (and their owners) can be recorded in the Benefit Register to receive reported information and updates on the delivery of those outputs, if that is required. An example of how the outputs can be recorded in the Benefit Register is shown at Image 55.

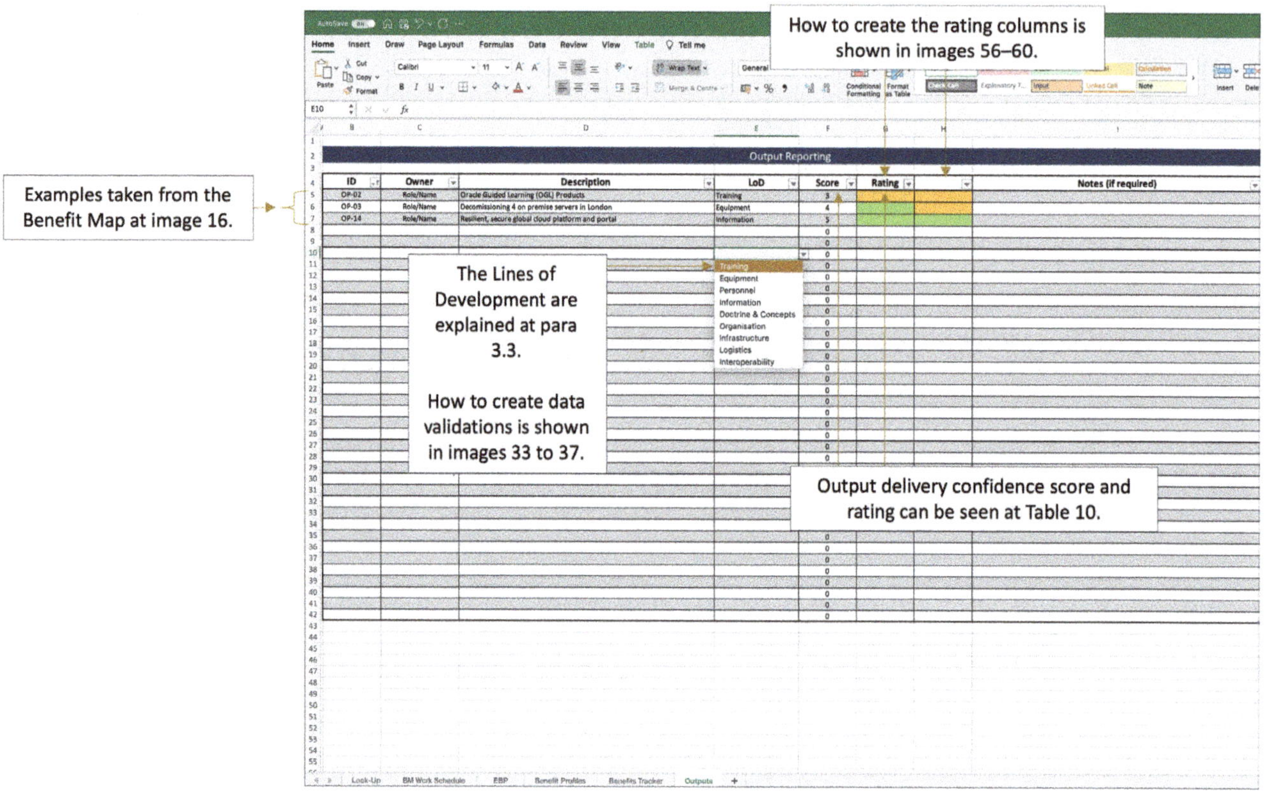

IMAGE 55 *Recording the Outputs in the Benefit Register.*

5.8.4 Images 56 to 60 show how to create new rules so the ratings Columns G and H auto populate when the outputs have been scored in Column F. Score, ratings and their descriptions can be seen at Table 10.

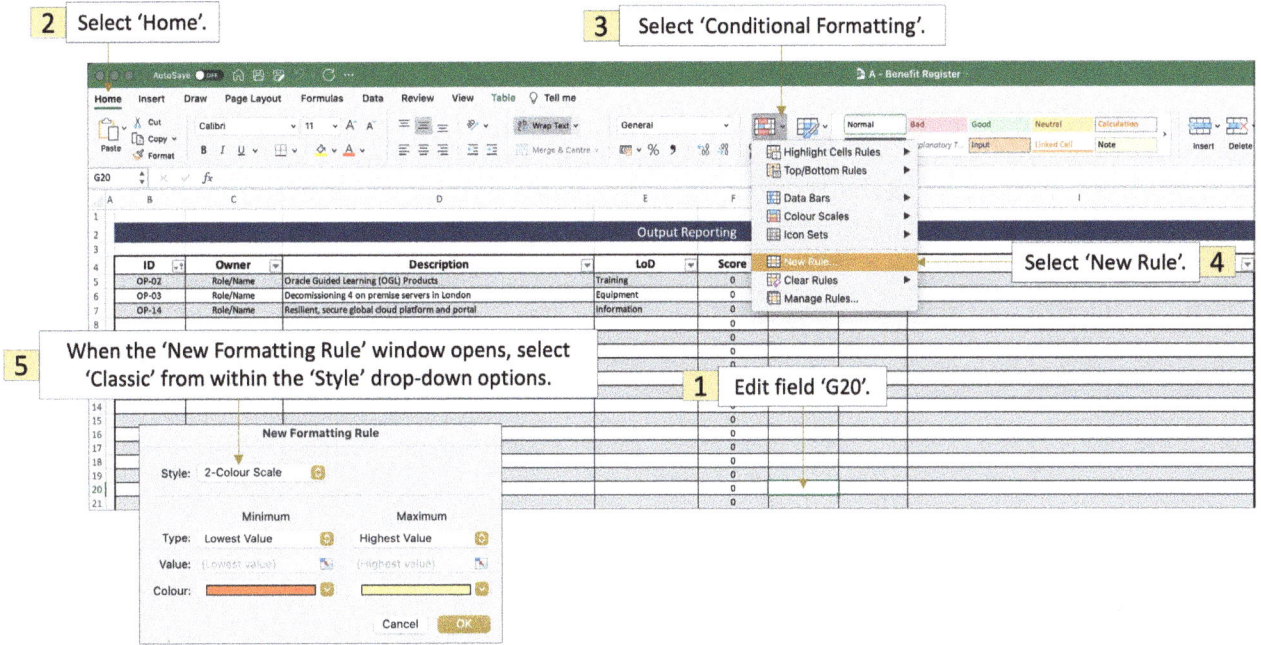

IMAGE 56 *Create a New Rule – field G20.*

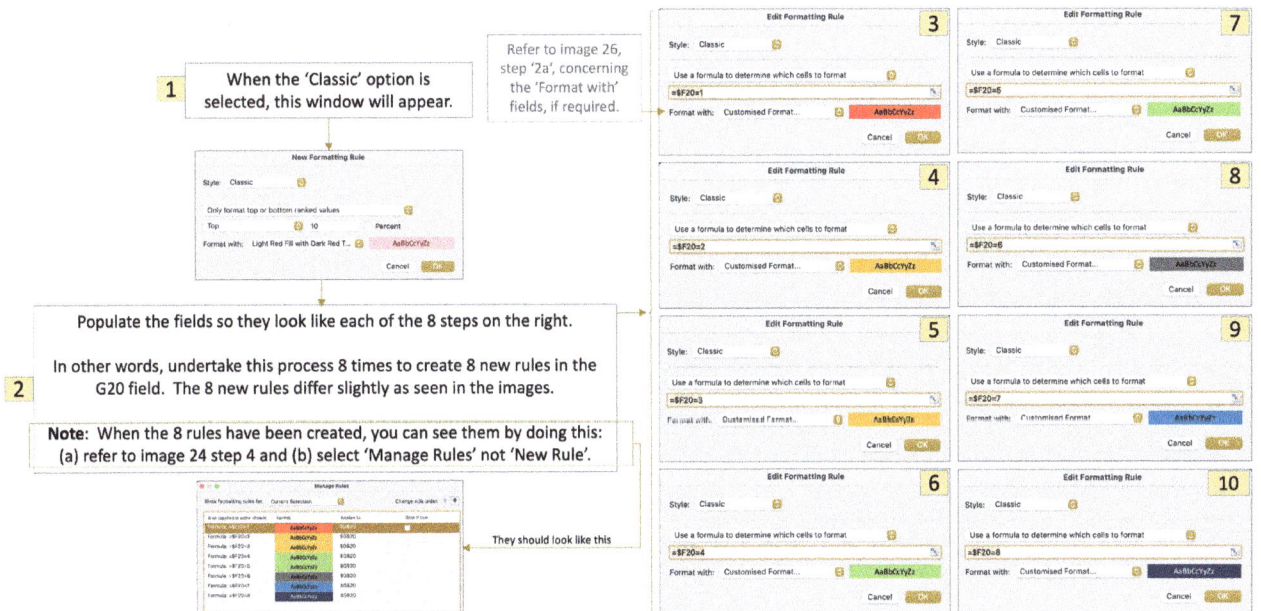

IMAGE 57 *Create 8 New Rules – field G20.*

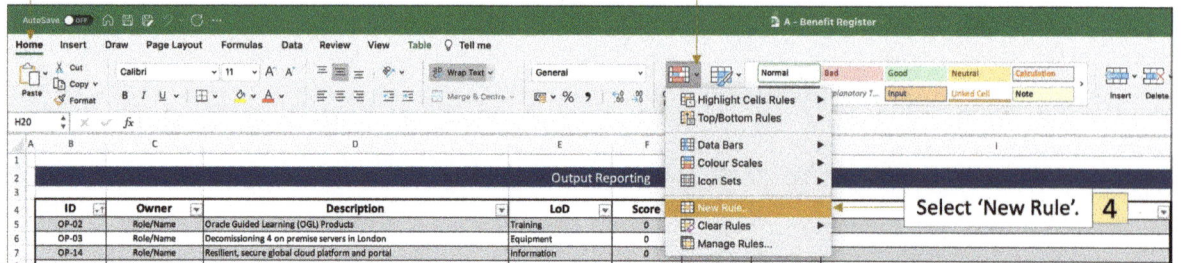

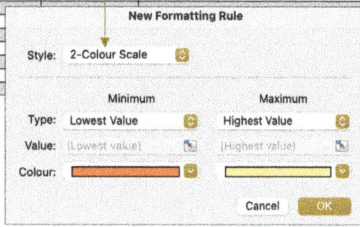

IMAGE 58 *Create a New Rule – field H20.*

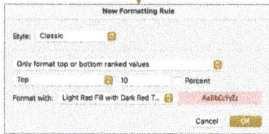

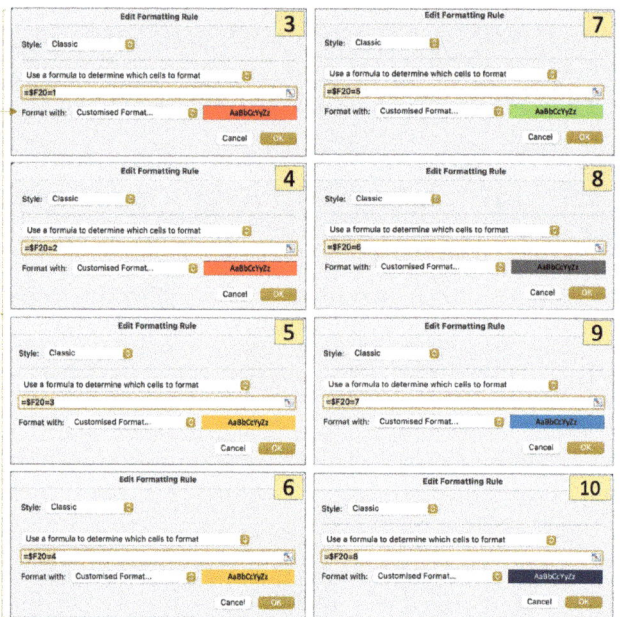

IMAGE 59 *Create 8 New Rules – field H20.*

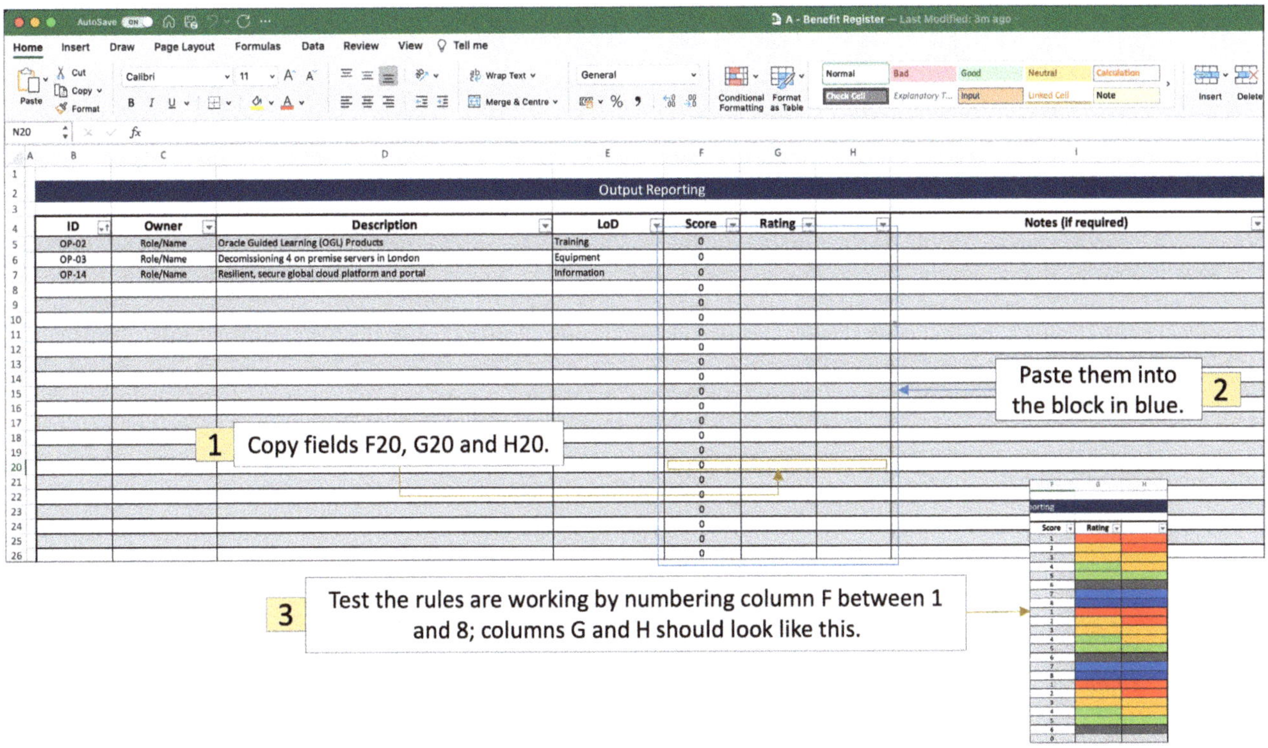

IMAGE 60 *Review.*

SECTION 6

Reporting

6.1 Introduction

6.1.1 It is important to document the approach to reporting, in the CI's BRP that is circulated to stakeholders both in/out of the CI for support and endorsement. A simple approach is more likely to succeed for the reasons explained below. There are 3 key areas for consideration: (a) reporting of the Benefits themselves (b) Benefit Report thresholds and (c) output reporting. Each is explained in this section with examples and templates to assist the BM.

6.2 Benefit Reporting

6.2.1 The reporting of Benefits can be undertaken in different ways and formats. Of course, a retained email, for example, from the Owner of a Benefit Profile could be sufficient. But a slightly formal approach could be seen to be more acceptable. The template and approach articulated below have been successfully used in the HO and the FCDO because they are not intrusive[64].

6.2.2 Benefit Profiles are recorded in a Benefit Register so they can be managed and reported. Each Benefit is tagged with a BRRD. The BRRD is confirmed by the owner of the Benefit Profile who is assisted by the BM. The BRRD triggers the owner of the Benefit Profile to submit a Benefit Realisation Report to the BM. The BM monitors BRRDs using a tracker in the Benefit Register; see para 5.7.

---

64 A previous SRO stated: 'we do not have the time, resource or capacity to undertake reporting, and this looks far too complicated'. The comment was in reference to a developing Benefit Report Template. It resulted in further engagements with Owners of Benefit Profiles that resulted in the simple template receiving support from the SRO.

6.3 Benefit Report Template

6.3.1 The Benefit Report template consists of an Excel document containing 2 worksheets. Worksheet 1 is the report itself. It intentionally contains only salient information so the reader is not presented with too much information when opening the document. Worksheet 2 is a cut/paste of the full Benefit Profiles from the master Benefit Register, comprising those Benefits being reported in worksheet 1. Worksheet 2 is a reference to remind the owner of the Benefit Profiles what was agreed when the Benefit Profiles were created then subsequently reviewed with the BM. The template is as follows[65]:

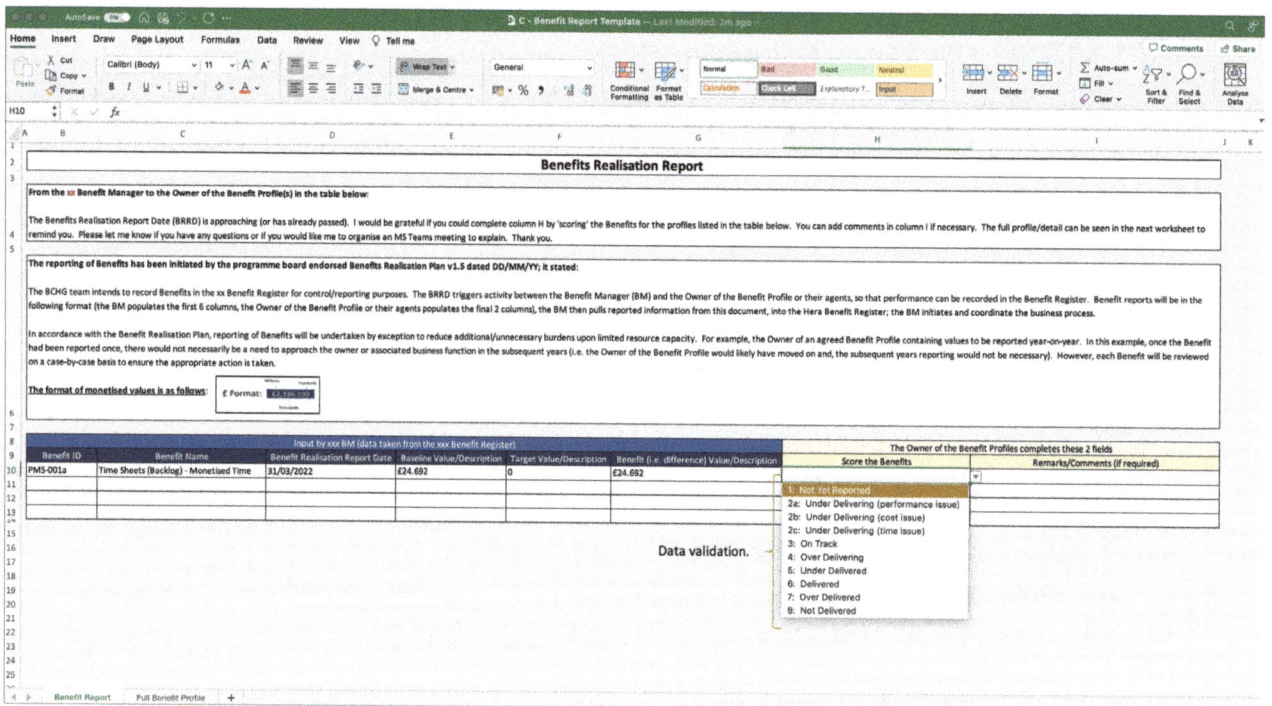

IMAGE 61 *Example – Benefit Realisation Report Template.*

6.3.2 The BRRD triggers activity between the BM and the owner of the Benefit Profiles, so that performance can be recorded in the Benefit Register. The BM populates the first 6 columns of the Benefit Report, the owner of the Benefit Profiles populates the final 2 columns. The BM then files the report that was completed by the owner of the Benefit Profiles and records the reported information into the master Benefit Register. This is a quick/simple process that is auditable. The BM initiates and coordinates the business process.

6.3.3 Owners of Benefit Profiles are to be informed in advance of their reporting milestones, and their reporting requirements. This will allow time for appro-

---

65 The template Benefit Report can be provided if requested by emailing this address: BRM.Mngr@hotmail.com

priate arrangements to be put in place by them to be able to track and monitor the performance of their Benefits in year. The Benefit Tracker within the master Benefit Register enables the BM to monitor and coordinate reporting activity.

6.3.4 The 'Score the Benefits' column consists of the 'Benefit Report Status'; see para 4.15. It contains a drop-down data validation field to simplify and reduce the reporting burdens upon the owner of the Benefit Profiles. When this reported information has been transferred into the Benefit Profiles in the Benefit Register by the BM, PivotTables and/or visualisations can be generated from it to provide insights and structured information for reporting purposes. See para 9.8.

6.3.5 Reporting can be undertaken by exception[66] to further reduce the reporting burdens placed on limited resource capacity. For example, the owner of an agreed Benefit Profile containing values to be reported year-on-year. In this example, once the Benefit had been reported once, there would not necessarily be a need to approach the owner or associated business function in the subsequent years (i.e. the owner of the Benefit Profile would likely have moved on and, the subsequent years reporting would not be necessary). However, each Benefit will be reviewed on a case-by-case basis to ensure the appropriate action is taken.

6.3.6 When the Benefit reporting regime has been implemented successfully, the process can be reviewed and ramped up/down as required. This guidance seeks to put a process in place to initiate reporting. The owner of the Benefit Profiles retains the source information that led to their determination when scoring the Benefits.

6.4 Schema

6.4.1 The 3 schemas help the BM and others to understand the processes involved when (a) planning Benefit Management activities for reporting, (b) scoring the Benefits, and (c) reporting Benefit Status by exception.

---

66 If this approach was mentioned within the CI's BRP that was subsequently supported, the BM can implement it.

Plan Benefits Management Activities for Reporting

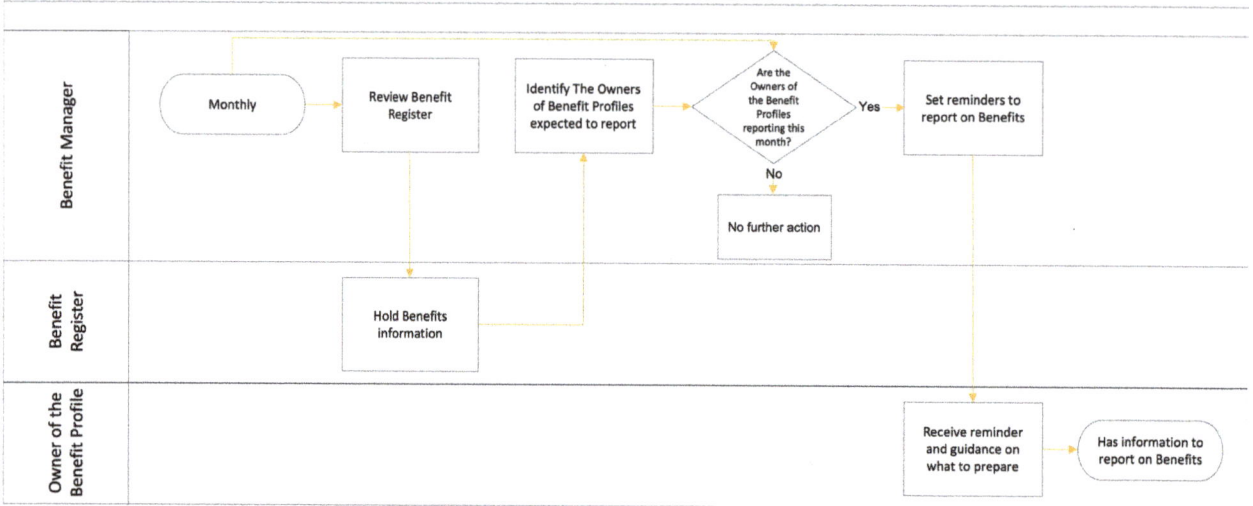

IMAGE 62 *Planning Benefit Management Activity for Reporting.*

Report/Score Benefits

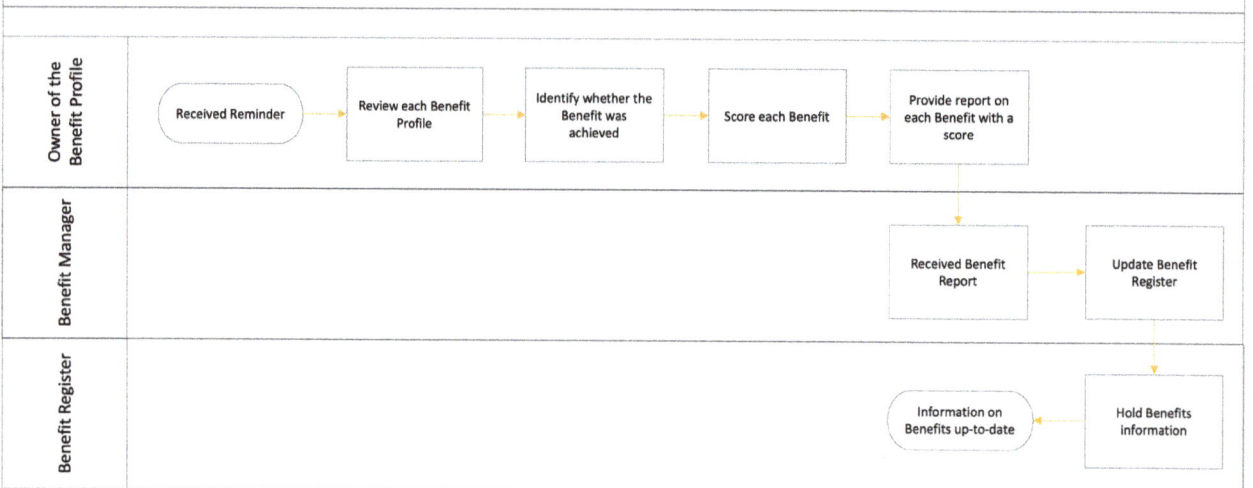

IMAGE 63 *Scoring the Benefits.*

Report deviations from Benefit Status to Programme Board by Exception

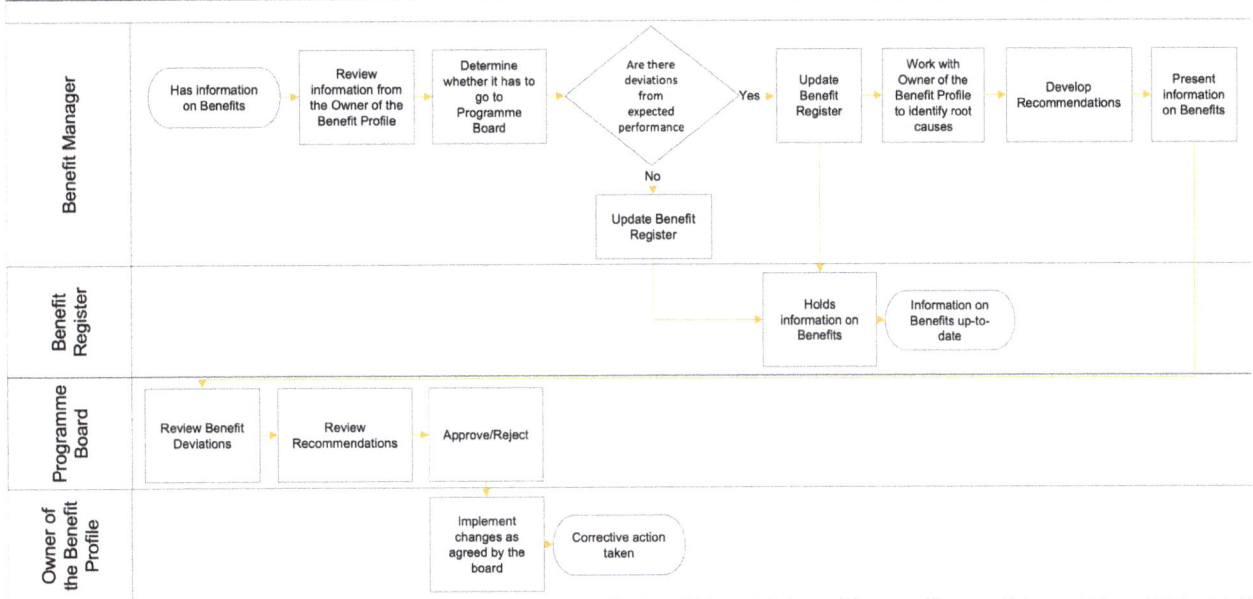

IMAGE 64 *Reporting Benefit Status by Exception.*

6.5 Benefit Report Thresholds

6.5.1 P3Os will wish to be aware of changes in financial profiles made in the period following a quarterly report, for example. Table 8 provides examples of thresholds that when breached require escalation/explanation to the portfolio office in particular. When used, the approach demonstrates a degree of oversight across the P3Os that may result in an action/treatment in the event of a breach. The thresholds can be adapted as required and it may not be necessary to use all of them:

Subject	Description	Threshold
(a)	(b)	(c)
Gross Benefit Forecast.	Revised 10-year forecast compared with previous quarter.	Forecast change of more than 10% **or** forecast change of more than £20m.
Value Erosion (*used by those organisations employing the Risk and Maturity Approach at* para 2.11).	Risk adjustment compared to previous quarter.	Risk adjustment change of more than +15% **or** risk adjustment change of more than £20m.
Investment (Run and Implementation Costs) over 10 years.	Investment over 10 years variance.	Investment change of more than 10% **or** investment change of more than £10m.

Subject	Description	Threshold
(a)	(b)	(c)
Realisation.	Variance between actual Benefit Realisation for the Year to Date (YtD) compared with YtD forecast.	Realisation change of more than 10% **or** realisation change of more than £10m.

TABLE 8 *Benefit Reporting Thresholds.*

6.5.2 The thresholds can be built as a formula into the Benefit Register to enable the P3Os to easily spot a breach; the BM is then more likely to have time to prepare the next report incorporating explanations with inputs from associated stakeholders if required. Benefit Report thresholds can assist the reporting function, better coordinate actions in the event of a breach and provide learning outcomes.

6.6 Output Reporting

6.6.1 A CI may direct its work packages to report confidence in the delivery of their outputs. If reporting is not currently being undertaken (i.e. via a schedule or plan) this section of the guide provides a simple option for consideration.

6.6.2 Output reporting is likely to start in the delivery phase, stopping when they have been delivered. The frequency of reporting can be weekly/monthly as governed by the CI.

6.6.3 Reporting of the outputs provides management oversight. Reporting has been undertaken in the MOD and the HO using the simple format at Table 9 using Excel. The BM populates Columns a–d by pulling the information from the 'outputs worksheet' in the Benefit Register; the owner of the outputs populates Columns e–g[67]; and the BM records reported information into the Benefit Register. The BM usually initiates and coordinates the business process.

---

67 When the owners of the outputs have scored them, the rating columns auto populate. How this is achieved is shown at images 56–60.

ID	Owner	Description	LoD	Score	Rating		Narrative if necessary (i.e. if confidence is Amber/Amber or worse)
(a)	(b)	(c)	(d)	(e)	(f)		(g)
OP-02	Role/Name	Oracle Guided Learning (OGL) Products	Training	4			

TABLE 9 *Example – Output Report Format*

6.7 Output Scoring

6.7.1 Delivery Confidence rating is drawn from the approach and criteria used in the IPA Gateway Review process[68]; they have been slightly adapted as follows:

Rating		Score	Description
(a)		(b)	(c)
Open Reporting			
		1	Successful delivery appears to be unachievable. There are major issues which at this stage do not appear to be manageable or resolvable. The Project/Programme may need re-baselining and/ or overall viability re-assessed.
		2	Successful delivery is in doubt with major risks or issues apparent in a number of key areas. Urgent action is needed to ensure these are addressed, and whether resolution is feasible.
		3	Successful delivery appears feasible but significant issues already exist requiring management attention. These appear resolvable at this stage and, if addressed promptly, should not present a cost/ schedule overrun.
		4	Successful delivery appears probable. However, constant attention will be needed to ensure risks do not materialise into major issues threatening delivery.
		5	Successful delivery to time, cost and quality appears highly likely and there are no major outstanding issues that at this stage appear to threaten delivery.

---

68 Guidance here (www): https://assets.publishing.service.gov.uk/government/uploads/system/uploads/ attachment_data/file/638436/delivery_confidence_guide_for_review_teams.pdf

Rating		Score	Description
(a)		**(b)**	**(c)**
Closed Reported			
		6	The Output has not been delivered.
		7	The Output has been partially delivered.
		8	The Output has been delivered.

TABLE 10 *Outputs Scoring.*

SECTION 7

Resource

7.1 Benefit Hierarchy

7.1.1 The Benefit Profiles must be owned to ensure that responsibilities and accountability are clear. A new system's reach/use is likely to span the entirety of the organisation; with numerous holders of delegated budgets/management account functions involved, it has proven necessary to expand on the traditional structure of Benefit roles as shown below.

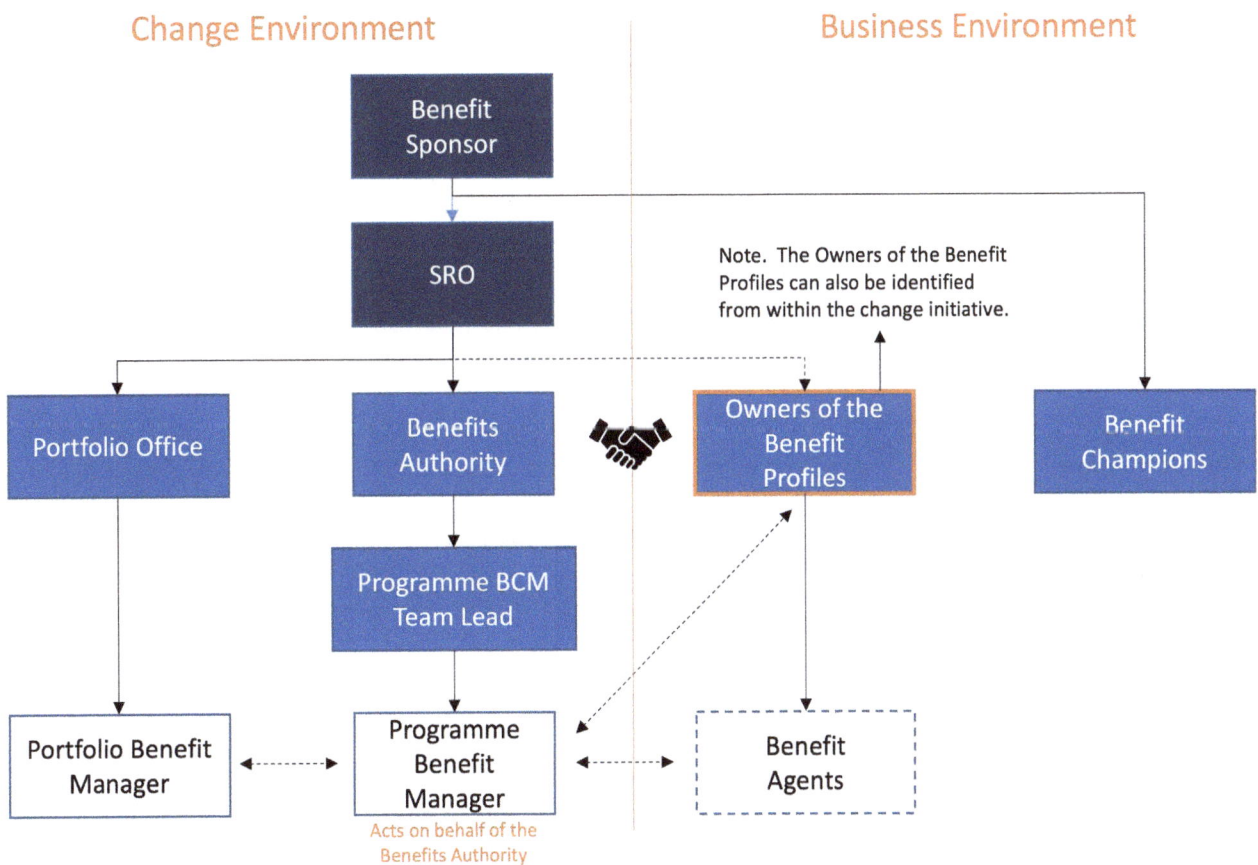

IMAGE 65 *Benefits Hierarchy*[69].

---

69 The 'virtual' concept of the handshake was explained at footnote 26.

a. The Portfolio Office. Benefits Management policy, direction and reporting requirements are received from the portfolio office.

b. Benefit Authority. The Benefit authority (i.e. Programme Manager or Deputy Director) is responsible to the SRO in a Benefit Management context.

c. Owner of the Benefit Profiles. Assists the BM to quantify the Benefits; the owner accepts the Benefit Profiles for delivery/reporting and agrees that they are realistic and deliverable. They can nominate and empower Benefit Agents (if necessary) to act on their behalf by delegating activities and tasks. The owner of the Benefit Profiles are recorded in the Benefit Profiles themselves. Owners and agents are assisted by the BM who coordinates the processes, leads on the development of the Benefit Profiles and helps to develop a Benefit Management Capability inside the organisation.

d. Benefit Manager. Responsible to the Benefits Authority, for development and maintenance of the Benefit artefacts (Strategy, Map, Register, Profiles, Plan) and, Benefit identification, quantification and tracking. The BM is the first port of call for Benefit-related matters. Attributes of the BM: Self-starter; team worker; negotiator; influencer; listener; communicator; confident; persuasive; industrious; energetic; resilient. Good with PowerPoint; Excel; and Word.

e. Benefit Champions. The Benefit Champions are the heads of the Directorates inside the organisation (i.e. Directors or Deputy Directors) receiving change[70]; they are best placed to influence and facilitate the realisation of Benefits across their area of responsibility by championing the Benefits on behalf of the Benefits Sponsor. Prior to closure of the CI, the BM can extract from the Benefit Register 'via PivotTables and visuals' the aggregated Benefits associated with the Directorates (see example para 9.9). The Benefit Champions will wish to be aware of them so they can be received and accepted into BaU[71].

---

70 For example: people directorate (responsible for the people dimension such as retention, behaviours, skills); finance directorate (who track spend on the provision of services); information & digital directorate (responsible for improvements to the systems); and other. The BM will need a general understanding of the roles of these directorates to ensure Benefits associated with them are undertaken correctly. The BM can find the organisation's directorates on the BaU structure/organisation chart.

71 A note can be sent to the directors prior to closure of the CI to facilitate the handover/takeover process of residual Benefits into BaU.

7.2 Business Change Team

7.2.1 The Business Change (BCHG) team provides an intelligent customer capability with commensurate degree of corporate knowledge (change expertise, communication, business readiness, Benefits Management) and dedicated Business Change and Engagement Managers (BC&EMs) working alongside the business functions and change champions, supporting the development and articulation of 'as-is' and 'to-be' states and implementing the change and stakeholder engagement strategy and plan. Key responsibilities include, but are not limited to, the following:

a. Promote the CI right across the organisation and maintain meaningful communication and engagement (i.e. engage and inform others about important aspects of change, readiness, transition and respond to questions and concerns).

b. Work with business functions to identify the impact of change (i.e. technology, data, people, processes) to avoid barriers to change, inform/capture requirements, develop UAT scripts, plan for implementation, other.

c. Minimise operational disruption and ensure the End Users and associated stakeholders fully adopt 'system name' by taking advantage of the technological and support capabilities and services the platform has to offer.

d. Build awareness of the Benefits-focused approach and inform the Owners of the Benefit Profiles of the process[72].

e. Work with the End Users and others to identify Benefit Indicators, quantify and metricise them, establish realistic targets and build a Benefit Management Capability inside the organisation.

f. Liaise with other CIs to work together on Benefits capture.

7.2.2 An example of the functions of a BCHG team.

---

72 Schema at para 6.4 for example.

```
                    ┌─────────────────┐
                    │  Leader of the  │
                    │     Change      │
                    │   Initiative    │
                    └─────────────────┘
                            │
                    ┌─────────────────┐
                    │   BCHG Team     │
                    │    Manager      │
                    └─────────────────┘
```

Comms & Engagement	Business Change & Engagement	Business Change Analyst	Benefits Management	Learning

Learning Content Developers

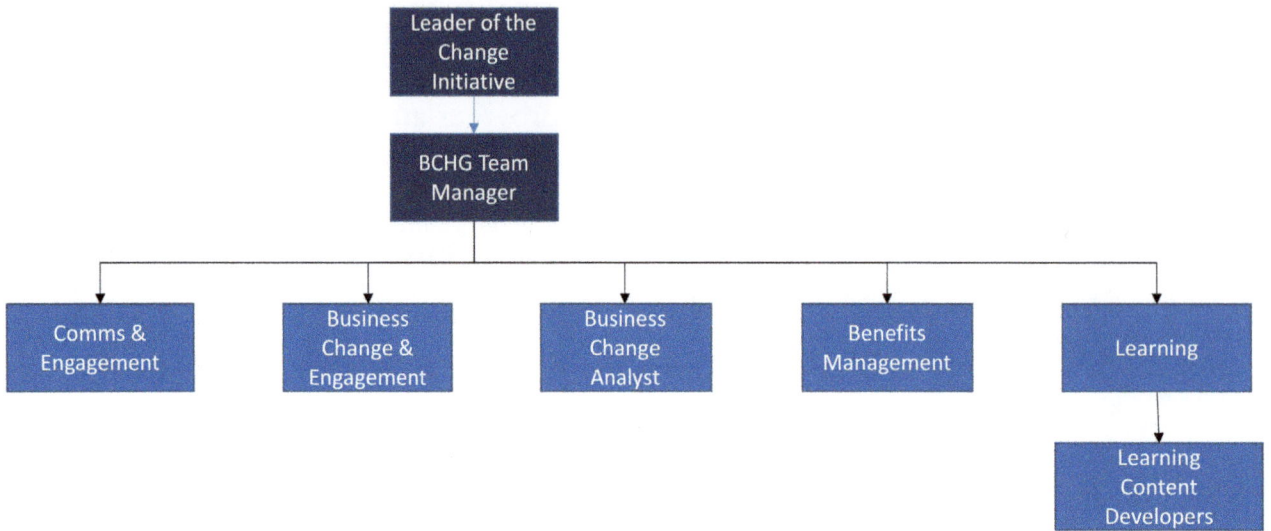

IMAGE 66 *BCHG Team/Functions.*

SECTION 8

Transition to BaU

8.1 Introduction

8.1.1 The CI Leadership and BM should work with 'in-service boards'(i.e. the Capability User Board; Efficiency Board; other) to incorporate and report information about Benefits, including the Benefits achieved to date and forecast Benefits. The Benefit Champions and/or Senior Leadership Team can help to achieve it. Without this there is a risk that insufficient attention is given by the business to Benefits Realisation and subsequent optimisation. Lack of communication can result in senior stakeholders being unclear about the status of Benefits in and around their area of responsibility.

8.2 Duplication

8.2.1 The CI Business Case represents the Benefits that occur because of the investment set out in the Business Case.

8.2.2 The BaU area receiving the Benefits Management function when the CI closes is likely to think about continuous improvement/investment opportunities and what other Benefits could be derived from the new system, subject to further investment beyond that set out in the initial CI's Business Case. Ideas for draft further Benefits will require investment, and this investment would be subject to a Business Case approval as it is beyond that set out in the earlier CI's Business Case.

8.2.3 The point being, the authors of the subsequent Business Case are to be cognisant with the former Business Case to avoid duplication of work and double counting the Benefits.

8.3 Closure of the CI

8.3.1 When the CI closes, residual Benefits that remain open and identification of subsequent emergent/new Benefits and Dis-Benefits will transition to the in-service, BaU BM/Function. There is little evidence of this happening for a few reasons. For example: resource constraints; an under-developed BRM capability at the receiving end; lack of communication and engagement earlier in the Benefit Management process.

8.3.2 The outgoing CI BM works with the in-service/BaU BM to transition the Benefits identification/reporting activities and associated artefacts into the business and provide appropriate guidance as required.

8.3.3 Benefits are likely to degrade in time (i.e. capability gaps emerge and risks materialise). This will inform the development of new CIs in the pipeline/ portfolio thus continuing the cycle of change and improvement, ensuring End Users needs are fulfilled in the form of new products and services, required by them, to deliver outputs efficiently/effectively and the organisation is able to deliver its SOs.

SECTION 9

Visualisations/Management Information

9.1 Introduction

9.1.1 The EBP and Benefit Profiles worksheets mature as the BM continues to identify, quantify and record Benefits data in the Benefit Register. The work has the effect of organising data into one place to make it work for you. The 3 Benefit Profiles from 1 (para 1.2) and, year-on-year frequency of the Benefits (para 1.4) mean the EBP and Benefit Profiles worksheets in the Benefit Register will increase in size and detail quickly.

9.1.2 The BM can aggregate the information using visualisations, charts and tables to (a) develop, inform and improve the quality of the BRP, (b) demonstrate and monitor the progress of Benefits capture, and (c) report Benefits data to in-service boards as mentioned previously at para 8.1.1, so they can draw insights from the information to inform decision making and improve performance.

9.1.3 The following examples will help the BM to shape data into information, identify learning outcomes and help to improve the BM's knowledge and experience using Excel.

9.2 Combination Charts (Costs and Benefits)

9.2.1 Combination charts are used to visually highlight differences between sets of data and make it easy to see one set of information presented in relation to other data. Let's start by creating 2 combination charts consisting of lines and bars that look at both costs and Benefits. We will do this by manually creating a small data table that pulls information from the EBP worksheet. The steps to create them can be seen in Images 67–76 incl. para 9.2.3.

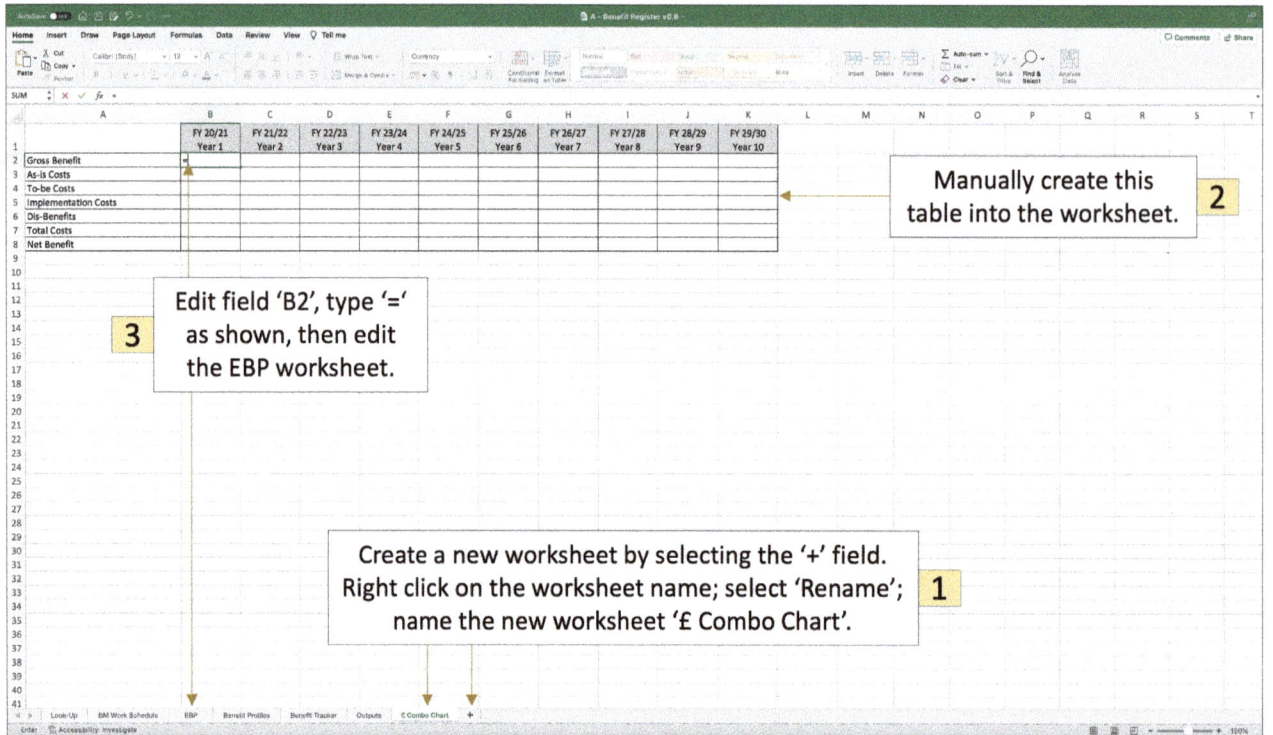

IMAGE 67 *Create Data Table.*

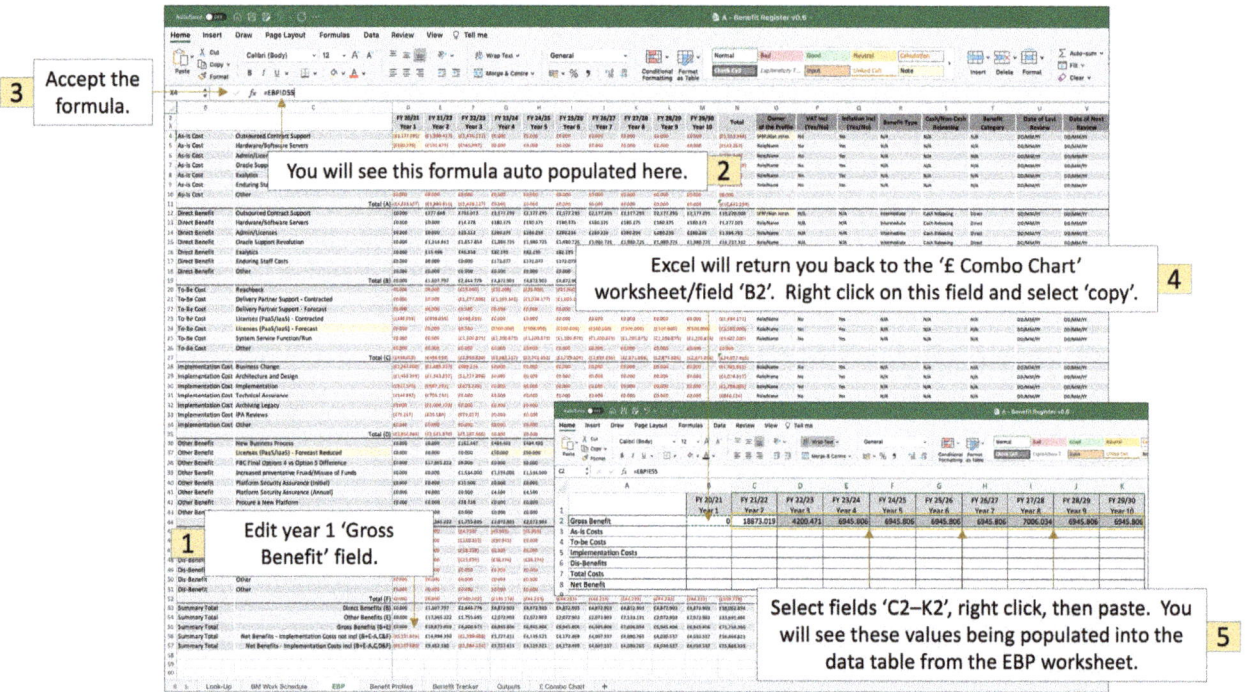

IMAGE 68 *Example – How to Populate the Data Table.*

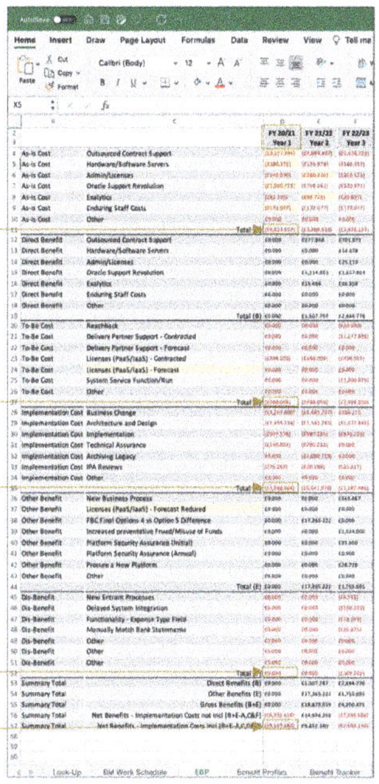

IMAGE 69 *Populate the Remaining Fields of the Data Table.*

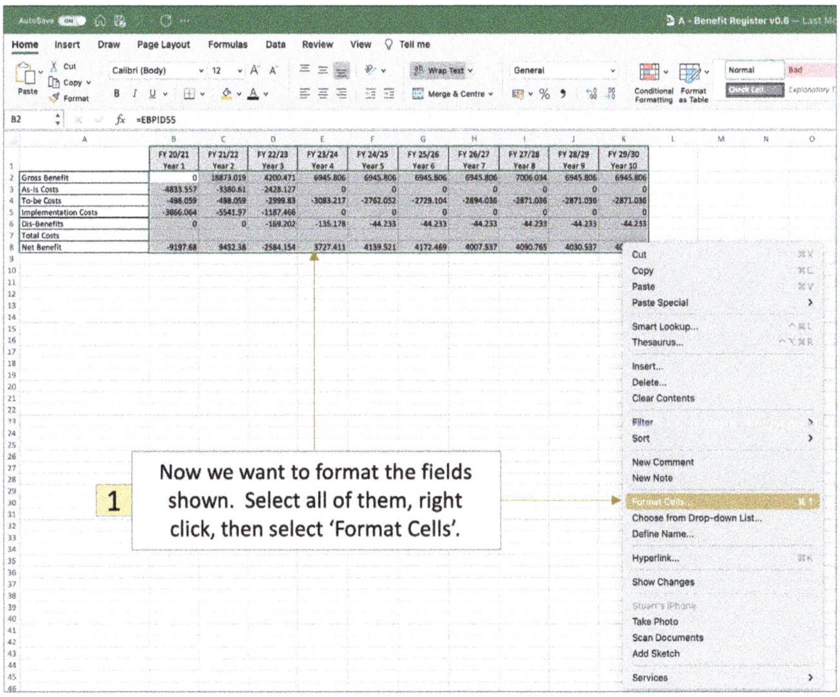

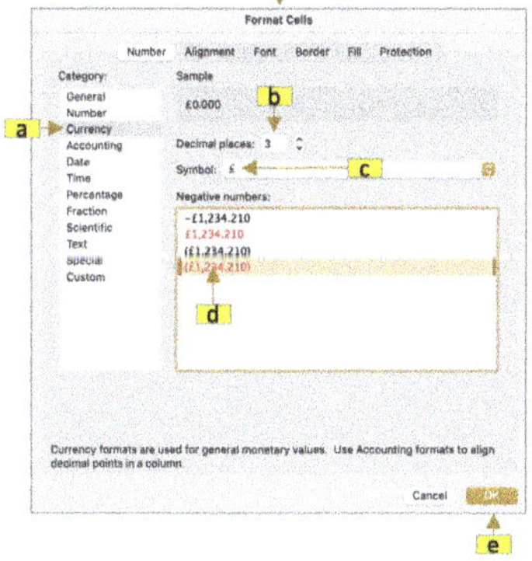

IMAGE 70 *Format Data Table.*

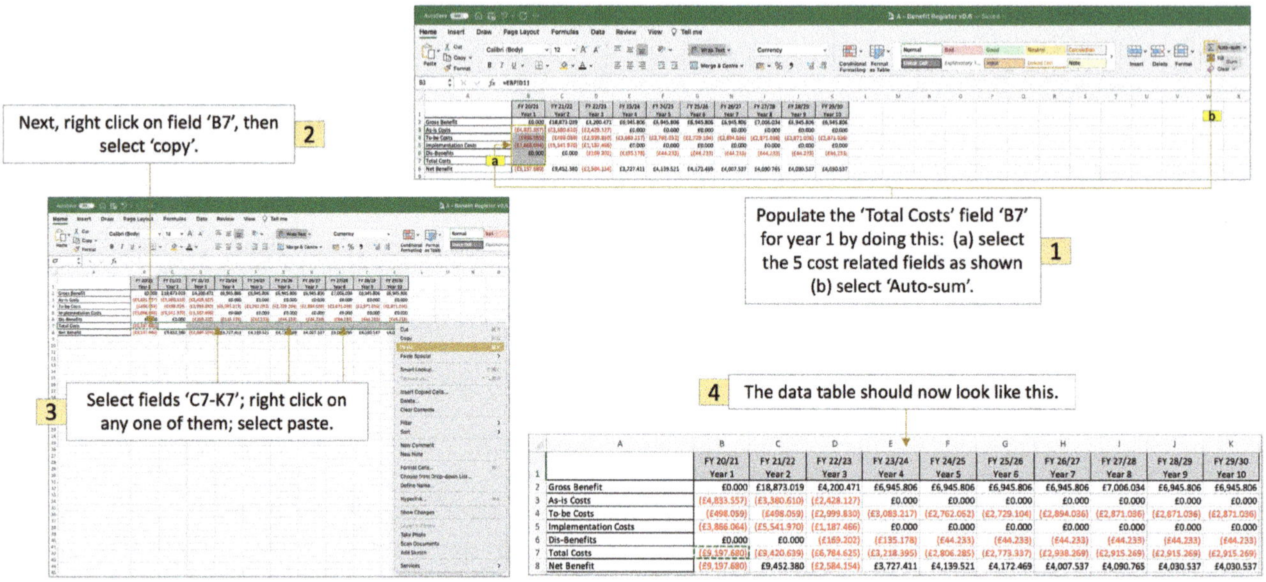

IMAGE 71 *Populate the Total Cost.*

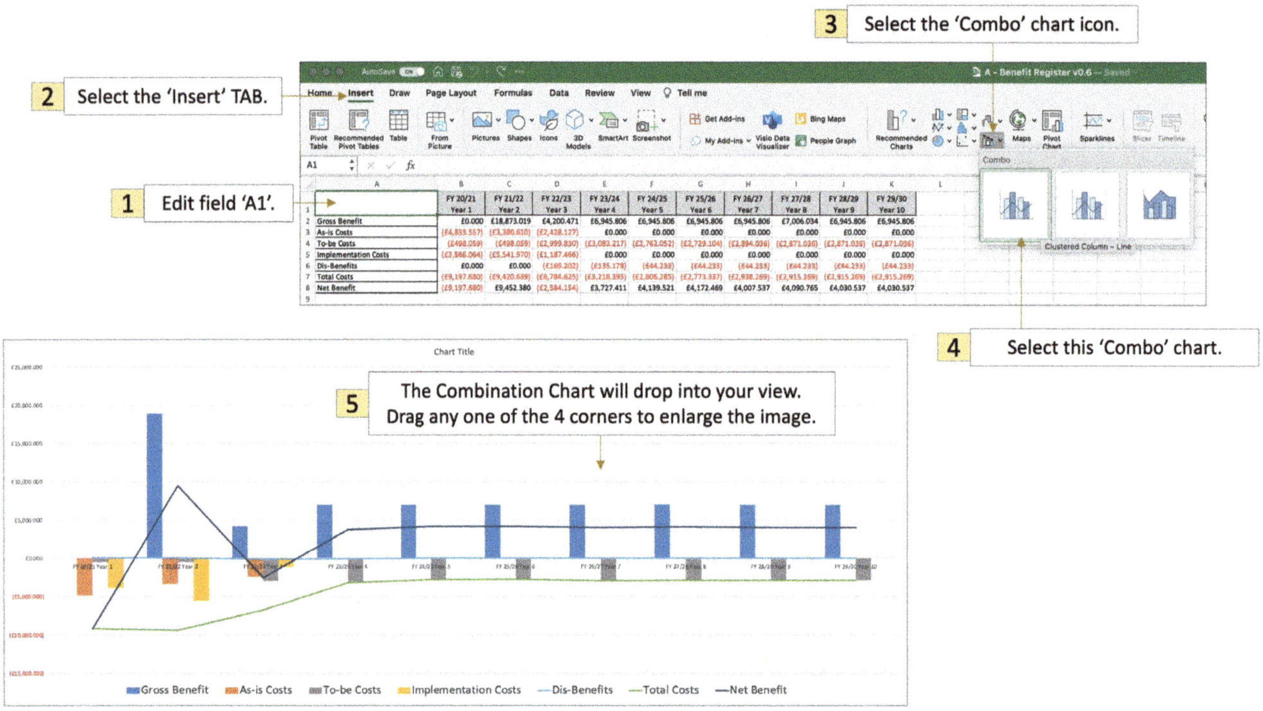

IMAGE 72 *Insert Combination Chart.*

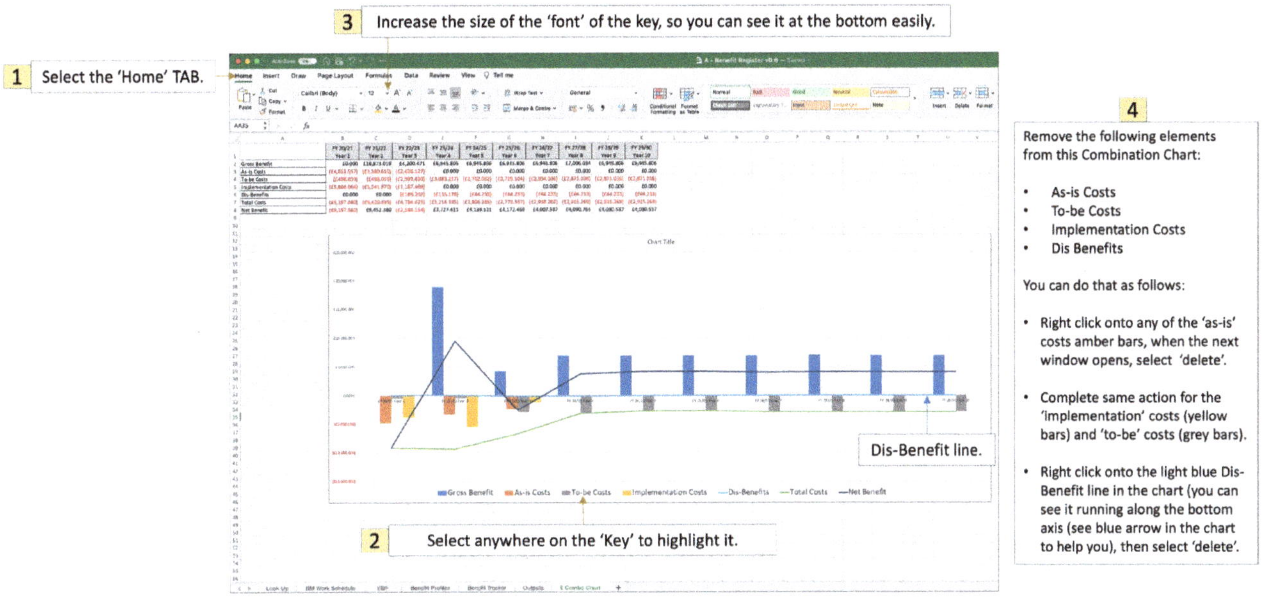

IMAGE 73 *Structure the Combination Chart.*

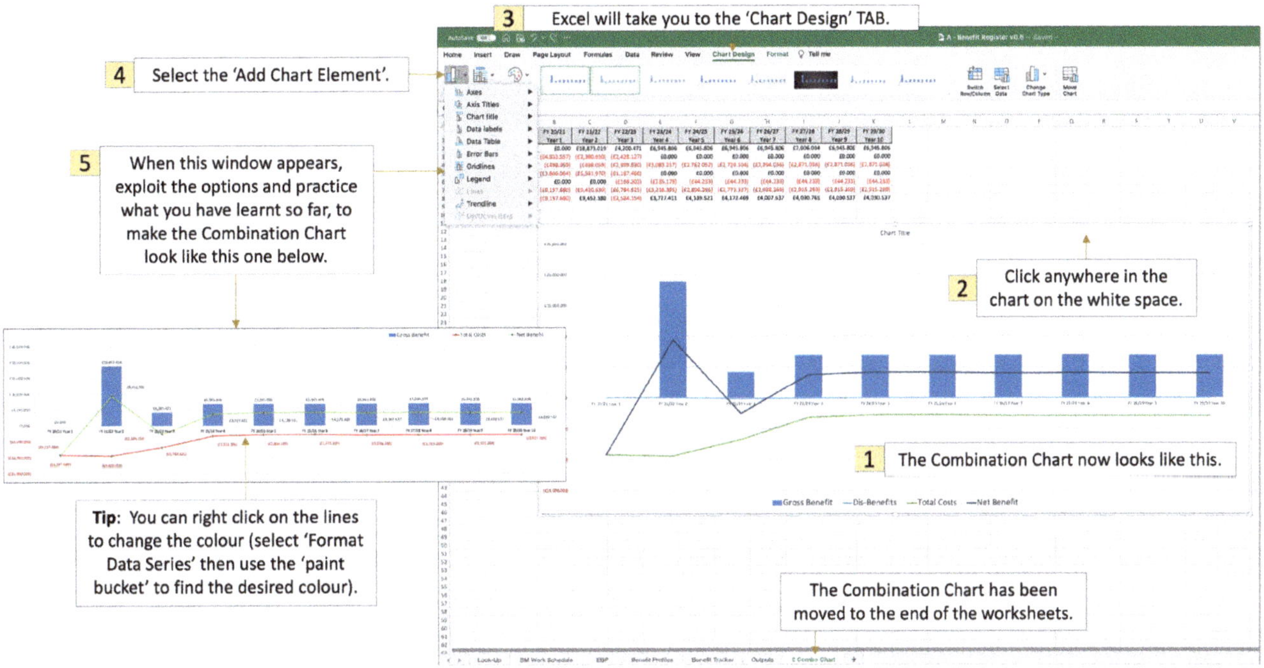

IMAGE 74 *Format the Combination Chart.*

9.2.2 This first combination chart looks at the Gross Benefits, Total Costs and Net Benefits across the life of the CI. The chart can easily be copied into a PowerPoint slide or dashboard for reporting purposes.

IMAGE 75 *Gross Benefits, Total Costs and Net Benefits Across the Life of the CI*[73].

9.2.3 We can use the same data table to create a second combination chart. This time, the second chart will consist of the individual elements of the Cost Profiles across the life of the CI. Follow these steps:

a. Using the same data table, complete the same actions as in Image 72 to create the second chart.

b. Complete same actions as in Image 73 but this time, at step 4, remove these bars/lines instead: (a) Gross Benefit (b) Total Costs (c) Net Benefit (d) Dis-Benefits.

c. Edit the new image; using the knowledge you have learnt so far and exploit the options shown in Image 74, the second Chart could look like this:

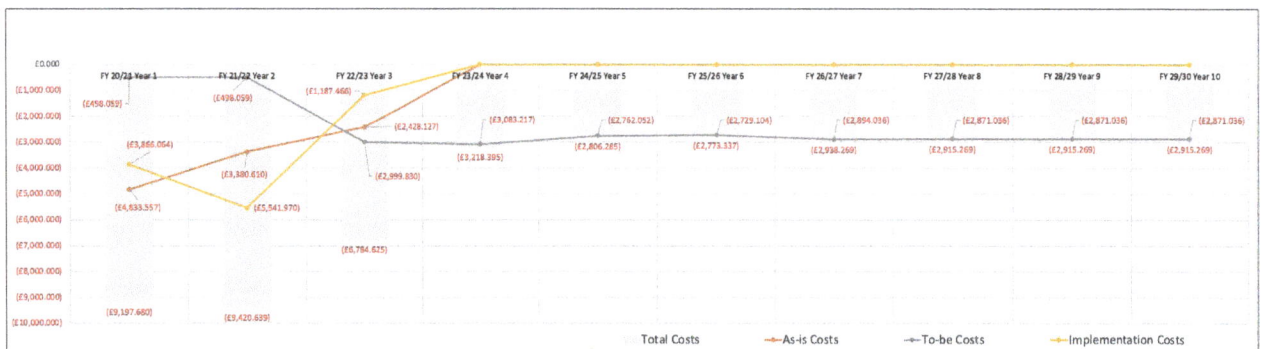

IMAGE 76 *Individual Elements of the Cost Profiles Across the Life of the CI.*

9.2.4 Both charts may not satisfy the P3O's/BM's information needs; the idea is to demonstrate what can be achieved quite quickly using data in the Excel Benefit Register as a starter to stimulate thinking.

---

73 **Tip**: When inserting the data labels seen in Image 75, they can be manually/individually positioned by clicking on a data label slowly twice, then dragging/moving it to the desired location.

9.3 PivotTables (Summary Views of the Economic Benefits)

9.3.1 A PivotTable is a pleasing way to summarise large amounts of data. You can use a PivotTable to analyse data in detail and answer unanticipated questions or draw insights from it. We are going to create 2 PivotTables to summarise alternative views of the Gross Benefits in the EBP. We will do this by creating a simple PivotTable that pulls information from the EBP worksheet, then we copy and tweak it to create a second. The steps to create both summarised views of the Economic Benefits can be seen in Images 77–83.

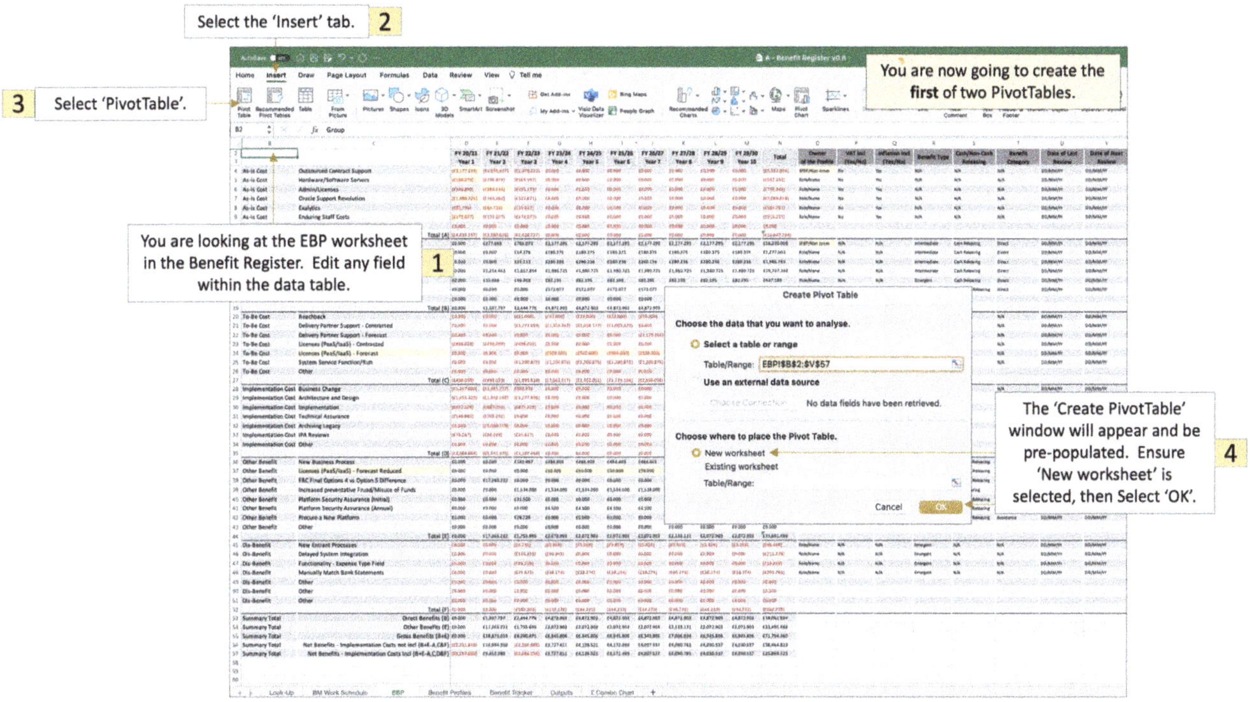

IMAGE 77 *Create the First PivotTable From the EBP Worksheet.*

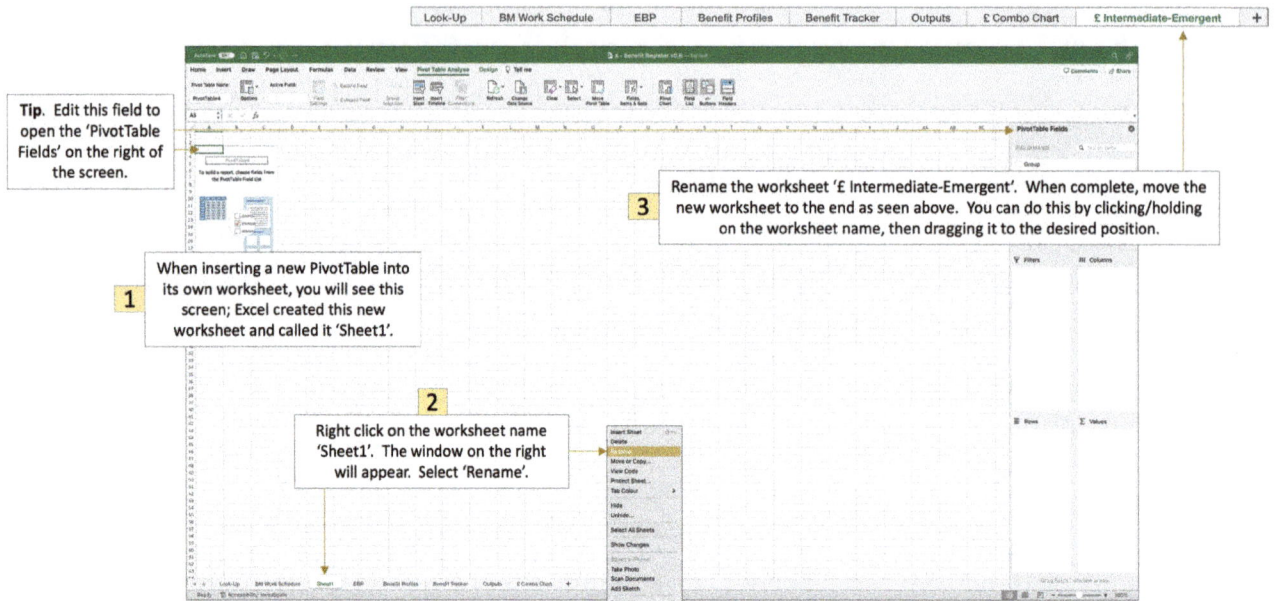

IMAGE 78 *Name and Position the PivotTable.*

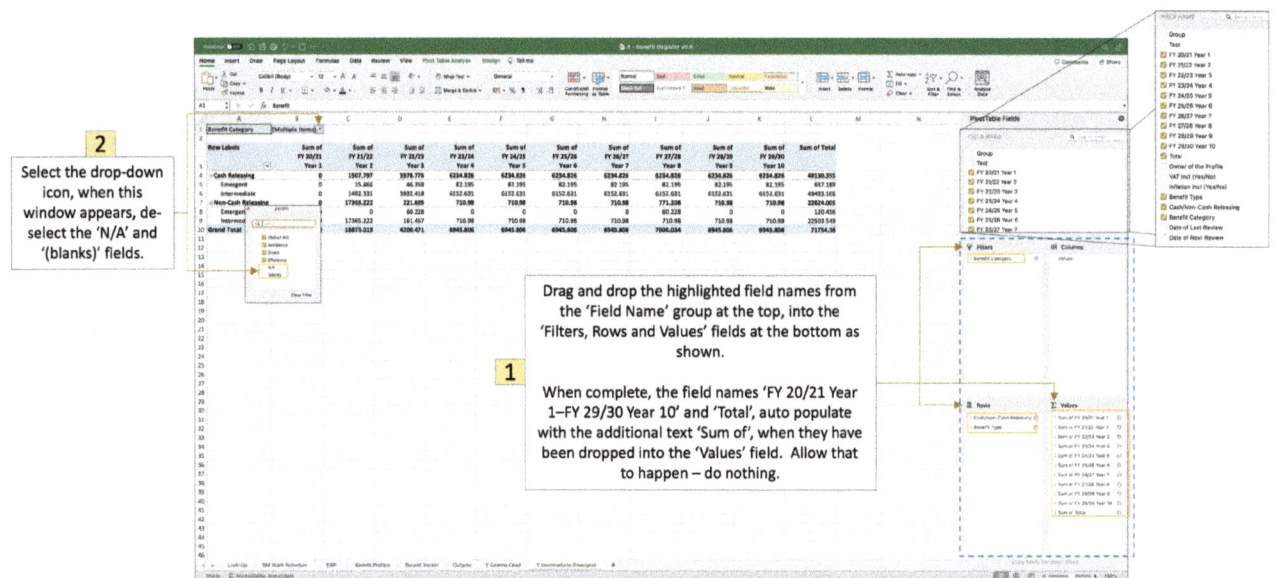

IMAGE 79 *Populate the PivotTable.*

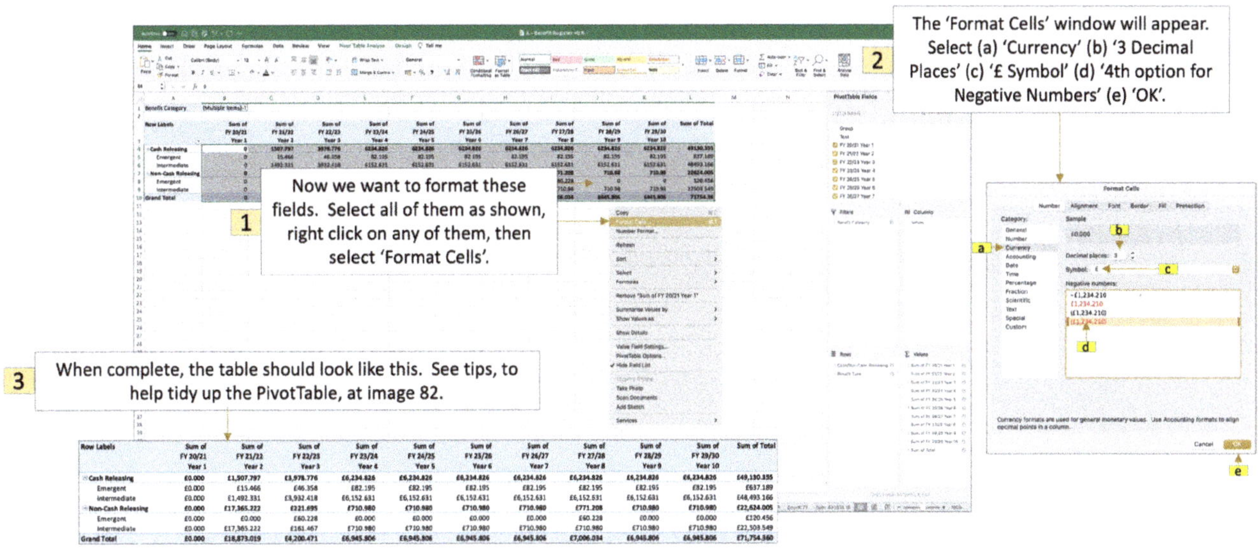

IMAGE 80 *Format the PivotTable.*

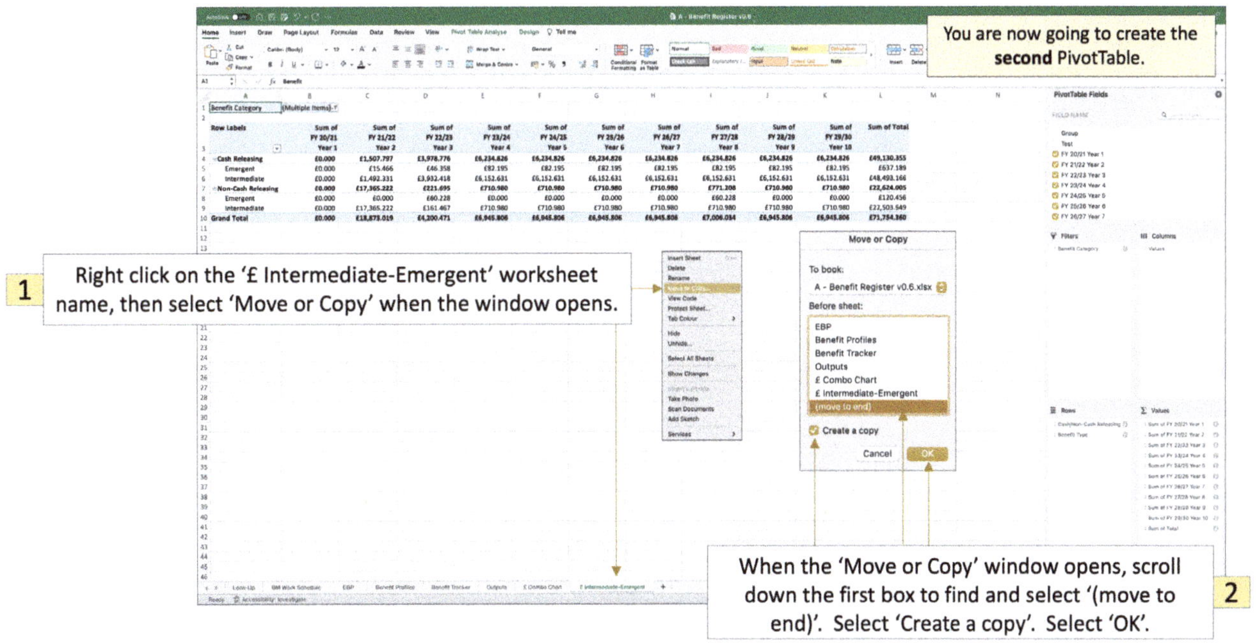

IMAGE 81 *Copy and Position the second PivotTable.*

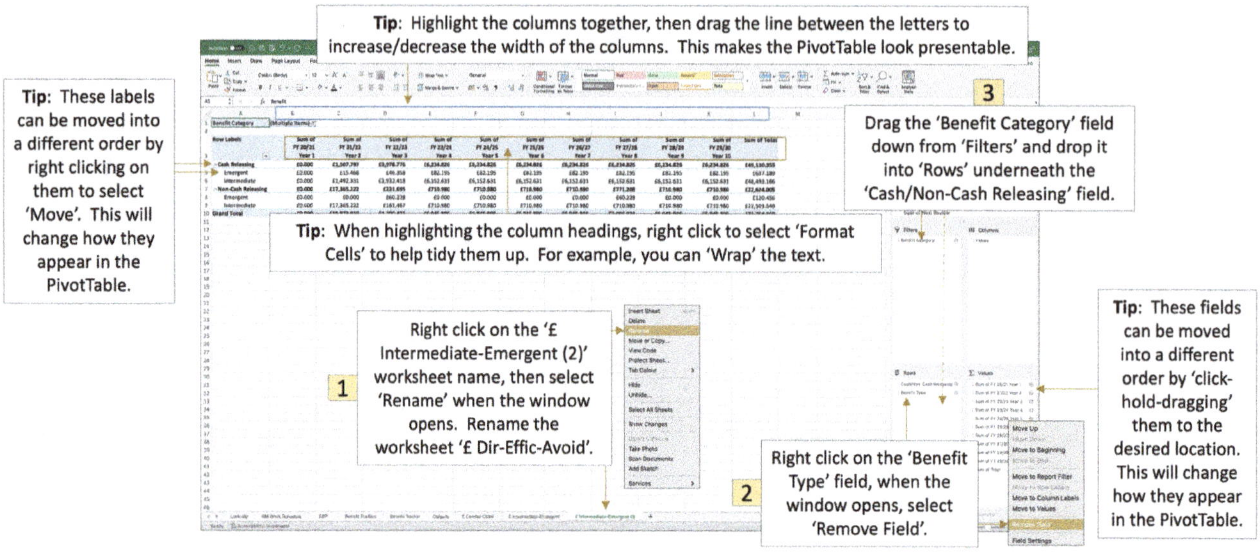

IMAGE 82 *Name, Update and Format the second PivotTable.*

The aggregated, low-level Intermediate/Emergent Benefits are used to inform and quantify, the Economic End Benefit on the CI's Benefit Map. See para 1.1.1.

Gross Direct, Efficiency & Avoidance Benefits that are Cash/Non-Cash Releasing across the life of the CI

Row Labels	Sum of FY 20/21 Year 1	Sum of FY 21/22 Year 2	Sum of FY 22/23 Year 3	Sum of FY 23/24 Year 4	Sum of FY 24/25 Year 5	Sum of FY 25/26 Year 6	Sum of FY 26/27 Year 7	Sum of FY 27/28 Year 8	Sum of FY 28/29 Year 9	Sum of FY 29/30 Year 10	Sum of Total
⊟ Cash Releasing	£0.000	£1,507.797	£3,978.776	£6,234.826	£6,234.826	£6,234.826	£6,234.826	£6,234.826	£6,234.826	£6,234.826	£49,130.355
Direct	£0.000	£1,507.797	£2,444.776	£4,700.826	£4,700.826	£4,700.826	£4,700.826	£4,700.826	£4,700.826	£4,700.826	£36,858.355
Avoidance	£0.000	£0.000	£1,534.000	£1,534.000	£1,534.000	£1,534.000	£1,534.000	£1,534.000	£1,534.000	£1,534.000	£12,272.000
⊟ Non-Cash Releasing	£0.000	£17,365.222	£221.695	£710.980	£710.980	£710.980	£710.980	£771.208	£710.980	£710.980	£22,624.005
Direct	£0.000	£0.000	£0.000	£172.077	£172.077	£172.077	£172.077	£172.077	£172.077	£172.077	£1,204.539
Efficiency	£0.000	£0.000	£161.467	£484.403	£484.403	£484.403	£484.403	£484.403	£484.403	£484.403	£3,552.288
Avoidance	£0.000	£17,365.222	£60.228	£54.500	£54.500	£54.500	£54.500	£114.728	£54.500	£54.500	£17,867.178
Grand Total	£0.000	£18,873.019	£4,200.471	£6,945.806	£6,945.806	£6,945.806	£6,945.806	£7,006.034	£6,945.806	£6,945.806	£71,754.360

Gross Intermediate & Emergent Benefits that are Cash/Non-Cash Releasing across the life of the CI

Row Labels	Sum of FY 20/21 Year 1	Sum of FY 21/22 Year 2	Sum of FY 22/23 Year 3	Sum of FY 23/24 Year 4	Sum of FY 24/25 Year 5	Sum of FY 25/26 Year 6	Sum of FY 26/27 Year 7	Sum of FY 27/28 Year 8	Sum of FY 28/29 Year 9	Sum of FY 29/30 Year 10	Sum of Total
⊟ Cash Releasing	£0.000	£1,507.797	£3,978.776	£6,234.826	£6,234.826	£6,234.826	£6,234.826	£6,234.826	£6,234.826	£6,234.826	£49,130.355
Intermediate	£0.000	£1,492.331	£3,932.418	£6,152.631	£6,152.631	£6,152.631	£6,152.631	£6,152.631	£6,152.631	£6,152.631	£48,493.166
Emergent	£0.000	£15.466	£46.358	£82.195	£82.195	£82.195	£82.195	£82.195	£82.195	£82.195	£637.189
⊟ Non-Cash Releasing	£0.000	£17,365.222	£221.695	£710.980	£710.980	£710.980	£710.980	£771.208	£710.980	£710.980	£22,624.005
Intermediate	£0.000	£17,365.222	£161.467	£710.980	£710.980	£710.980	£710.980	£710.980	£710.980	£710.980	£22,503.549
Emergent	£0.000	£0.000	£60.228	£0.000	£0.000	£0.000	£0.000	£60.228	£0.000	£0.000	£120.456
Grand Total	£0.000	£18,873.019	£4,200.471	£6,945.806	£6,945.806	£6,945.806	£6,945.806	£7,006.034	£6,945.806	£6,945.806	£71,754.360

End Benefit-02 (Reduced Expenditure): On premise servers removed; fewer contracts; cost optimisation; fewer licences; integration; convergence; monetised time savings; value for money.

FBC Target: £125.6M.
Current value: £71,754.360M.

IMAGE 83 *Both New PivotTables Side-by-Side*[74].

9.4 Data Table (Output Scores and Rating)

9.4.1 The outputs worksheet created at para 5.8 has been populated with more information to generate the visual at Image 84. It consists of a simple, easy to use table that does not draw information from any another worksheet (i.e. it stands alone); the table has been sorted on the score column. The outputs are scored by inserting a numeric value (1–8) in the score column, the rating columns then auto populate themselves. The scores are provided by the owner of the outputs in accordance with para 6.6.3.

---

74 Remember: the Gross Benefit (£71,754.360M) in the PivotTables drawn from the EBP worksheet are to be like-for-like with the aggregated monetised values in the Benefit Profiles worksheet.

9.4.2 An organisation may initiate reporting by exception only, to reduce the information being presented to the board, or to simplify a dashboard, so they remain decision led (i.e. those outputs with a score of 1 (Red–Red) or 2 (Amber–Red) for management attention and oversight; they can be kept on a watch list until the situation improves). Reporting the outputs and Benefits (i.e. left and right sides of the Benefit Map) will draw confidence in the CI's approach to shoring up the outputs, outcomes and Benefits and demonstrates end-to-end reporting in a Benefits context.

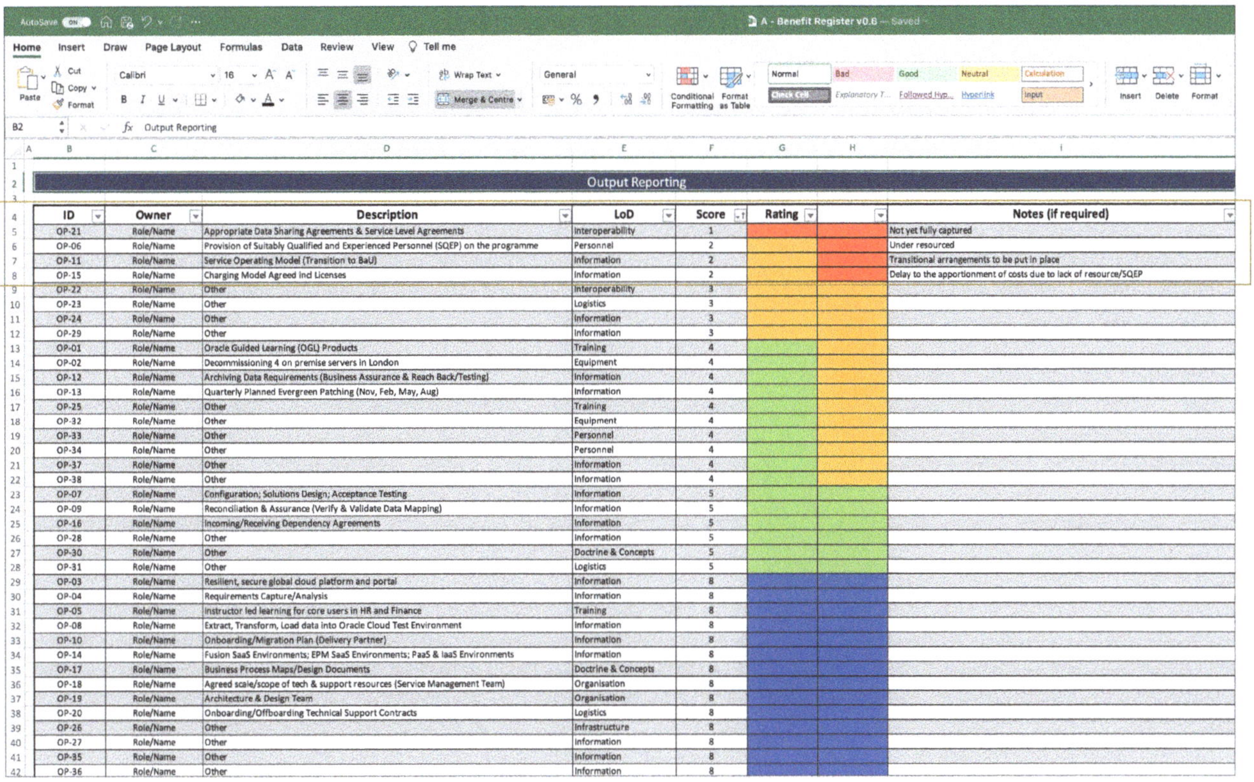

Output Reporting

ID	Owner	Description	LoD	Score	Rating		Notes (if required)
OP-21	Role/Name	Appropriate Data Sharing Agreements & Service Level Agreements	Interoperability	1			Not yet fully captured
OP-06	Role/Name	Provision of Suitably Qualified and Experienced Personnel (SQEP) on the programme	Personnel	2			Under resourced
OP-11	Role/Name	Service Operating Model (Transition to BaU)	Information	2			Transitional arrangements to be put in place
OP-15	Role/Name	Charging Model Agreed incl Licenses	Information	2			Delay to the apportionment of costs due to lack of resource/SQEP
OP-22	Role/Name	Other	Interoperability	3			
OP-23	Role/Name	Other	Logistics	3			
OP-24	Role/Name	Other	Information	3			
OP-29	Role/Name	Other	Information	3			
OP-01	Role/Name	Oracle Guided Learning (OGL) Products	Training	4			
OP-02	Role/Name	Decommissioning 4 on premise servers in London	Equipment	4			
OP-12	Role/Name	Archiving Data Requirements (Business Assurance & Reach Back/Testing)	Information	4			
OP-13	Role/Name	Quarterly Planned Evergreen Patching (Nov, Feb, May, Aug)	Information	4			
OP-25	Role/Name	Other	Training	4			
OP-32	Role/Name	Other	Equipment	4			
OP-33	Role/Name	Other	Personnel	4			
OP-34	Role/Name	Other	Personnel	4			
OP-37	Role/Name	Other	Information	4			
OP-38	Role/Name	Other	Information	4			
OP-07	Role/Name	Configuration; Solutions Design; Acceptance Testing	Information	5			
OP-09	Role/Name	Reconciliation & Assurance (Verify & Validate Data Mapping)	Information	5			
OP-16	Role/Name	Incoming/Receiving Dependency Agreements	Information	5			
OP-28	Role/Name	Other	Information	5			
OP-30	Role/Name	Other	Doctrine & Concepts	5			
OP-31	Role/Name	Other	Logistics	5			
OP-03	Role/Name	Resilient, secure global cloud platform and portal	Information	8			
OP-04	Role/Name	Requirements Capture/Analysis	Information	8			
OP-05	Role/Name	Instructor led learning for core users in HR and Finance	Training	8			
OP-08	Role/Name	Extract, Transform, Load data into Oracle Cloud Test Environment	Information	8			
OP-10	Role/Name	Onboarding/Migration Plan (Delivery Partner)	Information	8			
OP-14	Role/Name	Fusion SaaS Environments; EPM SaaS Environments; PaaS & IaaS Environments	Information	8			
OP-17	Role/Name	Business Process Maps/Design Documents	Doctrine & Concepts	8			
OP-18	Role/Name	Agreed scale/scope of tech & support resources (Service Management Team)	Organisation	8			
OP-19	Role/Name	Architecture & Design Team	Organisation	8			
OP-20	Role/Name	Onboarding/Offboarding Technical Support Contracts	Logistics	8			
OP-26	Role/Name	Other	Infrastructure	8			
OP-27	Role/Name	Other	Information	8			
OP-35	Role/Name	Other	Information	8			
OP-36	Role/Name	Other	Information	8			

IMAGE 84 *Scored Outputs.*

9.5 PivotTables (Summarised Views of Time and FTE Savings)

9.5.1 We are going to create 2 further PivotTables to summarise views of the Gross Time Savings and Gross FTE savings. We will do this by creating a PivotTable as before but, this time, it will pull information from the Benefit Profiles worksheet. We can then copy and tweak it slightly to create the second PivotTable[75]. The steps to create both summarised views of the Gross Time savings and Gross FTE savings can be seen in Images 85–92.

75 In addition to the 8 Time and 8 FTE savings populated into the Benefit Profiles worksheet at Image 42, additional 'dummy' Benefit Profiles in the context of Time and FTE savings have been added to inform both PivotTables.

Select the 'Insert' tab. **2**

3 Select 'PivotTable'.

You are now going to create the **first** of two PivotTables.

You are looking at the Benefit Profiles worksheet in the Benefit Register. Edit field 'A3' within the data table. **1**

Create Pivot Table

Choose the data that you want to analyse.

- Select a table or range

  Table/Range: 'Benefit Profiles'!$A$3:$AC$237

- Use an external data source

  Choose Connection... No data fields have been retrieved.

Choose where to place the Pivot Table.

- New worksheet
- Existing worksheet

  Table/Range:

Cancel OK

The 'Create PivotTable' window will appear and be pre-populated. Ensure 'New worksheet' is selected, then Select 'OK'. **4**

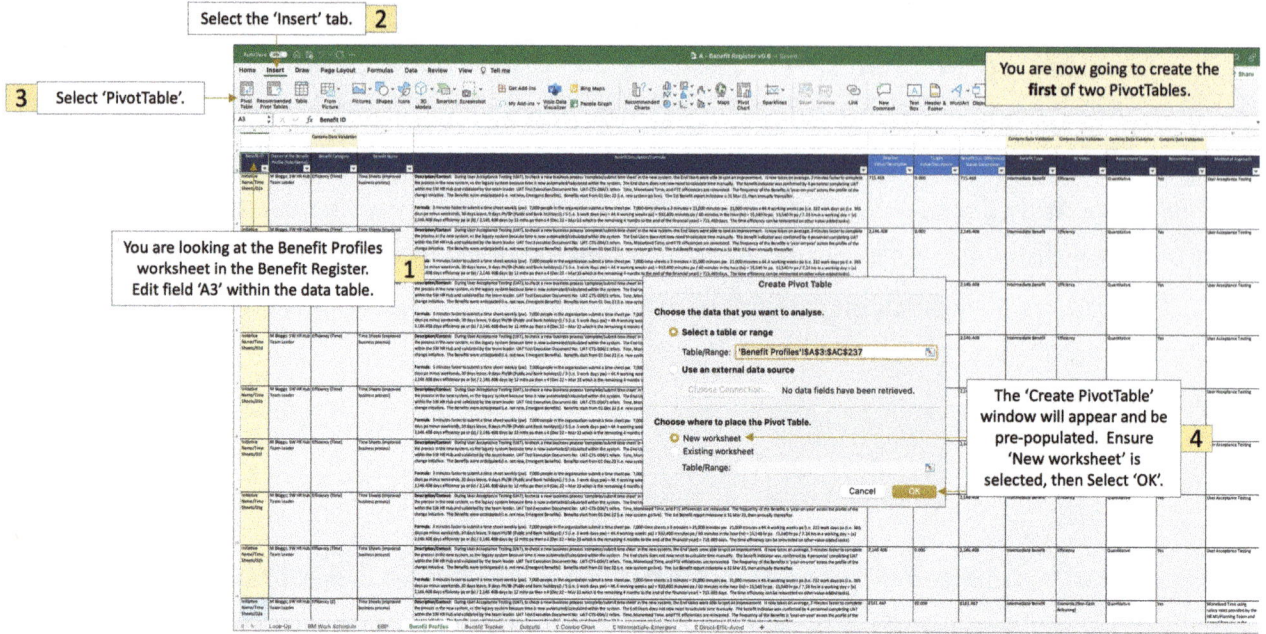

IMAGE 85 *Create the first PivotTable from the Benefit Profiles worksheet.*

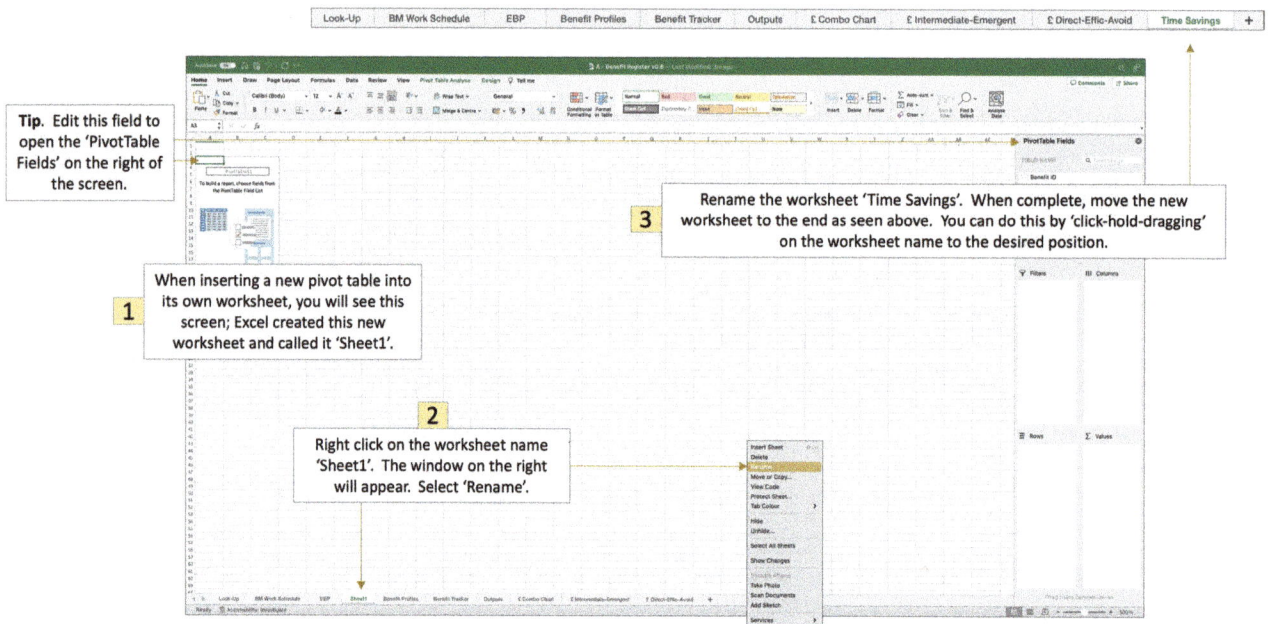

Tip. Edit this field to open the 'PivotTable Fields' on the right of the screen.

PivotTable Fields

Rename the worksheet 'Time Savings'. When complete, move the new worksheet to the end as seen above. You can do this by 'click-hold-dragging' on the worksheet name to the desired position. **3**

When inserting a new pivot table into its own worksheet, you will see this screen; Excel created this new worksheet and called it 'Sheet1'. **1**

2

Right click on the worksheet name 'Sheet1'. The window on the right will appear. Select 'Rename'.

Filters Columns

Rows Values

IMAGE 86 *Name and Position the PivotTable.*

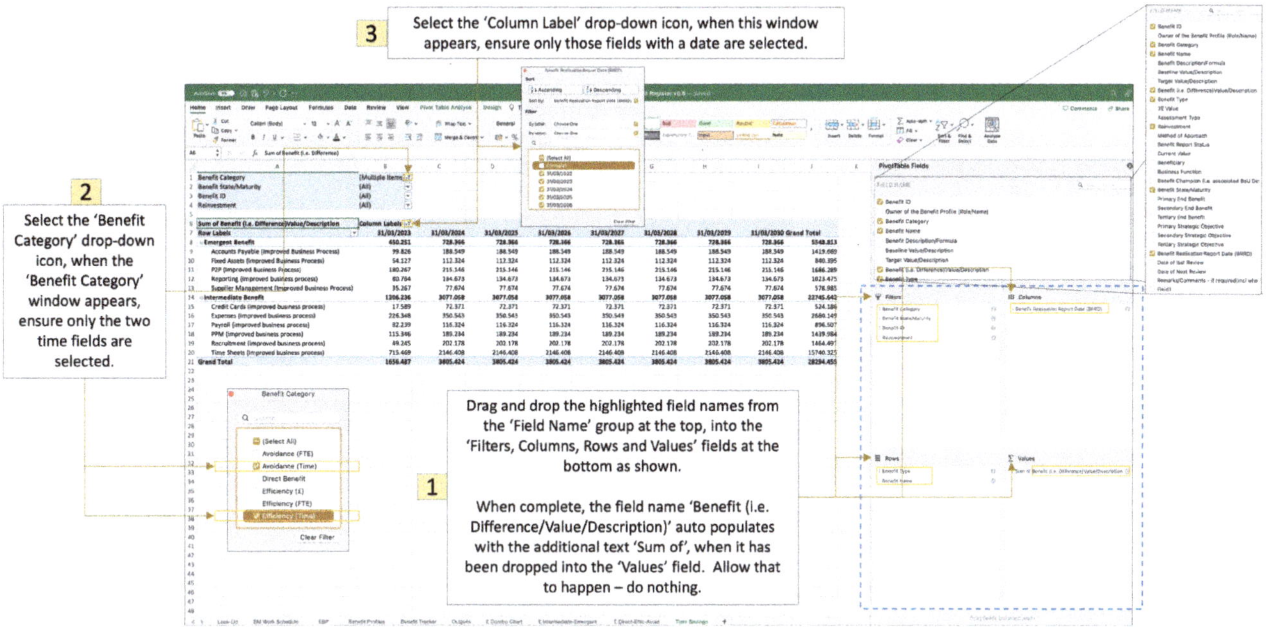

IMAGE 87 *Populate the PivotTable.*

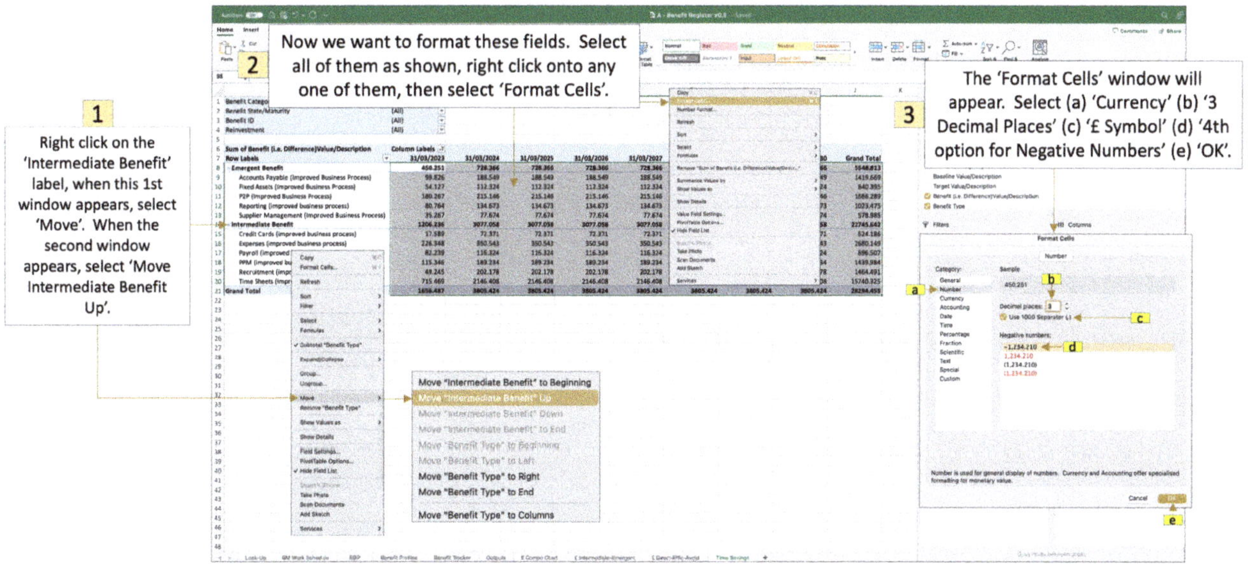

IMAGE 88 *Format the PivotTable.*

1   The formatting is nearly complete. Select the columns as shown, then click/drag the column dividing line between the letters, so the width of each column is the same and, makes the PivotTable look presentable.

2   Align the heading text to the right.

3   The PivotTable should now look like this.

Sum of Benefit (i.e. Difference)Value/Description	Column Labels								
Row Labels	31/03/2023	31/03/2024	31/03/2025	31/03/2026	31/03/2027	31/03/2028	31/03/2029	31/03/2030	Grand Total
Intermediate Benefit	1,206.236	3,077.058	3,077.058	3,077.058	3,077.058	3,077.058	3,077.058	3,077.058	22,745.642
Credit Cards (improved business process)	17.589	72.371	72.371	72.371	72.371	72.371	72.371	72.371	524.186
Expenses (improved business process)	226.348	350.543	350.543	350.543	350.543	350.543	350.543	350.543	2,680.149
Payroll (improved business process)	82.239	116.324	116.324	116.324	116.324	116.324	116.324	116.324	896.507
PPM (improved business process)	115.346	189.234	189.234	189.234	189.234	189.234	189.234	189.234	1,439.984
Recruitment (improved business process)	49.245	202.178	202.178	202.178	202.178	202.178	202.178	202.178	1,464.491
Time Sheets (improved business process)	715.469	2,146.408	2,146.408	2,146.408	2,146.408	2,146.408	2,146.408	2,146.408	15,740.325
Emergent Benefit	450.251	728.366	728.366	728.366	728.366	728.366	728.366	728.366	5,548.813
Accounts Payable (Improved Business Process)	99.826	188.549	188.549	188.549	188.549	188.549	188.549	188.549	1,419.669
Fixed Assets (Improved Business Process)	54.127	112.324	112.324	112.324	112.324	112.324	112.324	112.324	840.396
P2P (Improved Business Process)	180.267	215.146	215.146	215.146	215.146	215.146	215.146	215.146	1,686.289
Reporting (improved business process)	80.764	134.673	134.673	134.673	134.673	134.673	134.673	134.673	1,023.475
Supplier Management (Improved Business Process)	35.267	77.674	77.674	77.674	77.674	77.674	77.674	77.674	578.985
Grand Total	1,656.487	3,805.424	3,805.424	3,805.424	3,805.424	3,805.424	3,805.424	3,805.424	28,294.455

IMAGE 89   *Format the PivotTable – Continued.*

Tip. Remember, the data in this PivotTable is pulled from the Benefit Profiles worksheet. When the Benefit Profiles are being updated, some Benefits may be reported to be 'Cancelled' in the Benefit State/Maturity column. The cancelled Benefits can be de-selected using the 'Benefit Category' drop-down icon.

You are now going to create the **second** PivotTable.

Tip: Select Yes or No from this field, to see what Time savings can or cannot be reinvested. See para 1.8.

1   Right click on the 'Time Saving' worksheet name, then select 'Move or Copy' when the window opens.

2   When the 'Move or Copy' window opens, scroll down the first box to find and select '(move to end)'. Select 'Create a copy'. Select 'OK'.

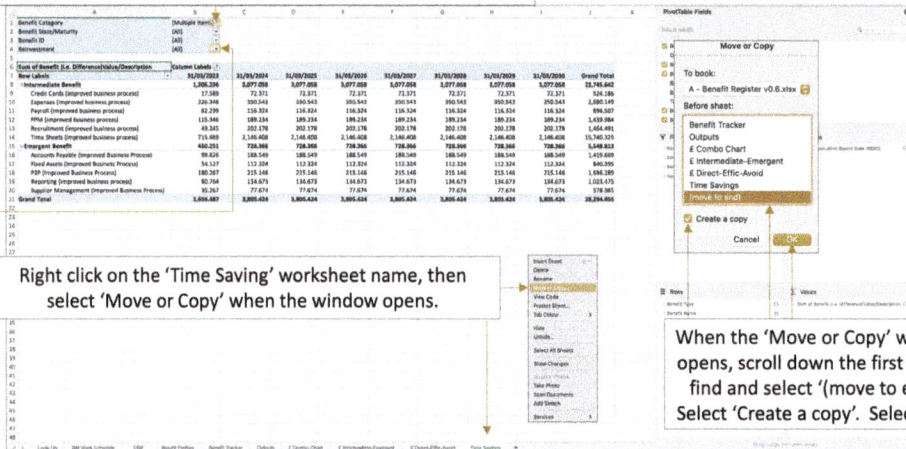

IMAGE 90   *Copy and Position the Second PivotTable.*

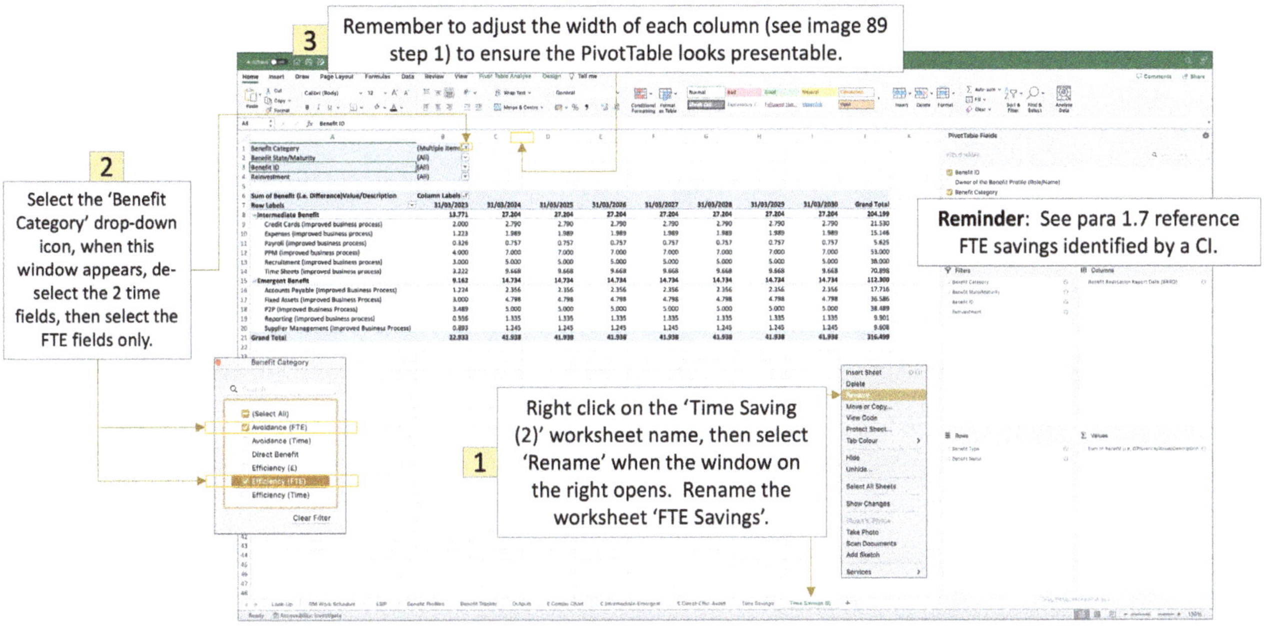

IMAGE 91 *Name, Update and Format the Second PivotTable.*

The aggregated, low-level Intermediate/Emergent Benefits are used to inform and quantify the Efficiency End Benefits on the CI's Benefit Map. See para 1.1.1.

Gross Intermediate/Emergent Time Savings across the life of the CI

Sum of Benefit (i.e. Difference)Value/Description	Column Labels								
Row Labels	31/03/2023	31/03/2024	31/03/2025	31/03/2026	31/03/2027	31/03/2028	31/03/2029	31/03/2030	Grand Total
⊟Intermediate Benefit	1,206.236	3,077.058	3,077.058	3,077.058	3,077.058	3,077.058	3,077.058	3,077.058	22,745.642
Credit Cards (improved business process)	17.589	72.371	72.371	72.371	72.371	72.371	72.371	72.371	524.186
Expenses (improved business process)	226.348	350.543	350.543	350.543	350.543	350.543	350.543	350.543	2,680.149
Payroll (improved business process)	82.239	116.324	116.324	116.324	116.324	116.324	116.324	116.324	896.507
PPM (improved business process)	115.346	189.234	189.234	189.234	189.234	189.234	189.234	189.234	1,439.984
Recruitment (improved business process)	49.245	202.178	202.178	202.178	202.178	202.178	202.178	202.178	1,464.491
Time Sheets (improved business process)	715.469	2,146.408	2,146.408	2,146.408	2,146.408	2,146.408	2,146.408	2,146.408	15,740.325
⊟Emergent Benefit	450.251	728.366	728.366	728.366	728.366	728.366	728.366	728.366	5,548.813
Accounts Payable (Improved Business Process)	99.826	188.549	188.549	188.549	188.549	188.549	188.549	188.549	1,419.669
Fixed Assets (Improved Business Process)	54.127	112.324	112.324	112.324	112.324	112.324	112.324	112.324	840.395
P2P (Improved Business Process)	180.267	215.146	215.146	215.146	215.146	215.146	215.146	215.146	1,686.289
Reporting (improved business process)	80.764	134.673	134.673	134.673	134.673	134.673	134.673	134.673	1,023.475
Supplier Management (Improved Business Process)	35.267	77.674	77.674	77.674	77.674	77.674	77.674	77.674	578.985
Grand Total	**1,656.487**	**3,805.424**	**3,805.424**	**3,805.424**	**3,805.424**	**3,805.424**	**3,805.424**	**3,805.424**	**28,294.455**

End Benefit-01 (Time Savings):
Do something faster; less complicated; fewer steps in the process; resourceful; not wasting time.

FBC Target: 134,000 days.
Current value: 28,294.479 days.

Gross Intermediate/Emergent FTE Savings across the life of the CI

Sum of Benefit (i.e. Difference)Value/Description	Column Labels								
Row Labels	31/03/2023	31/03/2024	31/03/2025	31/03/2026	31/03/2027	31/03/2028	31/03/2029	31/03/2030	Grand Total
⊟Intermediate Benefit	13.771	27.204	27.204	27.204	27.204	27.204	27.204	27.204	204.199
Credit Cards (improved business process)	2.000	2.790	2.790	2.790	2.790	2.790	2.790	2.790	21.530
Expenses (improved business process)	1.223	1.989	1.989	1.989	1.989	1.989	1.989	1.989	15.146
Payroll (improved business process)	0.326	0.757	0.757	0.757	0.757	0.757	0.757	0.757	5.625
PPM (improved business process)	4.000	7.000	7.000	7.000	7.000	7.000	7.000	7.000	53.000
Recruitment (improved business process)	3.000	5.000	5.000	5.000	5.000	5.000	5.000	5.000	38.000
Time Sheets (improved business process)	3.222	9.668	9.668	9.668	9.668	9.668	9.668	9.668	70.898
⊟Emergent Benefit	9.162	14.734	14.734	14.734	14.734	14.734	14.734	14.734	112.300
Accounts Payable (Improved Business Process)	1.224	2.356	2.356	2.356	2.356	2.356	2.356	2.356	17.716
Fixed Assets (Improved Business Process)	3.000	4.798	4.798	4.798	4.798	4.798	4.798	4.798	36.586
P2P (Improved Business Process)	3.489	5.000	5.000	5.000	5.000	5.000	5.000	5.000	38.489
Reporting (improved business process)	0.556	1.335	1.335	1.335	1.335	1.335	1.335	1.335	9.901
Supplier Management (Improved Business Process)	0.893	1.245	1.245	1.245	1.245	1.245	1.245	1.245	9.608
Grand Total	**22.933**	**41.938**	**41.938**	**41.938**	**41.938**	**41.938**	**41.938**	**41.938**	**316.499**

End Benefit-03 (FTE Savings):
Spare capacity; structured; organised; reinvestment; prioritisation, productivity, better use of resources.

FBC Target: 700 FTE.
Current value: 316.499 FTE.

IMAGE 92 *Both PivotTables Side-by-Side.*

9.6 Bar Chart (Intermediate, Emergent and Dis-Benefits Associations With the CI's End Benefits)

9.6.1 As mentioned previously, a direct relationship between the Intermediate, Emergent and Dis-Benefits with a CI's End Benefits are primary associations. Indirect relationships are secondary and tertiary associations. The same is true of the relationships between the End Benefits and SOs. The point being the BM can see (a) how Intermediate/Emergent Benefits and Dis-Benefits contribute to the wider End Benefits of the CI 'reducing work in the long run' and how that can be achieved at pace, and (b) how the End Benefits contribute to the wider SOs 'reducing work in the long run' and how that can be achieved at pace.

9.6.2   When the associations have been 'connected' in the Benefit Profiles in the Benefit Register, visualisations can be generated from it to provide useful information. For example (a) quantifying the End Benefits, (b) counting associations between the Intermediate/Emergent Benefits, Dis-Benefits, and the End Benefits, (c) quantifying the SOs, (d) counting associations between the End Benefits and the SOs, and (e) identifying those End Benefits or SOs with fewer associations 'suggesting more work can be done on them' so appropriate action/prioritisation can be taken.

9.6.3   We are going to create a Bar Chart summary of these associations. We can do this by creating a PivotTable that pulls information from the Benefit Profiles worksheet. The PivotTable will be copied twice. The second and third copies will be tweaked slightly. The BM can then easily see the information required to create the Bar Chart. The steps to achieve it can be seen in Images 93–101.

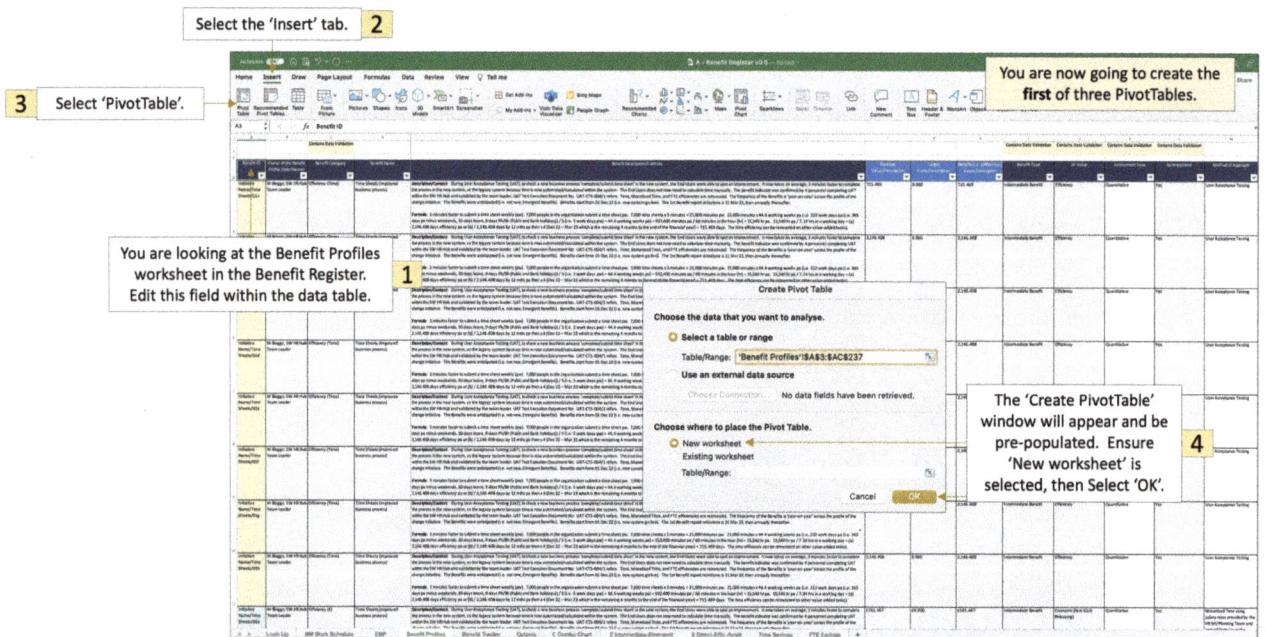

IMAGE 93 *Create the First PivotTable From the Benefit Profiles Worksheet.*

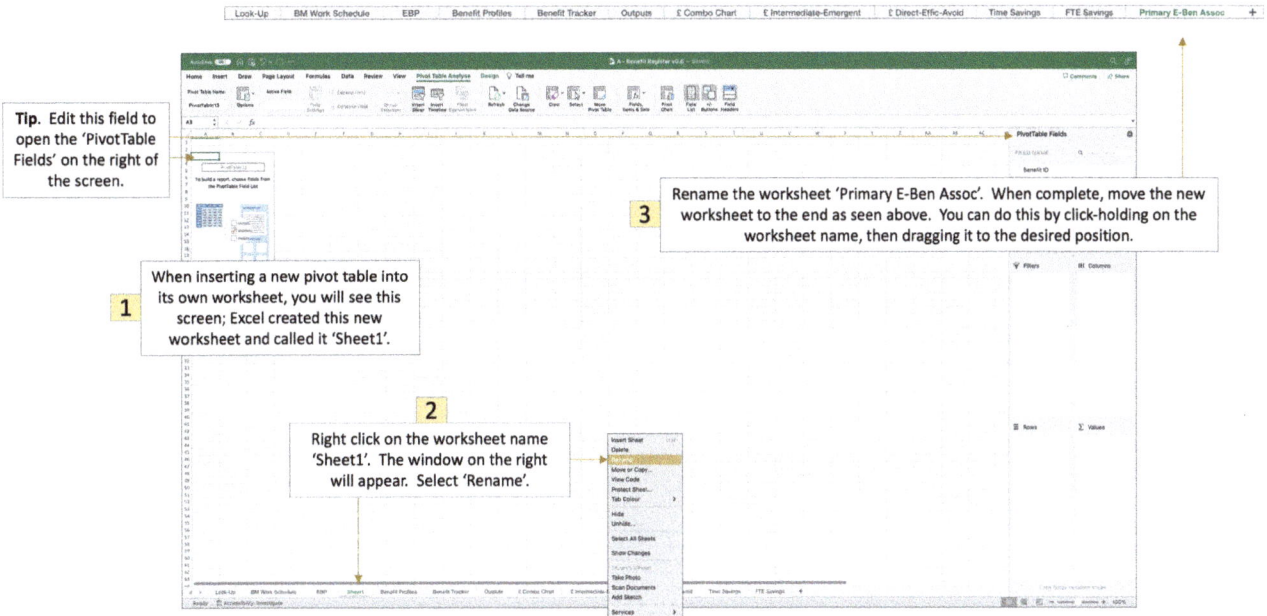

IMAGE 94 *Name and Position the PivotTable.*

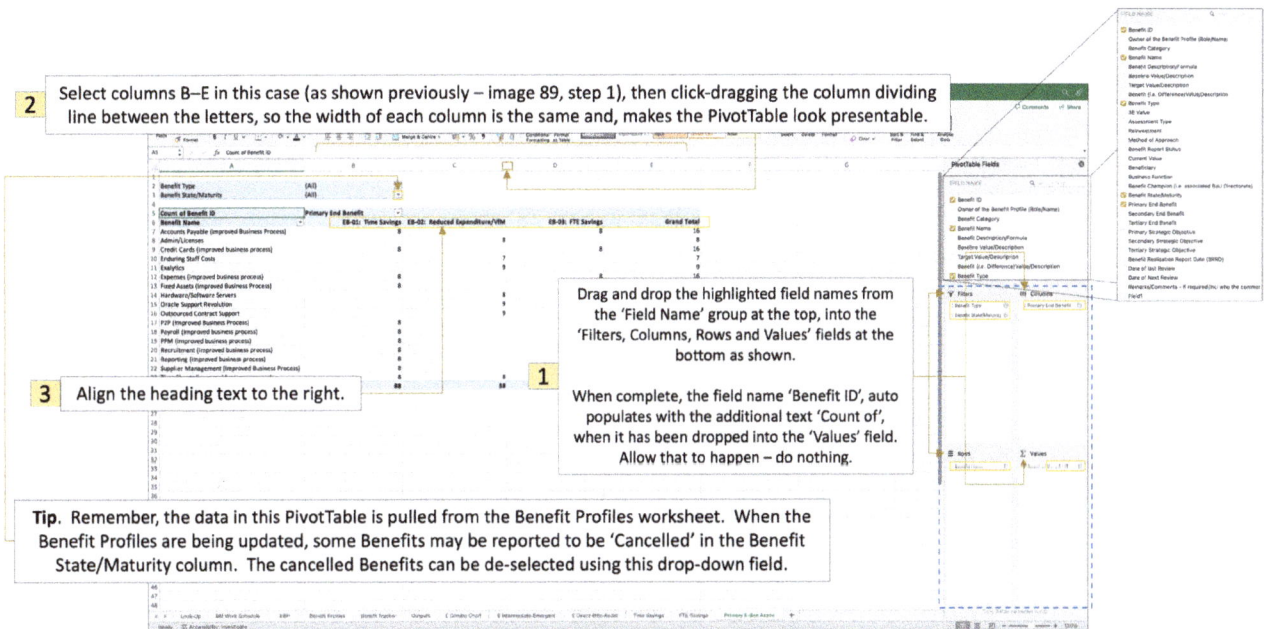

IMAGE 95 *Populate the PivotTable.*

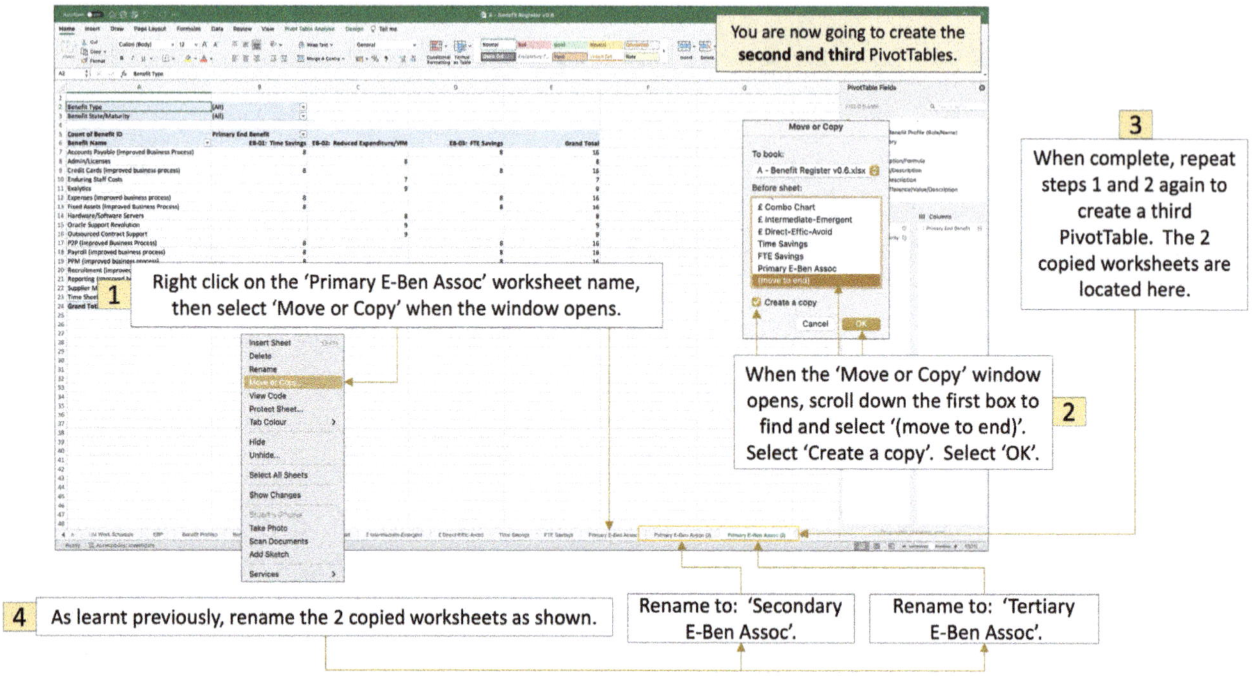

IMAGE 96 *Copy and Name the Second and Third PivotTables.*

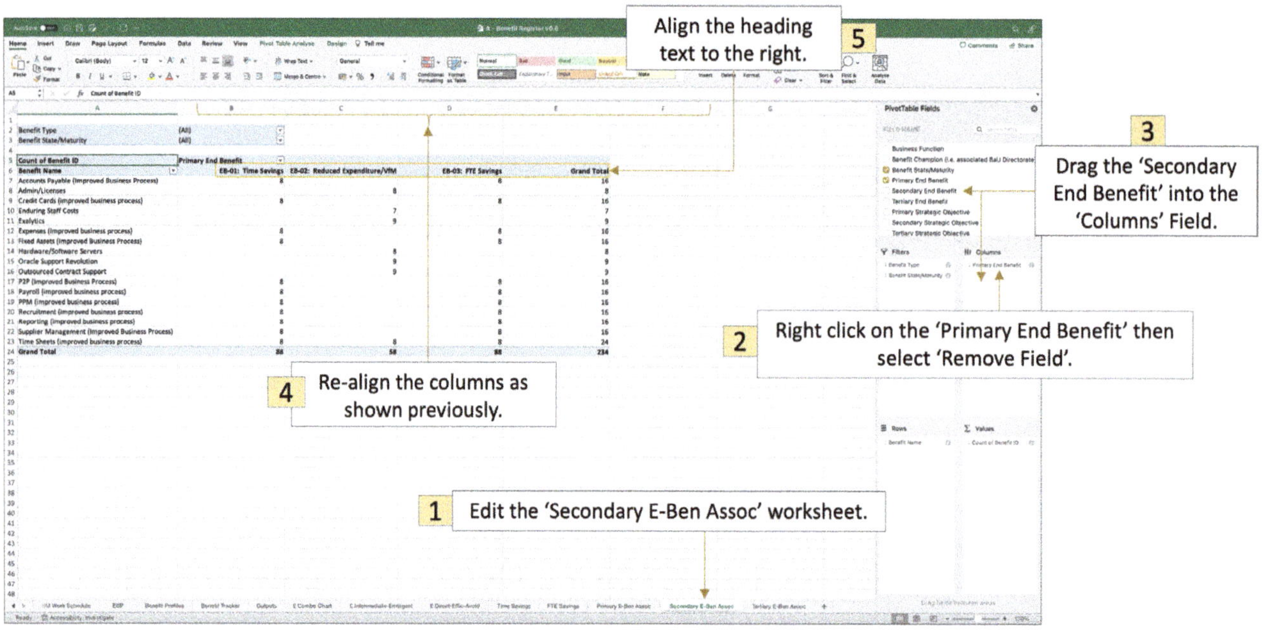

IMAGE 97 *Update and Format the Second PivotTable.*

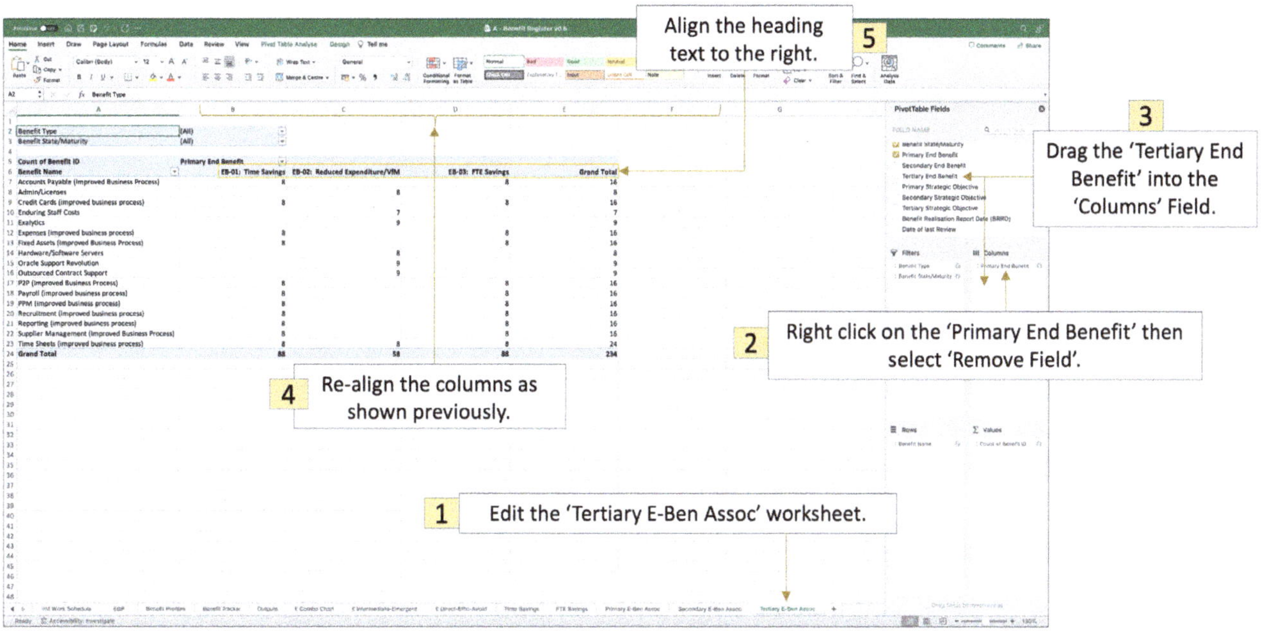

IMAGE 98 *Update and Format the Third PivotTable.*

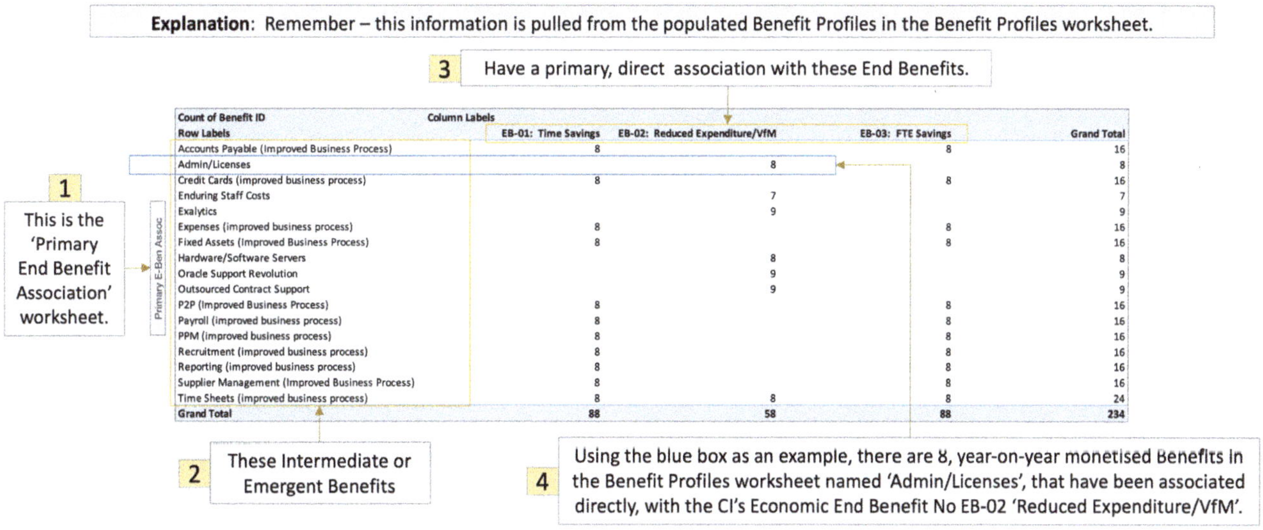

IMAGE 99 *Explanation of the Numeric Values.*

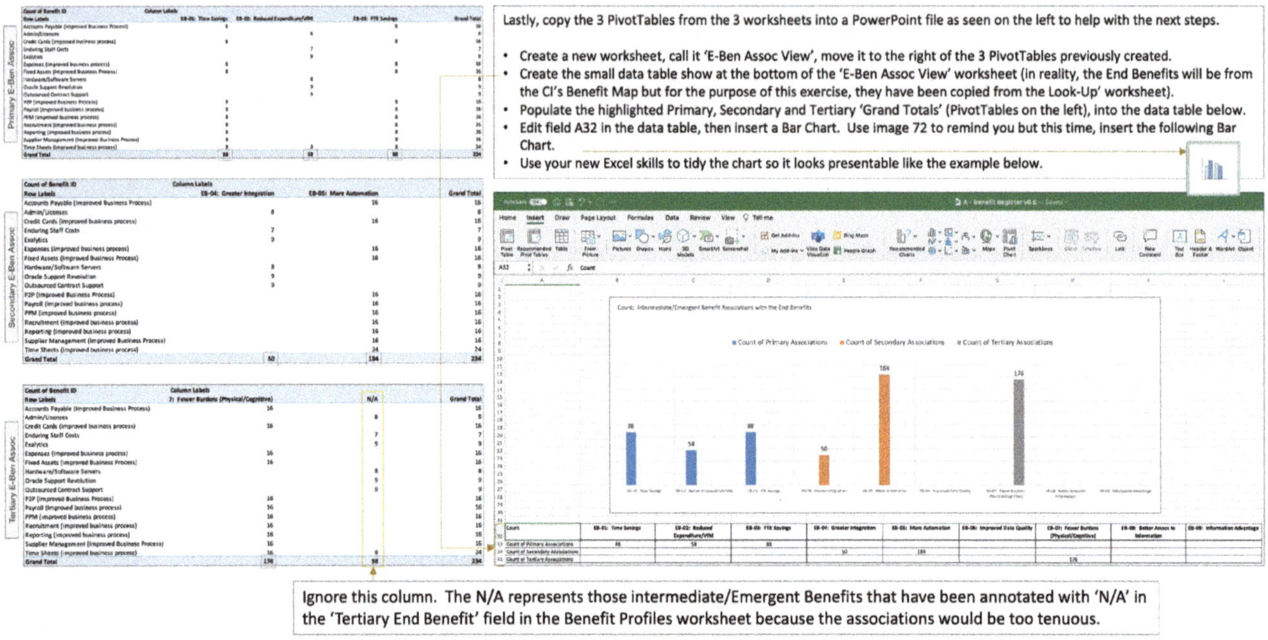
Lastly, copy the 3 PivotTables from the 3 worksheets into a PowerPoint file as seen on the left to help with the next steps.
• Create a new worksheet, call it 'E-Ben Assoc View', move it to the right of the 3 PivotTables previously created.
• Create the small data table show at the bottom of the 'E-Ben Assoc View' worksheet (in reality, the End Benefits will be from the CI's Benefit Map but for the purpose of this exercise, they have been copied from the Look-Up' worksheet).
• Populate the highlighted Primary, Secondary and Tertiary 'Grand Totals' (PivotTables on the left), into the data table below.
• Edit field A32 in the data table, then insert a Bar Chart. Use image 72 to remind you but this time, insert the following Bar Chart.
• Use your new Excel skills to tidy the chart so it looks presentable like the example below.
Primary E-Ben Assoc
Secondary E-Ben Assoc
Tertiary E-Ben Assoc
Ignore this column. The N/A represents those intermediate/Emergent Benefits that have been annotated with 'N/A' in the 'Tertiary End Benefit' field in the Benefit Profiles worksheet because the associations would be too tenuous.

IMAGE 100 *Create 'E-Ben Assoc View' Worksheet.*

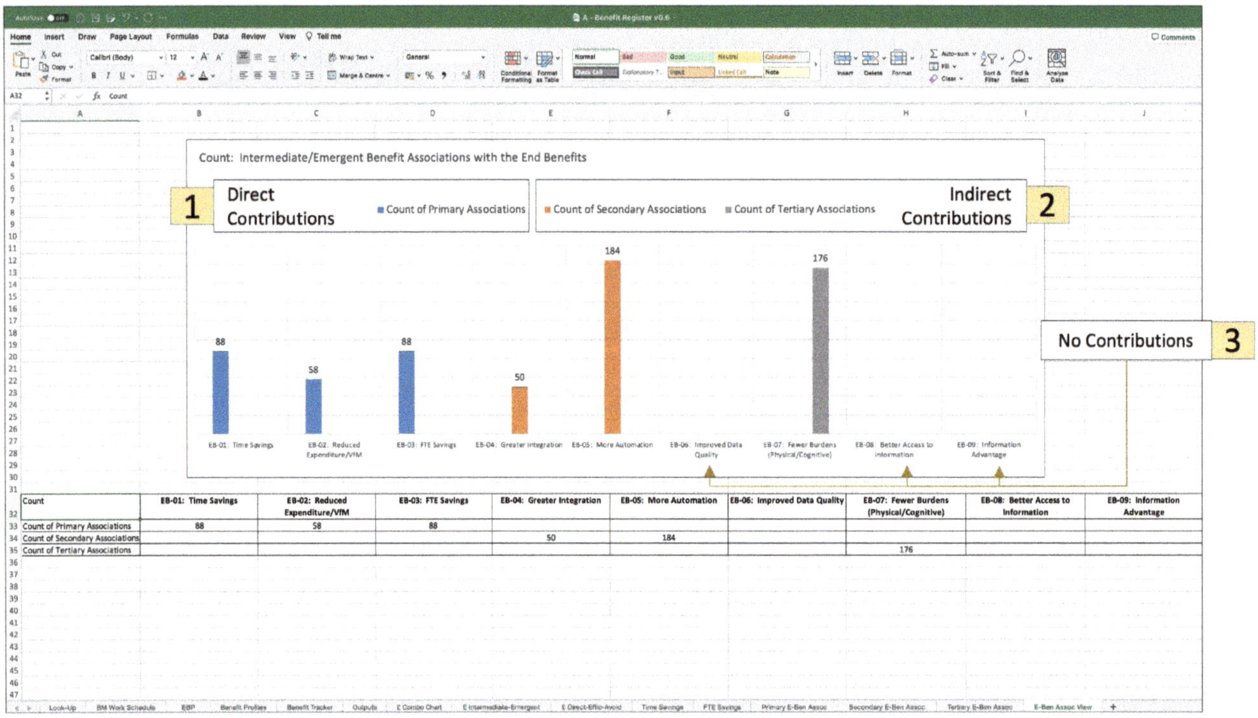
Count: Intermediate/Emergent Benefit Associations with the End Benefits
1
Direct Contributions
Count of Primary Associations
Count of Secondary Associations
Count of Tertiary Associations
Indirect Contributions
2
No Contributions
3
88
58
88
50
184
176
EB-01: Time Savings
EB-02: Reduced Expenditure/VfM
EB-03: FTE Savings
EB-04: Greater Integration
EB-05: More Automation
EB-06: Improved Data Quality
EB-07: Fewer Burdens (Physical/Cognitive)
EB-08: Better Access to Information
EB-09: Information Advantage
Count
Count of Primary Associations
Count of Secondary Associations
Count of Tertiary Associations

IMAGE 101 *Bar Chart – Count of Intermediate and Emergent Benefit Associations (Primary, Secondary and Tertiary) With the CI's End Benefits.*

9.6.4 Insights.

    a. Without this approach, the primary associations (blue bars[76]) would be captured only. This is one third of the CI's 9 End Benefits.

    b. With this approach, a wider contribution to the End Benefits can be seen. The BM can then prioritise work by capturing Benefit Indicators to be associated with the 3 End Benefits without a contribution if that is necessary to do so now. See para 3.8.3.

    c. The BM is having a positive impact because wider associations are being demonstrated using the Benefit Profiles worksheet, saving time and money. The work is being delivered at pace.

    d. We know already that the 3 blue bars with primary associations are being quantified through time, monetised time and the FTE. The same information can be used as an indirect quantification of those End Benefits with secondary and tertiary contributions; this is particularly useful if those End Benefits are difficult to quantify directly. This is not a doubling-up of Gross Benefit values, and reference to this in a supported BRP leaves no doubt.

9.7 Bar Chart (End Benefit Associations With the SOs)

9.7.1 A similar though faster approach can be undertaken to see the associations between the CI's End Benefits and the SOs. This will help to provide the ability to close in and resolve a significant problem at the portfolio level. For example, the portfolio office should see more of their objectives being quantified by the CIs across the portfolio.

9.7.2 To achieve it, we copy and rename the worksheets created from para 9.6. Tweaking them slightly enables the next view that counts the End Benefit associations with the SOs. The insights at para 9.6.4 also apply. The resulting view is as follows:

---

76 Remember, the blue bars added together represent the 234 individual Benefit Profiles in the Benefit Register. Each have a primary association with one of the CI's End Benefits. All of them have a secondary association (orange bars). Only 176 of them have a tertiary association.

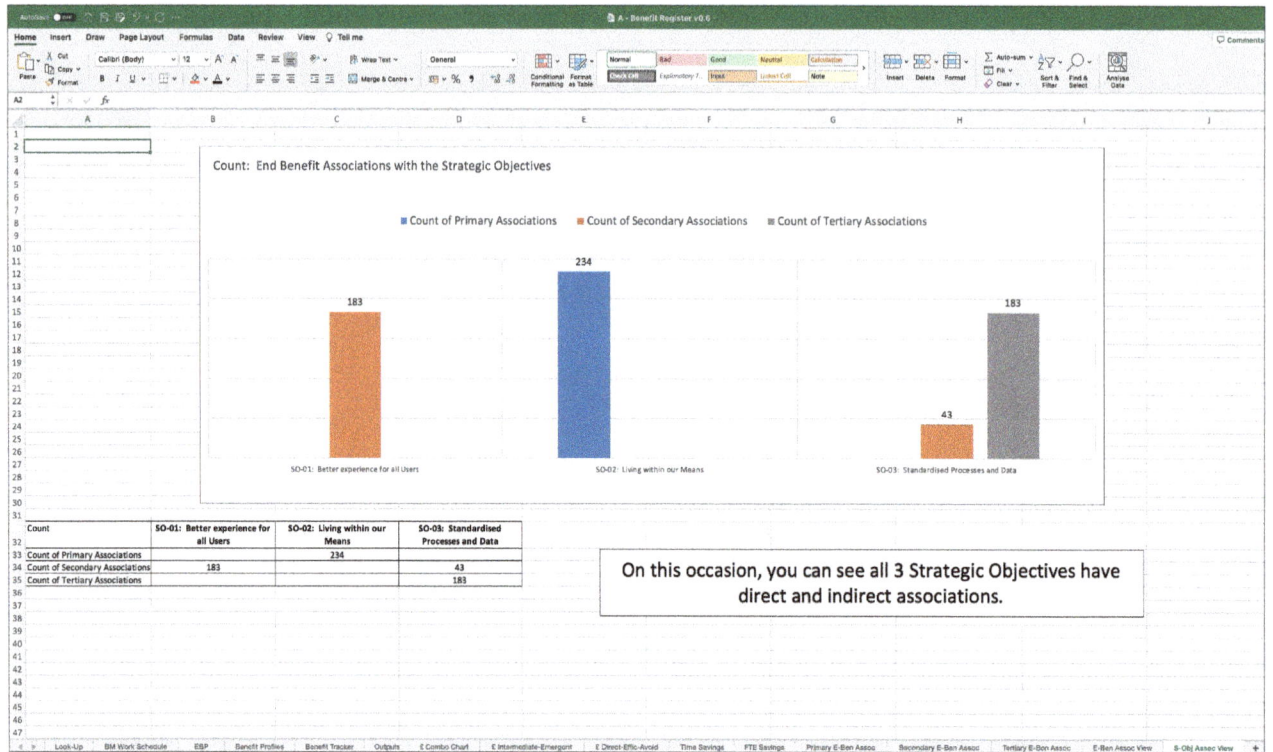

IMAGE 102 *Count of associations between the CI's End Benefits and the Strategic Objectives.*

9.7.3 The view is achieved by implementing the following actions:

Ser	Worksheet Name	Action
(a)	(b)	(c)
1	Primary E-Ben Assoc	• Copy 'Primary E-Ben Assoc' worksheet then Rename: 'Primary S-Obj Assoc'. • Move the 'Primary S-Obj Assoc' worksheet to the desired location in the Benefit Register. • Edit the 'Primary S-Obj Assoc' worksheet. • Remove 'Benefit Name' from PivotTable 'Rows' Field. • Move the 'Primary End Benefit' from the PivotTable 'Columns' Field, to the PivotTable 'Rows' Field. • Insert 'Primary Strategic Objective' into PivotTable 'Columns' Field.

Ser	Worksheet Name	Action
(a)	(b)	(c)
2	Secondary E-Ben Assoc	• Copy 'Secondary E-Ben Assoc' worksheet then Rename: 'Secondary S-Obj Assoc'. • Move the 'Secondary S-Obj Assoc' worksheet to the desired location in the Benefit Register. • Edit the 'Secondary S-Obj Assoc' worksheet. • Remove 'Benefit Name' from PivotTable 'Rows' Field. • Move the 'Secondary End Benefit' from the PivotTable 'Columns' Field, to the PivotTable 'Rows' Field. • Insert 'Secondary Strategic Objective' into PivotTable 'Columns' Field.
3	Tertiary E-Ben Assoc	• Copy 'Tertiary E-Ben Assoc' worksheet then Rename: 'Tertiary S-Obj Assoc'. • Move the 'Tertiary S-Obj Assoc' worksheet to the desired location in the Benefit Register. • Edit the 'Tertiary S-Obj Assoc' worksheet. • Remove 'Benefit Name' from PivotTable 'Rows' Field. • Move the 'Tertiary End Benefit' from the PivotTable 'Columns' Field, to the PivotTable 'Rows' Field. • Insert 'Tertiary Strategic Objective' into PivotTable 'Columns' Field.

Ser	Worksheet Name	Action
(a)	(b)	(c)
4	E-Ben Assoc View	• Copy 'E-Ben Assoc View' worksheet then Rename: 'S-Obj Assoc View'. • Move the 'S-Obj Assoc View' worksheet to the desired location in the Benefit Register. • Edit the 'S-Obj Assoc View' worksheet. • Manually update the data table so it looks like the table below (i.e. populate the SOs across the top, then populate the values as shown, using the values in the 3 new worksheets created at serials 1–3 above).

Count	SO-01: Better experience for all Users	SO-02: Living within our Means	SO-03: Standardised Processes and Data
Count of Primary Associations		234	
Count of Secondary Associations	183		43
Count of Tertiary Associations			176

• Right click on the Bar Chart; select 'Select Data'; ensure the columns and rows in the updated data table are selected only; select 'OK'.

TABLE 11 *View the Associations Between the CI's End Benefits and the SOs.*

9.7.4 If we wanted to, we could then interrogate the Benefit Profiles worksheet using the sort fields (i.e. the drop down selections in the column headings at the top) to generate views of the aggregated, quantified values from the Intermediate, Emergent and Dis-Benefits, through to the End Benefits and SOs. This can be achieved because the structure/categorisations (Image 32 and Table 4) of the Benefit Profiles worksheet enable it. This activity ought to be undertaken by the BM at the CI level to inform the portfolio office BM if the latter requires the information. This should not be achieved the other way round because the burden would be too great for the portfolio office BM to achieve it for all the CIs.

9.8 Line Chart (£ by Benefit State)

9.8.1 Stakeholders will want to know how the Benefits are progressing when the reporting regime has been established. When the BM receives a Benefit Report and can update the associated Benefit Profiles with the reported information, the following fields are likely to be updated:

a. Benefit Report Status (Column N): See paras 4.15.1–4.15.2.

b. Current Value (Column O): Column O wants to know the current value of the Benefit in Column H. For example, if Column H stated the Benefit forecast is £2M, and if the Benefit Report states the current value is £2M, insert £2M in Column O.

c. Benefit State/Maturity (Column S): See paras 4.20.1–4.20.2.

d. BRRD (Column Z): A new date will be required if the Benefit is to be reported again in the future.

e. Date of Last Review (Column AA): Ensure the last review date is correct.

f. Date of Next Review (Column AB): Ensure the next review date is correct. If reviews are no longer required (i.e. the Benefit is closed – see para 4.20.2), enter 'N/A' in this field.

g. Remarks/Comments (Column AC): As required.

9.8.2 We can use the reported information to create a Line Chart that summarises the status of the Intermediate and Emergent Benefits and Dis-Benefits with their values. We do this by creating a PivotTable that pulls information from the Benefit Profiles worksheet. Once formatted, the PivotTable can then be used to create the Line Chart. The steps to achieve it can be seen in Images 103–111.

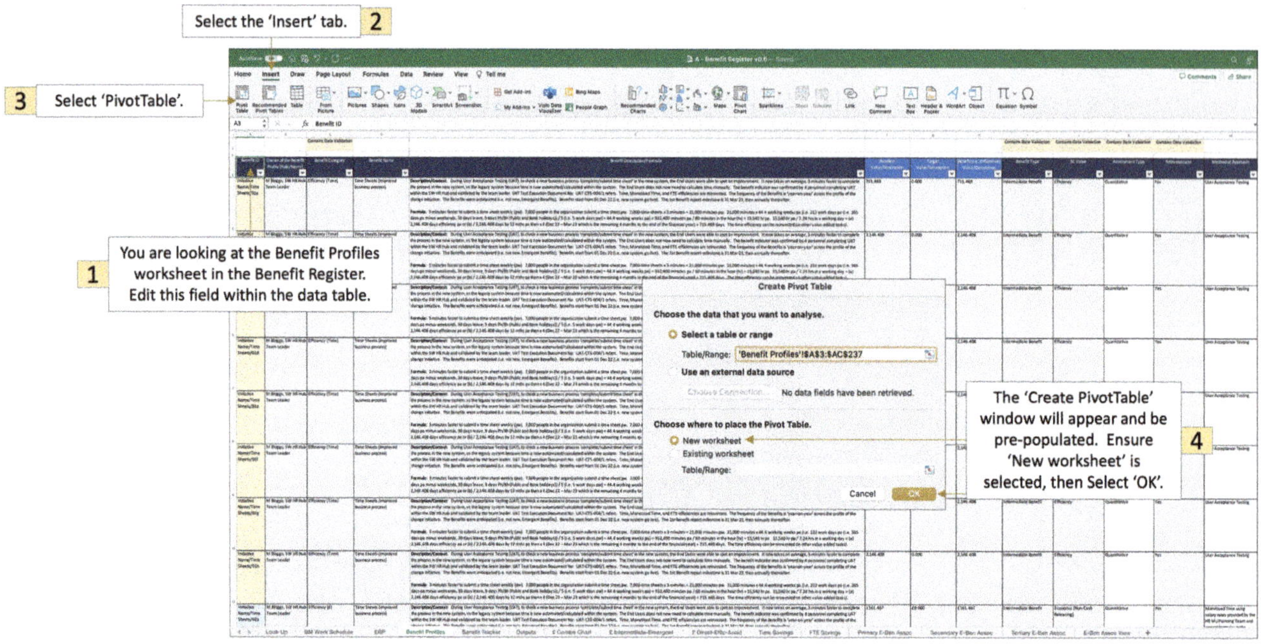

IMAGE 103 *Create the PivotTable from the Benefit Profiles Worksheet.*

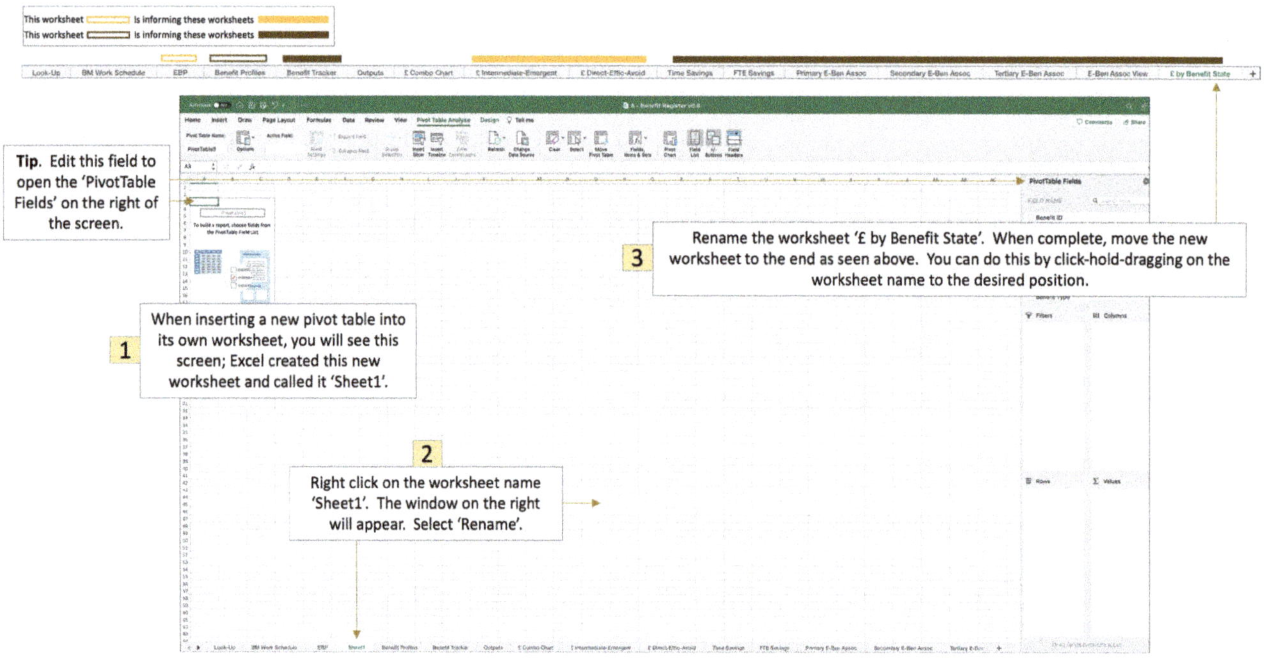

IMAGE 104 *Name and Position the PivotTable.*

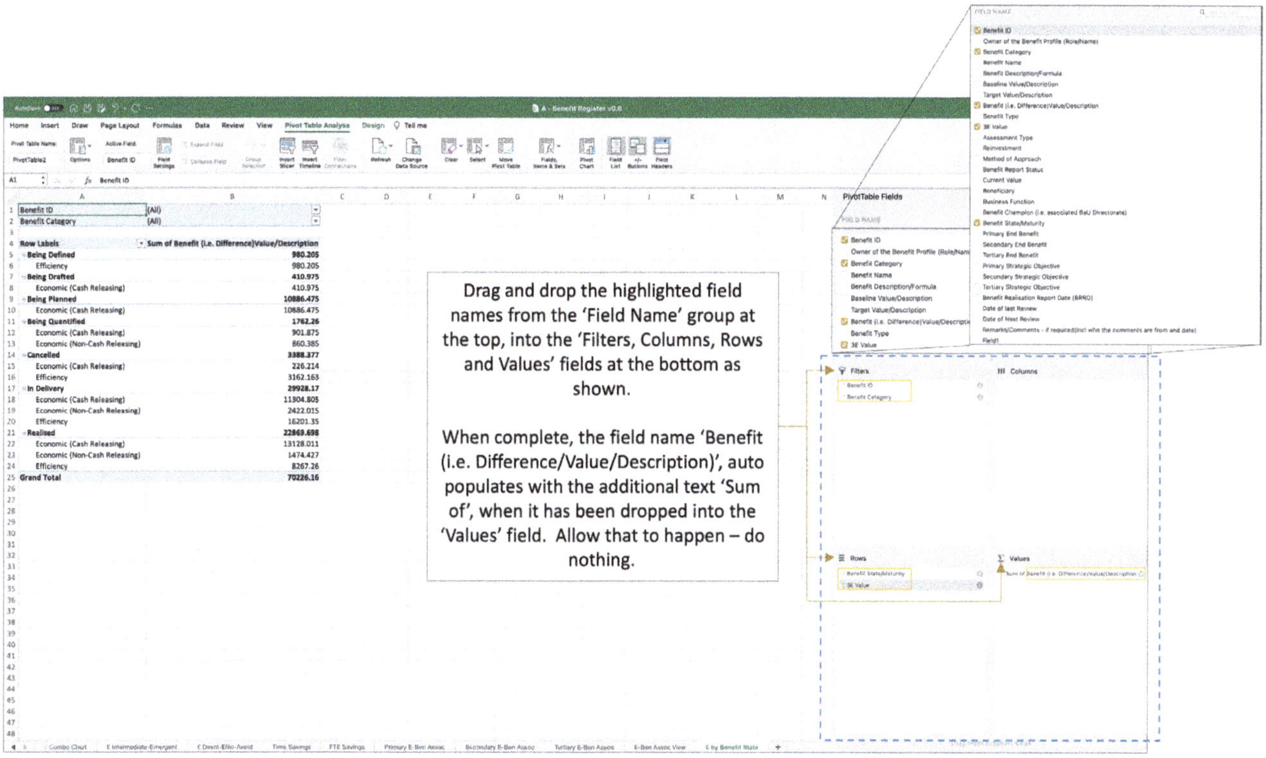

IMAGE 105 *Populate the PivotTable.*

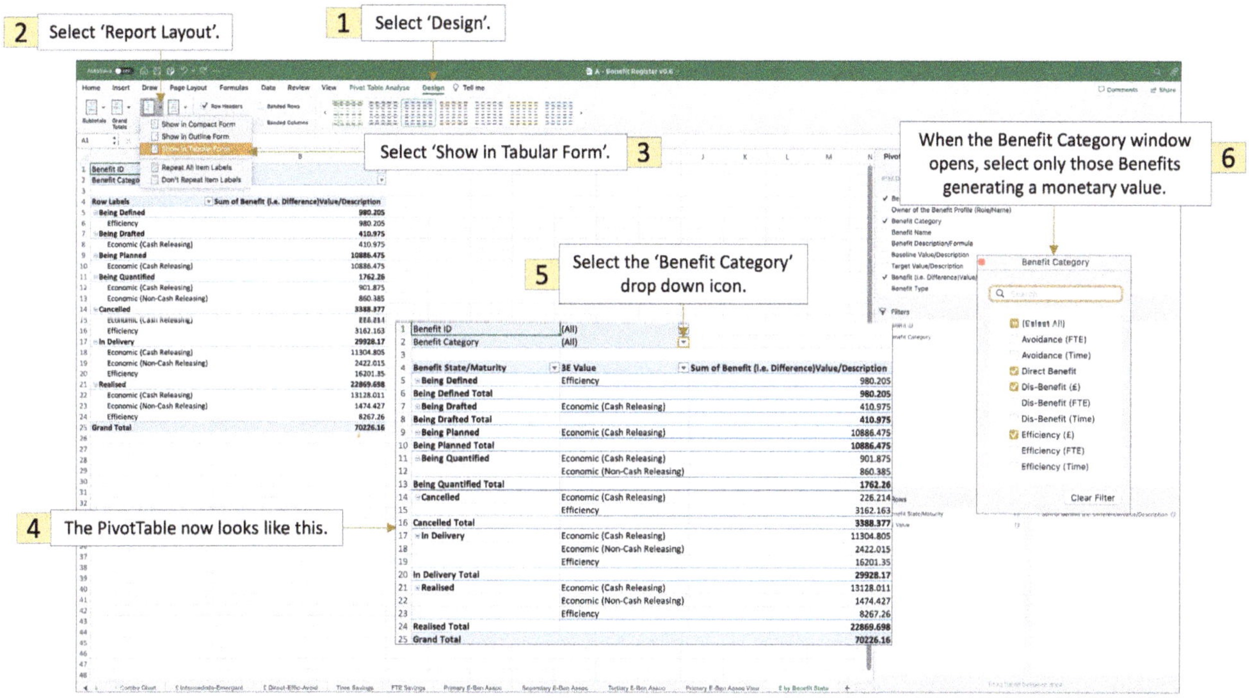

IMAGE 106 *Report Layout in Tabular Form.*

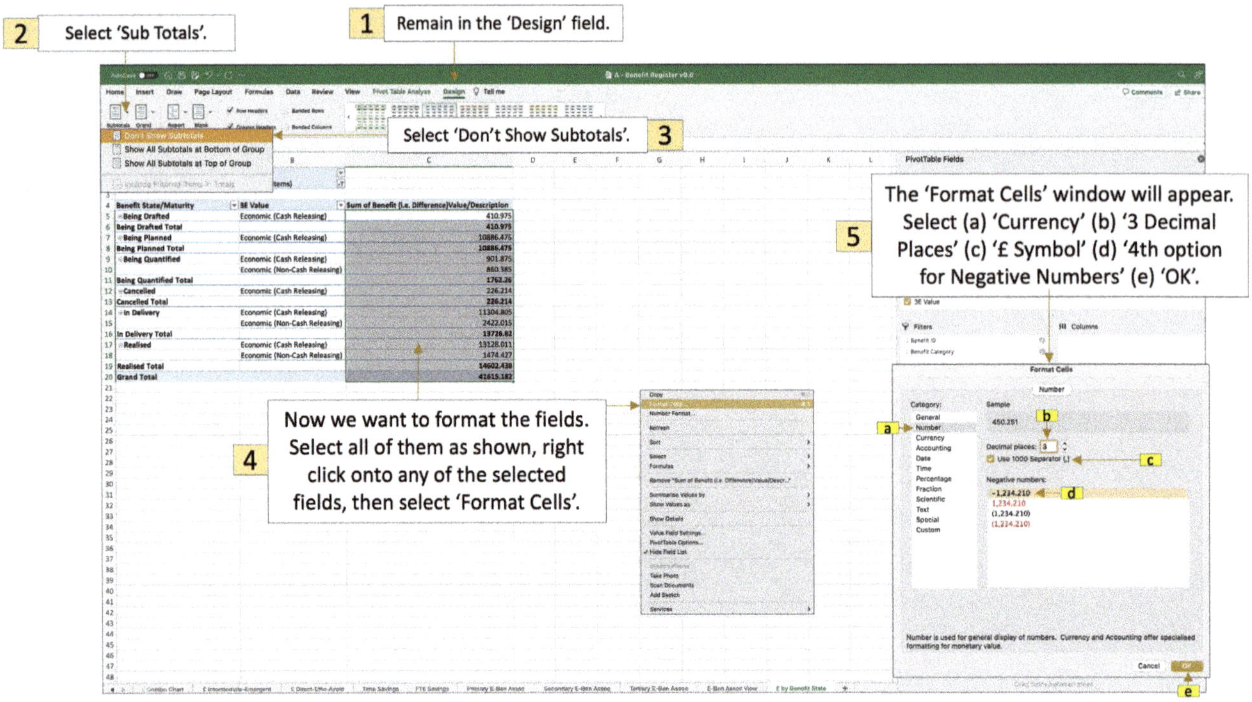

IMAGE 107 *Structure and Format the Monetised Values.*

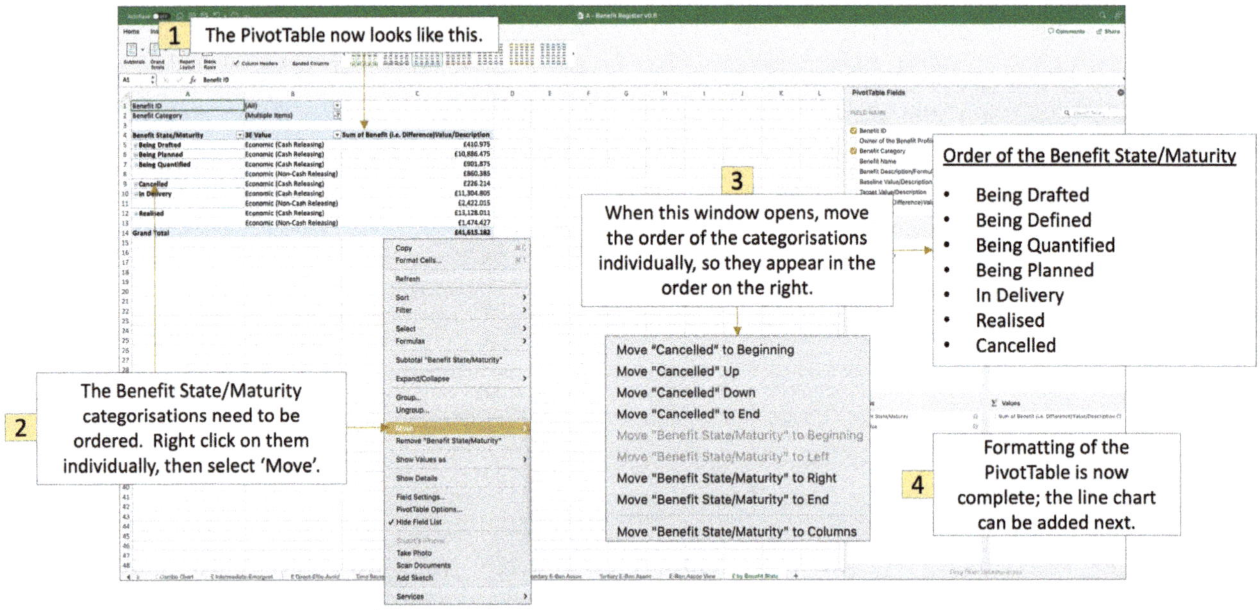

IMAGE 108 *Order of the Benefit State/Maturity.*

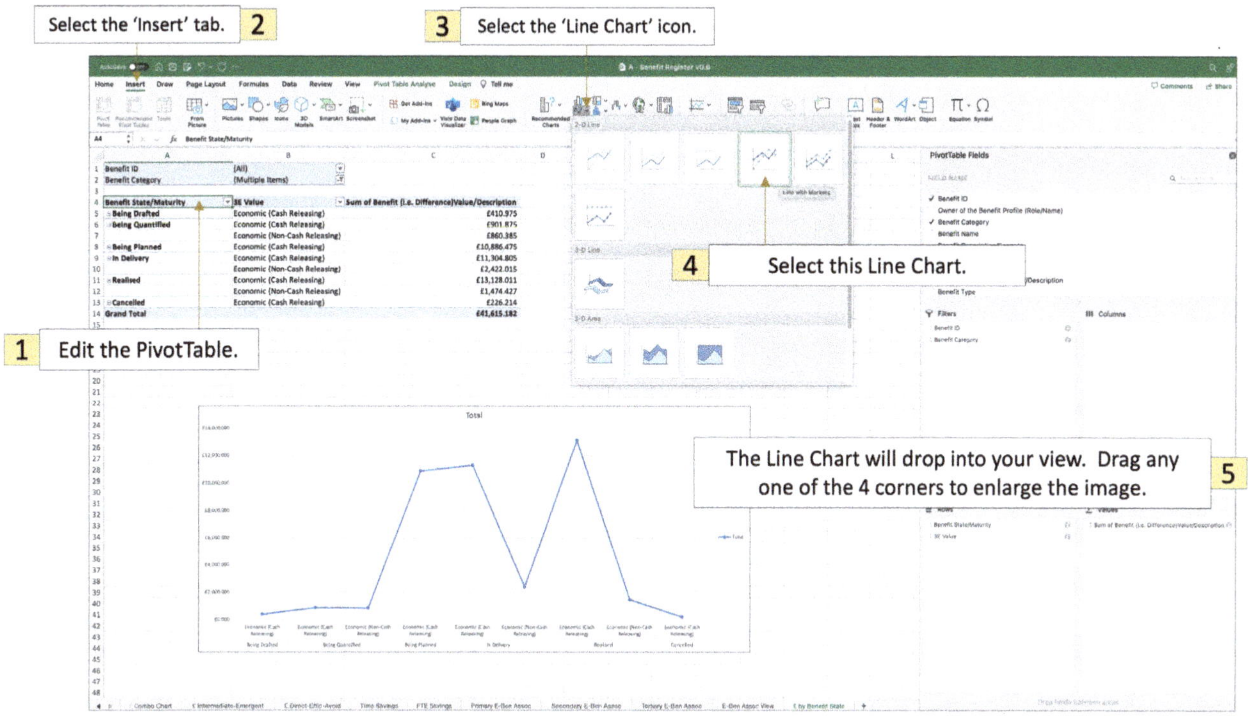

Select the 'Insert' tab. **2**

3 Select the 'Line Chart' icon.

4 Select this Line Chart.

1 Edit the PivotTable.

5 The Line Chart will drop into your view. Drag any one of the 4 corners to enlarge the image.

IMAGE 109 *Insert the Line Chart.*

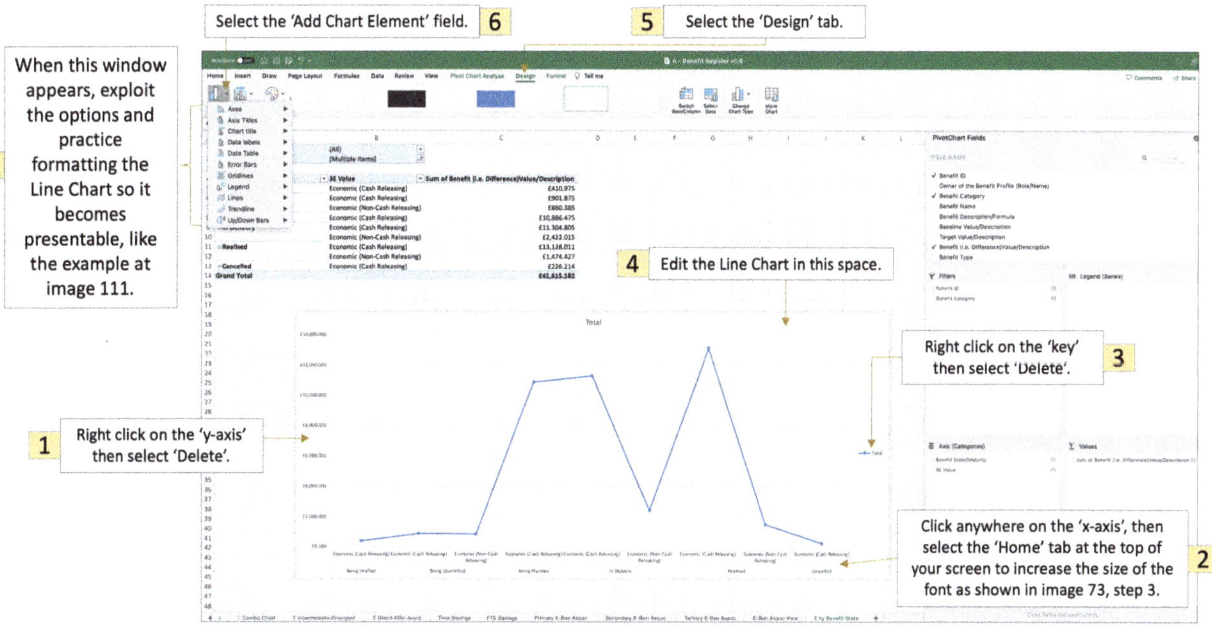

Select the 'Add Chart Element' field. **6**

5 Select the 'Design' tab.

7 When this window appears, exploit the options and practice formatting the Line Chart so it becomes presentable, like the example at image 111.

4 Edit the Line Chart in this space.

3 Right click on the 'key' then select 'Delete'.

1 Right click on the 'y-axis' then select 'Delete'.

2 Click anywhere on the 'x-axis', then select the 'Home' tab at the top of your screen to increase the size of the font as shown in image 73, step 3.

IMAGE 110 *Format the Line Chart.*

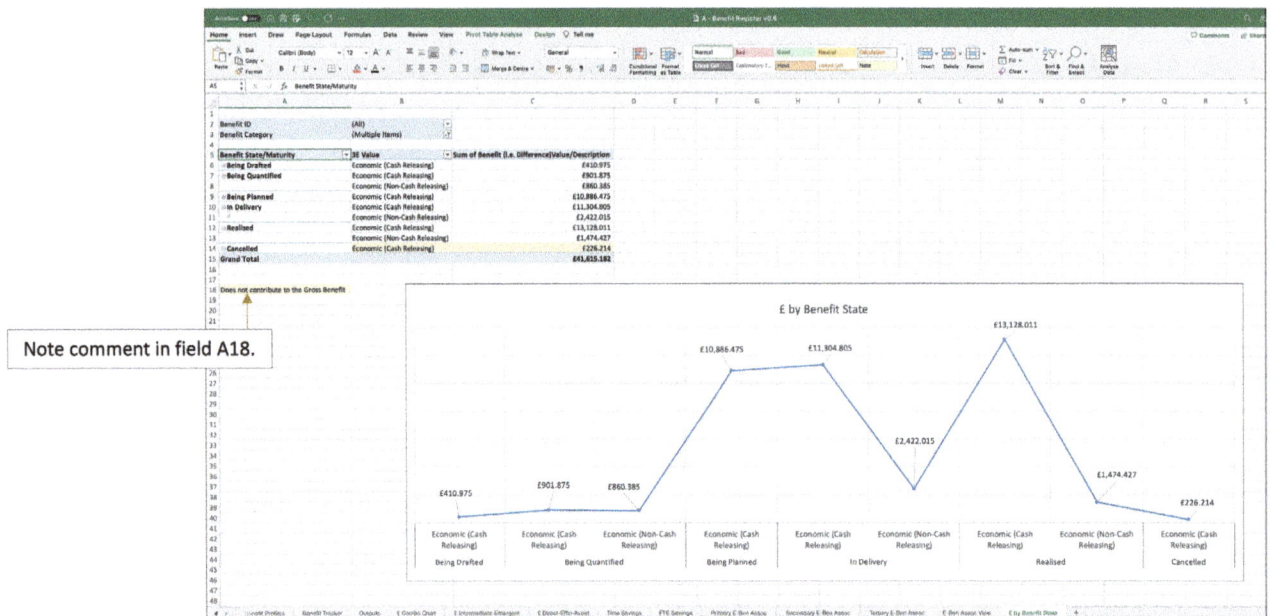

IMAGE 111 *Review.*

9.8.3 For completeness, and on this occasion the 'Grand Total' @ £41,615.182M is less than the Gross Benefit Profile in the EBP @ £71,754.360M because this is an exercise only, to demonstrate the use of the visual at Image 111. Footnote 74 remains the requirement.

9.9 PivotTable (Benefit Champions' Benefit Status)

9.9.1 The Benefit Champions will wish to be aware of the Benefits in their area of responsibility so they can champion and report them. The Benefit Champions are best placed to improve the culture of their workforce in a Benefits Management context by ensuring Benefit Indicators are identified and reported to the BM. This will go a long way to help ensure the organisation is Benefits Led; the organisations Efficiency Board will expect it and the IPA Gateway Review process will wish to see it. The BM can assist the Benefit Champions by educating the workforce on the key tenants of Benefits Management (see para 7.1.1 e).

9.9.2 Scenario: The BM is to generate a report for the Benefit Champions showing the status of Cash Releasing and Non-Cash Releasing Benefits in their area of responsibility. To do this, the BM follows these simple steps in Image 112.

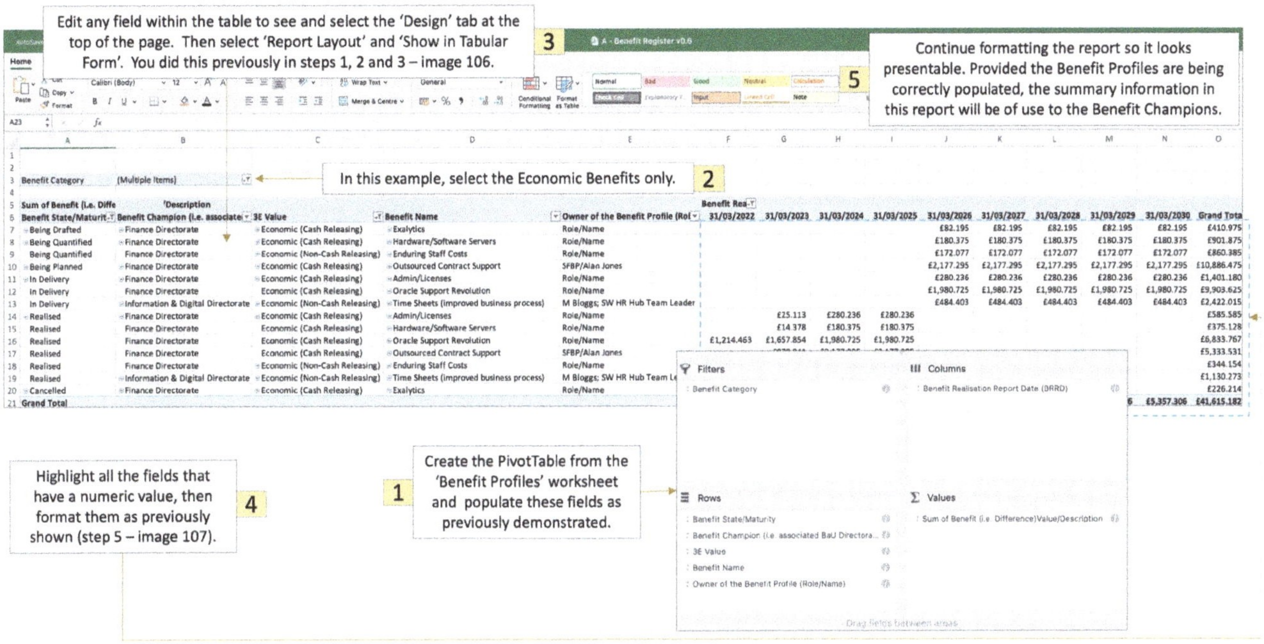

IMAGE 112 *Summary Report for the Benefit Champions.*

Roles and Responsibilities

10.1 Introduction

10.1.1 The roles and responsibilities described below are the result of wide engagements across public and private sector organisations. They represent the 'main thing'; unnecessary language has been removed. The roles should be recorded with assigned names so they can be easily identified.

10.2 SRO

10.2.1 Reports to the Transformation Board, for example, on the status of Benefits delivery.

10.2.2 Ensures the CI and business areas affected maintain a focus on Benefits delivery.

10.2.3 Ensures the BMS is created, reviewed, improved and applied.

10.2.4 Escalation route to the Management Board.

10.3 Benefit Champions

10.3.1 Head of business area that can/does influence and monitor the realisation of the Benefits on behalf of the Benefit Sponsor.

10.3.2 Provides a single point of oversight for the consolidation, influence and support of activities across their Functions.

10.3.3 Facilitates the issue and amendment of corporate policy and documentation to reflect process modifications required to transform the business.

10.3.4 Enables and champions business change to facilitate the realisation of the Benefits.

10.4 Benefits Authority

10.4.1 Ensures the development and implementation of the approach to Benefit Management (BMS, Map, BRP, Register and Profiles) on behalf of the SRO.

10.4.2 Ensures Benefit reviews are being undertaken during the life of the CI.

10.4.3 Reviews the Benefit Profiles prepared by the CI and BM.

10.4.4 Represents the CI side of the handshake.

10.5 Business Change Team

10.5.1 Defines and implements all aspects of operational change management/ transformational activities required for the transition and bedding in of the outcomes.

10.5.2 Ensures appropriate resource within the Business Change Team and the existence of a Change Network supporting the realisation of Benefits.

10.5.3 Validates Benefits and reviews the delivery schedule with the BM and associated stakeholders.

10.5.4 Identifies, resolves, and reports the double counting of Benefits in conjunction with the BM.

10.5.5 Confirms the effectiveness of the CI's deliverables supporting Benefit Realisation.

10.6 Benefit Manager (BM)

10.6.1 Develops, owns and maintains the BMS, Map, BRP, Register and Profiles.

10.6.2 Initiates Benefit reviews and reports on status of Benefits accrual and corrective actions.

10.6.3 Day-to-day management of the Benefit Management approach and process including review and update as required.

10.6.4 Facilitates individual Benefit Profile evaluations with the owner of the Benefit Profiles.

10.6.5 Identifies and raises risks and issues relating to realisation of the Benefits.

10.6.6 Responsible for maintaining a Benefits documentation library.

10.7 Owners of the Benefit Profiles

10.7.1 Accept the Benefit Profiles prepared by the BM and agree that they are realistic and deliverable.

10.7.2 Authorise any movement (of the Benefits) between the Benefit State/Maturity levels in conjunction with the BM.

10.7.3 Monitor the successful delivery of enabling and business changes upon which the realisation of the Benefits depends.

10.7.4 Appoint Benefit Agents if required (i.e. an End User, who uses the business processes in their day-to-day activities, and is best placed to report improvements, or otherwise, to the owner of the Benefit Profiles).

10.7.5 Report on the realisation of the Benefits.

10.7.6 Usually represent the business function side of the handshake but not exclusively.

10.8 Benefit Agents (If Established)

10.8.1 Measure the performance of the Benefits (i.e. in accordance with the Benefit Profiles prepared by the BM and owner of the Benefit Profiles).

10.8.2 Assist the BM and owner of the Benefit Profiles by maintaining the Benefit Profiles.

10.8.3 Report Benefit Realisation to the owner of the Benefit Profiles/BM.

10.9 Benefit Initiators

10.9.1 An entity (individual, group or area) who identifies an opportunity or requirement for a Benefit to be delivered. The Benefit initiators are likely to become the Owners of the Benefit Profiles or a Benefit Agent.

10.10 Benefit Receivers/Beneficiary

10.10.1 An entity (individual, group, area) who takes receipt of the Benefits and sees the effects of this into BaU.

10.11 Portfolio Office

10.11.1 Communicates the breadth of the organisation's CIs to provide understanding.

10.11.2 Provides validation of baseline assumptions and approach[77].

10.11.3 Confirms the accuracy of Benefits figures/confidence levels[78].

10.11.4 Standardises the use of formulas and measures across the portfolio.

10.11.5 Coheres the CIs and Benefit reporting, especially where combined Benefits and efficiencies exist.

10.11.6 Acts as the interlocutor across the portfolio on Benefits-related matters.

10.12 PMO (or the PSO)

10.12.1 Monitors the progress of Benefit realisation against the plan with the BM[79].

10.12.2 Facilitates the production of performance reports as directed.

10.12.3 Maintains Benefits Information under change control.

---

77 For example, a CIs alignment to SOs.

78 For example, a portfolio office in the MOD chaired a monthly Benefits Forum. The idea being to share ideas, learn lessons and improve performance. A single CI in the portfolio would be invited to provide an update during each forum. The updates went into some detail and provided insight to enable the portfolio team to assess confidence in the CIs Benefits and forecast.

79 For example, how is the PMO managing risks, dependencies, schedule and the associated impacts on the Benefits Forecast.

SECTION 11

Examples Benefit Profiles

11.1 Introduction

11.1.1 The below table consists of examples of Benefit Profiles that can help to inform a CI's EBP and Benefit Profiles worksheets. The author had first developed and used them with stakeholders in the HO and subsequently re-used/refined them in the FCDO where they had been accepted and owned. These profiles were mentioned earlier at para 1.13.5.

Benefit Short Code	Benefit Name	Measurement/ Description
(a)	(b)	(c)
Benefit Profiles drawn from the HO Approach		
Efficiency – Time	Cessation of [legacy system name] Enhancement work – Time Saving	**Context**: [legacy system name] Ops & Support work removed, resulting from closure of the system. The FTE (100% of their time) has been re-allocated/reinvested inside the organisation on other value-added tasks and priorities. **Formula**: No. of workdays for each FTE undertaking the work x frequency.
Efficiency – Monetised Time	Cessation of [legacy system name] Enhancement work – Monetised Time	**Context**: [legacy system name] Ops & Support work removed, resulting from closure of the system. The FTE (100% of their time) has been re-allocated/reinvested inside the organisation on other value-added tasks and priorities. **Formula**: No. of working days x daily cap rate for grade undertaking the work (i.e. average cap rate £ pa) / 222 work days pa (i.e. 365 days pa minus weekends, 30 days leave, 9 days Ph/Bh = £ pd) x frequency. Don't forget to include the organisation's contribution to the employee's National Insurance, Pension and Location Allowances.

Benefit Short Code	Benefit Name	Measurement/ Description
(a)	(b)	(c)
Efficiency – FTE	Cessation of [legacy system name] Enhancement work – FTE Saving	**Context:** [legacy system name] Ops & Support work removed, resulting from closure of the system. The FTE (100% of their time) has been re-allocated/reinvested inside the organisation on other value-added tasks and priorities. **Formula:** No of workdays / 222 overall workdays annually = number of FTE x frequency.
Avoidance – Time	Time to deliver an alternative Cloud Infrastructure in the absence of convergence – Time Saving	**Context:** [legacy system name] could have undertaken work to Design, Develop, Build, Test and Deploy (DDBTD) new cloud infrastructure (or purchase an alternative fully designed cloud infrastructure) at a point in time, if the decision to converge legacy systems into a single solution under [new system name] had not been taken. [new system name] enables the legacy system to move to an approved solution, to meet the Government Shared Services Strategy's data convergence priorities and future landscape. In doing so, significant time and effort is avoided. For example: (a) [new system name] brings SaaS/environments with packaged products fully supported by Oracle. Time and effort to DDBTD an alternative/equivalent new SaaS solution can be removed. (b) [new system name] brings a PaaS/IaaS solution that need only be configured for those systems migrating to [new system name]. Time and effort to DDBTD an alternative PaaS/IaaS solution would be significant. The profile/concept has been adopted from similar/agreed work in the HO/FCDO when converging numerous systems of varying sizes into a single cloud solution/architect saved time inside the organisation. *The organisation can determine the size and complexity of the work for each system by categorising them to be either small, medium or large bodies of work.* **Formula:** No of workdays for the internal FTEs and external SMEs and developers to undertake the work x frequency. **Frequency:** Twice (i.e. 01 Dec 23 & 01 Dec 28). The organisation could have undertaken the work twice in a 10-year period (i.e. current contract term 3+1+1)[80].

80 Commercial language. The average contract length for a medium/large system was determined to be 5 years during discussions with the commercial departments. The 3+1+1 (i.e. 3-year contract with 2 x 1 year extension options) means, during the life of a CI (typically 10-year profile) there could be 2 occasions when re-contracting could be necessary (i.e. a probable/likely scenario). The Benefit Profile in the example had been agreed/owned by a representative from each of the legacy systems converging to a new system. If the legacy system/owner of the Benefit Profile disagreed with the frequency, it was not forced upon them. The accuracy/validity of the Benefit Profile is periodically reviewed in the event that circumstances change (i.e. delivery of the new system is delayed, the avoidance Benefit profiles would also slip to the right).

Benefit Short Code	Benefit Name	Measurement/ Description
(a)	(b)	(c)
Avoidance – £	Time to deliver an alternative Cloud Infrastructure in the absence of convergence – Monetised Time	**Context**: [legacy system name] could have undertaken work to DDBTD new cloud infrastructure (or purchase an alternative fully designed cloud infrastructure) at a point in time, if the decision to converge legacy systems into a single solution under [new system name] had not been taken. [new system name] enables the legacy system to move to an approved solution, to meet the Government Shared Services Strategy's data convergence priorities and future landscape. In doing so, significant time and effort is avoided. For example: (a) [new system name] brings SaaS/environments with packaged products fully supported by Oracle. Time and effort to DDBTD an alternative/equivalent new SaaS solution can be removed. (b) [new system name] brings a PaaS/IaaS solution that need only be configured for those systems migrating to [new system name]. Time and effort to DDBTD an alternative PaaS/IaaS solution would be significant. The profile/concept has been adopted from similar/agreed work in the HO/FCDO when converging numerous systems of varying sizes into a single cloud solution/architect saved time inside the organisation. *The organisation can determine the size and complexity of the work for each system by categorising them to be either small, medium or large bodies of work.* **Formula**: No of working days x daily cap rate for FTEs/SMEs undertaking the work (i.e. average cap rate £ pa) / 222 work days pa (i.e. 365 days pa minus weekends, 30 days leave, 9 days Ph/Bh = £ pd) x frequency. Don't forget to include the organisation's contribution to the employee's National Insurance, Pension and Location Allowances for the Internal FTEs. See para 1.10.1 b ii for the average daily cap rate for outsourced resource. **Frequency**: Twice (i.e. 01 Dec 23 & 01 Dec 28). The organisation could have undertaken the work twice in a 10-year period (i.e. current contract term 3+1+1).

Benefit Short Code	Benefit Name	Measurement/ Description
(a)	(b)	(c)
Avoidance – FTE	Time to deliver an alternative Cloud Infrastructure in the absence of convergence – FTE Saving	**Context**: [legacy system name] could have undertaken work to DDBTD new cloud infrastructure (or purchase an alternative fully designed cloud infrastructure) at a point in time, if the decision to converge legacy systems into a single solution under [new system name] had not been taken. [new system name] enables the legacy system to move to an approved solution, to meet the Government Shared Services Strategy's data convergence priorities and future landscape. In doing so, significant time and effort is avoided. For example: (a) [new system name] brings SaaS/environments with packaged products fully supported by Oracle. Time and effort to DDBTD an alternative/equivalent new SaaS solution can be removed. (b) [new system name] brings a PaaS/IaaS solution that need only be configured for those systems migrating to [new system name]. Time and effort to DDBTD an alternative PaaS/IaaS solution would be significant. The profile/concept has been adopted from similar/agreed work in the HO/FCDO when converging numerous systems of varying sizes into a single cloud solution/architect saved time inside the organisation. *The organisation can determine the size and complexity of the work for each system by categorising them to be either small, medium or large bodies of work.* **Formula**: No of workdays / 222 overall workdays annually = number of FTE x frequency. **Frequency**: Twice (i.e. 01 Dec 23 & 01 Dec 28). The organisation could have undertaken the work twice in a 10-year period (i.e. current contract term 3+1+1).

Benefit Short Code	Benefit Name	Measurement/ Description
(a)	(b)	(c)
Avoidance – Time	**Procurement** (Re-engineering of the Oracle on-premise legacy system, hardware and protocols – Time Efficiency)	**Context**: Previous studies identified 2 options/solutions for the replacement or sustainment of [legacy system name]: (a) move/host [legacy system name] into a new cloud infrastructure solution or (b) undertake re-engineering of the Oracle on premise legacy system, hardware and non-standard protocols. The former was selected as the preferred option. This Benefit Profile captures the avoidance of time in a procurement context/body of work (i.e. documentation, requirements, approvals) to re-engineer the Oracle on-premise legacy system and protocols. *The organisation can determine the size and complexity of the work for each system by categorising them to be either small, medium or large bodies of work.* The profile/concept has been adopted from similar/agreed work in the HO/FCDO when converging numerous systems of varying sizes into a single cloud solution/architect saved time inside the organisation. **Formula**: No of workdays for each FTE undertaking the work x frequency. **Frequency**: Twice (i.e. 01 Dec 23 & 01 Dec 28). Commercial could have undertaken the procurement activity twice in a 10-year period (i.e. current contract term 3+1+1).

Benefit Short Code	Benefit Name	Measurement/ Description
(a)	(b)	(c)
Avoidance – £	**Procurement** (Re-engineering of the Oracle on-premise legacy system, hardware and protocols – Monetised Time)	**Context:** Previous studies identified 2 options/solutions for the replacement or sustainment of [legacy system name]: (a) move/host [legacy system name] into a new cloud infrastructure solution or (b) undertake re-engineering of the Oracle on-premise legacy system, hardware and non-standard protocols. The former was selected as the preferred option. This Benefit Profile captures the avoidance of spend on resource in a procurement context/body of work (i.e. documentation, requirements, approvals) to re-engineer the Oracle on-premise legacy system and protocols. *The organisation can determine the size and complexity of the work for each system by categorising them to be either small, medium or large bodies of work.* The profile/concept has been adopted from similar/agreed work in the HO/FCDO when converging numerous systems of varying sizes into a single cloud solution/architect saved time inside the organisation. **Formula:** No of working days x daily cap rate for grade undertaking the work (i.e. average cap rate £ pa) / 222 work days pa (i.e. 365 days pa minus weekends, 30 days leave, 9 days Ph/Bh = £ pd) x frequency. *Don't forget to include the organisation's contribution to the employee's National Insurance, Pension and Location Allowances.* **Frequency:** Twice (i.e. 01 Dec 23 & 01 Dec 28). Commercial could have undertaken the procurement activity twice in a 10-year period (i.e. current contract term 3+1+1).

Benefit Short Code	Benefit Name	Measurement/ Description
(a)	(b)	(c)
Avoidance – FTE	**Procurement** (Re-engineering of the Oracle on-premise legacy system, hardware and protocols – FTE)	**Context**: Previous studies identified 2 options/solutions for the replacement or sustainment of [legacy system name]: (a) move/host [legacy system name] into a new cloud infrastructure solution or (b) undertake re-engineering of the Oracle on-premise legacy system, hardware and non-standard protocols. The former was selected as the preferred option. This Benefit Profile captures the avoidance of FTEs in a procurement context/body of work (i.e. documentation, requirements, approvals) to re-engineer the Oracle on-premise legacy system and protocols. *The organisation can determine the size and complexity of the work for each system by categorising them to be either small, medium or large bodies of work.* The profile/concept has been adopted from similar/agreed work in the HO/FCDO when converging numerous systems of varying sizes into a single cloud solution/architect saved time inside the organisation. **Formula**: No of workdays / 222 overall workdays annually = number of FTE x frequency. **Frequency**: Twice (i.e. 01 Dec 23 & 01 Dec 28). Commercial could have undertaken the procurement activity twice in a 10-year period (i.e. current contract term 3+1+1).
Other Profiles		
Efficiency – £	Re-negotiated Oracle Licensing Agreement	The FBC Stated: [paragraph number]: 'Since the OBC was approved, the organisation has re-negotiated the Oracle licensing agreement to get the licence charges for FY21 reduced by £xxxM, in return for the [organisation name] agreeing to extend the term of the licence agreement by a further year to May 25. This has served to significantly reduce the cost impact of "dual running".' The resulted to-be costs line/CT (Oracle Cloud Licences SaaS) saw a commensurate reduction during FY 20/21.
Avoidance – £	Underspend – Small Changes to the System	**Reference**: To-be cost line 'Contract Provision (5 years funded changes to the system) Contracted'. The £xxxk provision for small changes to the system was not spent in FY 21/22 due in part to the original go-live in Jun 21 moving to summer 22).

Benefit Short Code	Benefit Name	Measurement/ Description
(a)	(b)	(c)
Efficiency – £	CI's Implementation Costs – Underspend	**Context:** The current CI's implementation costs are forecast at £xxxM. This is £xxxM under the FBC forecast (£xxxM). This cash-releasing underspend has been agreed/captured within the Benefits calculation (i.e. this is the current, live forecast) during close liaison with the PMO finance business partner; subsequent engagements will ensure this information is kept up to date so as to not skew the Gross Benefit Forecast.
Avoidance – £	FBC Short-Listed Options/ Avoidance (difference between options 2/3)	**Context:** In consultation with the programme director and senior commercial SME, circ. £xxxM cost avoidance, Non-Cash Releasing Benefit is noted for inclusion in the Benefit Register. The circ. £xxxM is the difference between option 2 and option 3 on the basis that we are comparing against the approved option 5 vs the 'de facto' re-start option. The FBC acknowledged the 'predicted saving' comparator between options 2/3.
Avoidance – £	Disruptive upgrades – avoided	**Context:** [legacy system name] is dependent on the physical location of the data centres and network infrastructure in [location name] maintained by the Service Management team. Discussions with the software/support provided revealed: We could expect to refresh servers, firewalls and network switches, plus management and development LANS with 60 PCs with replacement storage arrays. The upgrade, in all probability (without another solution such as [new system name]), would have been undertaken at 5-yearly intervals. The associated effort @ circ. £xxxk in 2022 and again 2027 (reduce by 20% for conservatism) = £xxxk.

TABLE 12 *Examples – Benefit Profiles.*

SECTION 12

Summary

12.1 Coherence

12.1.1 Throughout *The Benefit Manager's Desktop Step-by-Step Guide,* there are important references for BMs to seek confirmation or direction on aspects of Benefits Management, so the CI's approach to it is cohered, aligned and confidence improves in reported information across the P3Os and beyond. Those references have been consolidated below for ease of access. BMs can use the information, and the CI's approach to it, in the BRP for circulation to the appropriate stakeholders for review and endorsement.

a. Tooling – Benefit Register – footnote 15.

b. Use of formulas – paras 1.10.1–1.10.3.

c. Format of Numeric and Monetised Values – para 1.10.4.

d. Format/Structure of the EBP – para 2.9.4.

e. Recording of VAT in the EBP – para 2.10.1.

f. Recording of Inflation in the EBP – para 2.10.2.

g. Recording of OB in the EBP (para 2.10.3) or the Risk and Maturity Approach (para 2.10.4).

h. Strategic Alignment – footnote 39.

i. Benefit Categorisations – paras 4.2–4.30.

j. Benefit Report Thresholds – paras 6.5.1–6.5.2.

12.2 End Note

12.2.1 *The Benefit Manager's Desktop Step-by-Step Guide* has merged the approaches to Benefits Management that have been successfully implemented across several large-scale organisations, into a single, coherent approach and reference, for use by P3O professionals, BMs and In-Service/Business as Usual Capability Managers working in private and public sector bodies and organisations.

12.2.2 It closes the knowledge gap between the significant information that already exists on this subject (i.e. the www; information and guidance received during formal/informal training; coffee shop chat), and the confusion so often seen in the workplace where its practical application and understanding is less clear or confused. BM practitioners can use it to accelerate, increase their knowledge, and boost performance.

12.2.3 It is hoped that this guide will have a positive contribution toward and help to improve, the Benefits Management Profession. A new approach to training personnel who aspire to be, or those already actively engaged in the profession and seeking further knowledge, can be drawn from it.

12.2.4 Please provide any feedback or questions you may have to BRM.Mngr@hotmail.com. Shared knowledge will raise our game, keep this guide current and better inform this quintessential aspect of project, programme, and portfolio delivery.

The approach to change should be 'Benefits-led' to ensure maximum value for the change, the End Users, and the Organisation as a whole. *Managing Benefits* by Steve Jenner (2nd edition) rightly stated: 'Benefits are not just another dimension of project and programme management (PPM) – rather, they are the rationale for the investment of taxpayers' and stakeholders' funds in change initiatives. As such, Benefits should be the driver behind all change initiatives from initiation through to, and indeed beyond, integration into Business as Usual (BaU).'

S C Wilde MBE
Director, Benefits Realisation Management Limited (BRM Ltd)
Company number 11672194

www.ingramcontent.com/pod-product-compliance
Lightning Source LLC
Chambersburg PA
CBHW041622220326
41599CB00043BA/7221